IAN MITCHELL is an historian, who recently gave up teaching to devote himself to writing full time. After graduating from university in his native Aberdeen in 1973, he did postgraduate research at Leeds. This was followed by a British Council scholarship in Berlin, where he studied German historiography. The author of articles in learned journals, and of a standard textbook on Bismarck, Ian taught for over twenty years at Clydebank College, mainly on German history. Increasingly interested in Scottish history and heritage, Ian has previously co-produced a book, *The First Munroist*, (with Pete Drummond) on the foundation period of Scottish mountaineering dealing with A.E. Robertson and his contemporaries. *Scotland's Mountains Before the Mountaineers* continues and develops this marriage between his historical training and his interests as a mountaineer.

Ian has been a lifelong hillwalker, beginning in the Cairngorms in the mid 1960s. He is familiar with the Scottish hills as a walker, bothier and climber, and completed his Munros several years ago. He has also visited the mountains of Iceland, Norway, the Pyrenees, Morocco and the Austrian Alps. His first two mountain books were co-written with Dave Brown. *Mountain Days and Bothy Nights* was an instant bestseller and is established as a classic of 60s mountain sub-culture, while *A View from the Ridge* won critical acclaim, and the prestigious Boardman-Tasker Prize in 1991. Since then, Ian has published three solo books, *Second Man on the Rope*, an account of his climbs and travels with Dave Brown, *Mountain Footfalls*, and most recently he published a volume of outdoor fiction, *The Mountain Weeps*. Ian also writes frequently on outdoor matters for climbing journals and the general media, and has a regular column in the *West Highland Free Press*. In addition, he gives talks and slide shows on his books; there is one to accompany *Scotland's Mountains Before the Mountaineers*.

First Published 1998
Reprinted 1999

The paper used in this book is recyclable. It is made from low chlorine
pulps produced in a low energy, low emission manner
from renewable forests.

Printed and bound by
Caledonian International Book Manufacturing Ltd., Glasgow

Typeset in 10.5 point Sabon by
S. Fairgrieve, Edinburgh 0131 658 1763

Cover reproduction Kilchurn Castle
with Cruachan Ben Mountains, noon, 1802 by J.M.W. Turner
(Plymouth City Museums & Art Gallery Collection)

Scotland's Mountains before the Mountaineers

IAN MITCHELL

Luath Press Limited

EDINBURGH

www.luath.co.uk

Contents

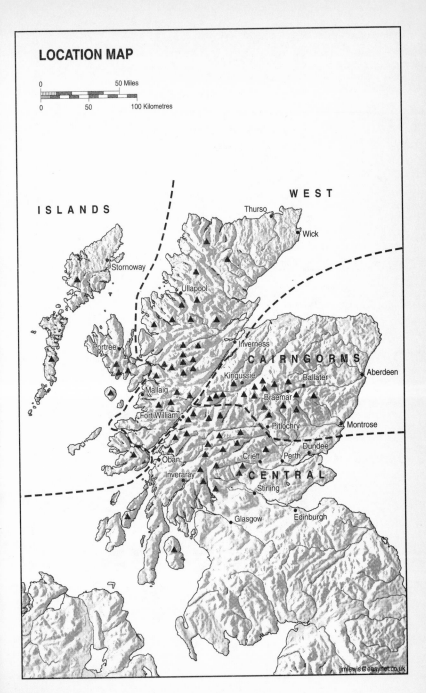

LOCATION MAP

0   50 Miles

0   50   100 Kilometres

ISLANDS

WEST

Thurso

Wick

Stornoway

Ullapool

Portree

Inverness

CAIRNGORMS

Mallaig

Kingussie

Ballater

Aberdeen

Braemar

Fort William

Pitlochry

Montrose

Oban

Dundee

Crieff

Perth

Inveraray

CENTRAL

Stirling

Glasgow

Edinburgh

jimlewis@easynet.co.uk

MAP 1 CENTRAL

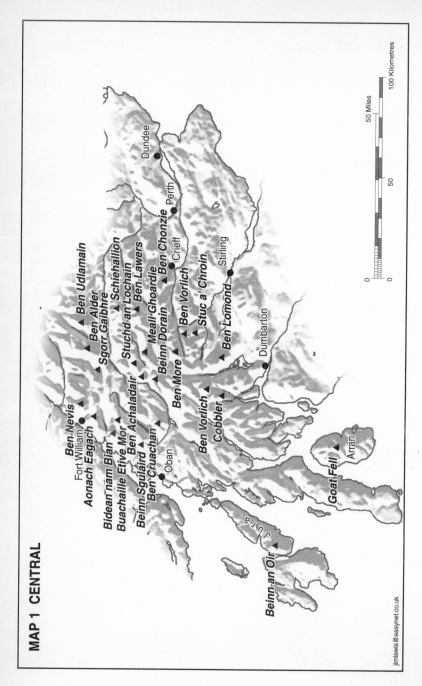

Fort William
Ben Nevis
Aonach Eagach
Bidean 'nam Bian
Buachaille Etive Mor
Ben Achaladair
Beinn Sgulaird
Ben Cruachan
Oban
Ben Vorlich
Cobbler
Ben Udlamain
Ben Alder
Sgorr Gaibhre
Schiehallion
Stuchd an Lochain
Ben Lawers
Meall Ghoardie
Beinn Dorain
Ben More
Ben Chonzie
Crieff
Ben Vorlich
Stuc a'Chroin
Ben Lomond
Perth
Stirling
Dumbarton
Dundee
Goat Fell
Arran
Beinn an Oir
Jura

0   50   100 Kilometres
0   50 Miles

jimlewis@easynet.co.uk

viii

MAP 2 CAIRNGORMS

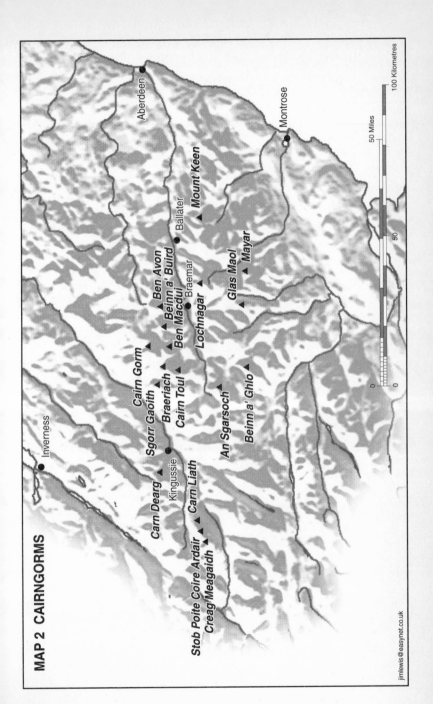

Inverness

Aberdeen

Kingussie

Carn Dearg ▲

Sgorr Gaoith ▲

Cairn Gorm ▲

Braeriach ▲

Cairn Toul ▲

Carn Liath ▲

Stob Poite Coire Ardair ▲

Creag Meagaidh ▲

Ben Avon ▲

Beinn a' Buird ▲

Ben Macdui ▲

Lochnagar ▲

Braemar

Ballater

Mount Keen ▲

Glas Maol ▲

Mayar ▲

An Sgarsoch ▲

Beinn a' Ghlo ▲

Montrose

jimlewis@easynet.co.uk

0   50   100 Kilometres
0   50 Miles

ix

MAP 3 WEST

0   50 Miles

0   50   100 Kilometres

Thurso

Ben Hope

Ben Klibreck

Ben More Assynt

Ullapool

Beinn Dearg

Sgurr Fiona

Slioch

Ben Wyvis

Beinn Alligin

Fionn Bheinn

Inverness

An Socach

Sgurr na Lapaich

Beinn Fhionnlaidh

Mam Sodhail

Sgurr Fhuaran

Sgurr nan Conbhairean

Sgurr na Ciste Dhubh

Carn Ghluasaid

Ben Sgritheall

A'Chralaig

Gairich

Sron a'Choire Ghairbh

Sgurr nan Coireachan

Sgurr Thuilm

Fort William

jimlewis@easynet.co.uk

x

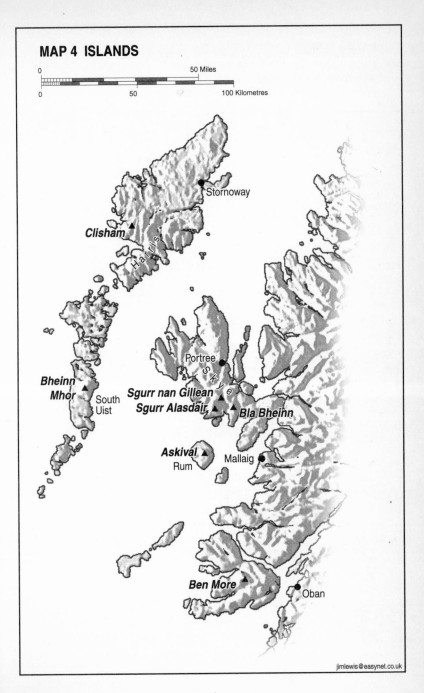

MAP 4 ISLANDS

0
50 Miles

0
50
100 Kilometres

Stornoway

Clisham ▲

Harris

Bheinn
Mhor ▲
South
Uist

Portree

S k y e

Sgurr nan Gillean ▲
Sgurr Alasdair ▲
Bla Bheinn ▲

Askival ▲
Rum
Mallaig

Ben More ▲
Oban

jimlewis@easynet.co.uk

xi

Foreword

THIS USEFUL BOOK RIGHTLY acknowledges that it picks up a story which began tentatively to be told in the pages of the *Scottish Mountaineering Club Journal* as early as 1894. That tentative beginning was only carried further over seventy years later by David Baye Horne, Professor of History in the University of Edinburgh. It is to Horn's 1966 article in the SMCJ on 'The Origins of Mountaineering in Scotland' that modern historians have hitherto turned when they needed information on early ascents of Scottish mountains. Inevitably, when concentrating on recorded ascents, the historian is pushed at first towards the conclusion that the Gael seldom if ever climbed the mountains of the *Gaidhealtachd*, and that knowledge of the Highland peaks and ridges is disproportionately a product of Victorian athletic tourism and late nineteenth and twentieth-century mountaineering for its own sake.

The detailed Gaelic nomenclature of nearly all Highland hills and mountain masses alone gives the lie to this assumption (with the infertile Cuillin of Skye being the exception which proves the rule). In this new book on 'pre-mountaineering' ascents and near-ascents in the Highlands, we have at last a work which does justice to those who lived and worked, travelled and fought, in the Highlands before Walter Scott. His writings had already made the Borders a tourist area, when his poetry did the same service for the Trossachs and Ben Lomond. Inevitably, even a sophisticated trawl of written sources can reveal only the tip of an iceberg. Nevertheless, this is an important new revision of a fascinating topic.

Professor Bruce P. Lenman
Professor of History, University of St Andrews
December 1997

Abbreviations

OCCASIONAL ABBREVIATIONS ARE EXPLAINED in location in the text. For the reader's convenience, the more frequent abbreviations are:

CCJ	*Cairngorm Club Journal*
DNB	*Dictionary of National Biography*
FASTI	*Fasti Ecclesiae Scoticanae*
NLS	National Library of Scotland (with ms. no.)
NSA	(Second) *Statistical Account of Scotland*
OSA	*Statistical Account of Scotland* (Original)
SGM	*Scottish Geographical Magazine*
SMCJ	*Scottish Mountaineering Club Journal*
TGSI	*Transactions of the Gaelic Society of Inverness*
WHFP	*West Highland Free Press*
Op. Cit.	Quote from a different page of the immediately preceding text referred to
Loc. Cit.	Quote from the same page of the immediately preceeding text referred to

Introduction

MOUNTAINEERING HAS PRODUCED a body of literature unrivalled by other sports. One need only check the shelves of any bookshop and compare the space allotted to mountaineering as opposed to, for example, fishing, yachting, cycling or other activities – most of whose productions are of a technical nature – to confirm the point. Mountaineering is unique not only in the volume, but also in the quality and range of its literary productions, which gain their superiority from their concern, not solely with the techniques, but with the general culture of the activity – the social histories, the intellectual biographies, the human relations which mountaineering is uniquely able to treat in literary form.

In Scotland, 'for a wee country', we are well supplied with mountaineering works of literary quality. James Bryce's *Memories of Travel*, though published in 1921, deals with the vanished world of Victorian and Edwardian times. Seton Gordon's books, especially his *Highways and Byways in the West Highlands* (1935) and its companion on the *Central Highlands* (1948) are fine studies on mountain culture. Then there is Alastair Borthwick's classic of 1930s sub-culture, *Always a Little Further*, and of course a work which has achieved scriptural status internationally, W.H. Murray's *Mountaineering in Scotland* (1947). J.H.B. Bell's *A Progress in Mountaineering* (1950) could be added to the list, as well as Hamish Brown's *Hamish's Mountain Walk* (1980). There is the fine biography of the Anglo-Scot, Norman Collie, by Christine Mill (1987), as well as I.D.S. Thomson's *Jock Nimlin* (1995). We have a delightful and scholarly 'biography' of our highest mountain, *Ben Nevis* by Ken Crocket (1986), and from the same imprint came the excellent, though mistitled anthology *A Century of Scottish Mountaineering* (1988) with its anthology of hill-climbing pioneers – the Naismiths, Raeburns and others – even though these pioneers were too closely identified therein as of necessity members of the Scottish Mountaineering Club (SMC). Other aspects of our culture have received attention both of scholarly and literary quality, for example in P. Drummond's *Scottish Hill and Mountain Names* (1991). This catalogue is of course selective and subjective, but it does give an idea of the enviable literary mountain culture of Scotland.

However, there is a serious gap in all this literary work, and that is in the pre-history of Scottish mountaineering: explorations, ascents, travels, social relations in the mountains, before mountaineering became an organised sport from the middle of the last century. There are more works on the opening up of Africa by Scots explorers than about the opening up of the Scottish Highlands, by Scots and others. An activity becomes a sport when it gains its own techniques, its own *mores* – or rules, its own specialised equipment, and its own institutions and publications, i.e. when it becomes separated off from the ordinary business of living. A trawlerman is not a sports fisherman, neither is a chamois hunter a mountaineer. Mountaineering began to coalesce into a sport around the middle of the last century, with the formation of the Alpine Club in London in 1857, and the publication of the *Alpine Journal* in 1863. This was paralleled by the emergence of guides, of both the human and the printed variety, and the manufacture of equipment designed for the activity, such as the Alpenstock and later ice-axe, and emergence of specialised techniques, such as belaying. The process was uneven, originating in the countries contiguous with the Alpine chain. In Scotland it took another few decades to come to fruition, with the formation of the Scottish Mountaineering Club, and its rival Cairngorm Club in the 1880s, and the appearance of their attendant *Journals*, and was encouraged by the appearance of improved maps, and guides, like A.P. Abraham's *Rock Climbing in Skye* (1908). One marvels and wonders at the exploits of the pioneers, so much so that it is easy to feel that they discovered – indeed invented – the mountains. But what of the pre-history of the mountains, their experiences before the mountaineers proper came along? For, before the mountaineers *proper* (whose fundamental aim, avowed and putting all other motives into the shade, was to climb mountains as an activity justified in itself), were the mountaineers *improper*, with which this account will deal. The process will be described in detail in what follows, but broadly speaking there were several stages before the quantum leap to mountaineer took place.

As with mountain areas elsewhere, the Scottish Highlands were originally viewed by outsiders as threatening, both in terms of the terrain and the inhabitants. Mountains were seen as ugly and sterile, and likely to be inhabited by bandits and even monsters and devils. In *Landscape and Memory* Simon Schama shows that this mountainphobia was a general aspect of European Christian civilisation till fairly modern times. For the medieval mind of Dante, Purgatory

4

was a mountain, a place of gloom, pain and ugliness. In England, the seventeenth-century poet Andrew Marvell hated the mountains:

> That do with your hook-shoulder'd height
> The Earth deform and Heaven fright.

As late as 1702, a Professor of Physics at Zurich University collected a list of dragons inhabiting the Swiss Alps! Indeed, Christian theology had to find a reason why God had created such abominations, why Eden had decayed into 'vast heaps of indigested stones', in the words of one authority. Often mountains were seen as results of the Flood, a punishment for man's wickedness. We are fortunate to have a splendid example of such an attitude from sixteenth-century Scotland, in the form of lines from David Lyndsay's *Ane Dialog Betuix Experience and ane Courteour*:

> The Erth, quhilk was so fair formit
> Wes, be that curious Flude, deformit;
> Quhare unquhyle were the plesand planes
> Wer holkit glennis, and hie montanes:
> (*Works* 1879, Vol II p. 269)

And an additional drawback of the Scottish mountains to the Lowlander, was the alien nature of its inhabitants and their culture. John of Fordun spoke for most when, after mentioning the domestic, decent, devout character of the Lowland Scots, he commented on the Scottish Highlands in 1380, (original in Latin), as follows:

> The highlanders and people of the islands, on the other hand, are a savage and untamed nation, rude and independent, given to rapine and easy living... comely in person yet unsightly in dress, hostile (to the Lowlanders) owing to diversity of speech... and exceedingly cruel. (Quoted in T.C. Smout, *A History of the Scottish People,* 1969, p. 39.)

Though travellers for curiosity and pleasure were not totally unknown, most people had to have a very good reason for visiting the area. And aside from the few traders and fishermen, the Scottish mountains were visited before pacification in the mid-eighteenth century by other people for vocational reasons: cartographers, military men, astronomers, geologists and so forth. Then they were visited, in the Romantic period of the later eighteenth and early nineteenth century, for the uplifting effects of the scenery; the view was the thing, and for the Ossianic and Fingalian romance associated with the bens and glens. Later – in the high Victorian era when robust manliness was in vogue – the invigorating effects of pedestrianism were seen as bringing one nearer to God, or to self-knowledge. Finally, the dialectical transformation was made in the later Victorian period to an early form of the 'because it is there' philosophy. Indeed, the wheel had come full circle, and for many the mountains became a solace, an escape, from the threatening world of Victorian industrialism, its problems, its ugliness, its inhabitants. Clearly, all these stages overlapped, often in the same individual; but there is a *fundamental* difference between the person who went on the mountain primarily to make a map, or look at the stars, and who also enjoyed his stroll, and the person who – even if making incidental glancing nods towards the idea of utility in some sense – basically is on the mountain because he is on the mountain. A revolution in 'ways of seeing' the mountains had taken place, in the mental maps people had of them.

This change in perception may have been summed up by the mid-Victorian author and art critic, John Ruskin, when he said that 'mountains are the beginning and end of all natural beauty'. But Ruskin was not *responsible* for this change in perception, as is often stated; he merely summed up a process of shifting focus which had been occurring for the best part of a century in the eyes of travellers to mountain areas, including the Scottish Highlands. This 'revolution in seeing' is partly what this work is about, though it does not exhaust its intention.

We are victims here of the 'Columbus discovered America' syndrome. People forget the Indians, and they forget the Highlanders. This is possibly understandable due to the attitude of today's Gael towards the mountains. It is no exaggeration to say that those of a Highland background are conspicuous by their absence from the Scottish hills; the vast majority of our climbers and walkers are either English or foreign, and the Scots contingent is made up almost entirely of Lowlanders. In the *Gaidhealtachd* itself things are no better. Today the ignorance of the vast majority of Highlanders about what lies beyond the Highland roads is staggering; only a few shepherds and gamekeepers are the exception. But with modern techniques of their job, their knowledge of the hills is of necessity less than that of their forebears; few actually live in the mountains now, and the Argocat has replaced Shanks's Pony in their work. It is hardly surprising, therefore, that this impression has been transferred back in time, and the assumption made that the Gael of yesterday had little interest in the mountains which surrounded him.

And unlike in Ireland, myth does not come much to the Gael's aid. Various Irish holy men are reputed to have scaled the peaks of the Emerald Isle, sometimes on their knees, including St Brendan – taking time off from discovering America – who gave his name to Mount Brandon. But none of the Scottish Celtic saints appear to have ascended the peaks. Ronald Black assures me (personal communication 17.12.97) that *Beinn Chaluim* is named after Saint Columba, but there is no tale of his having ascended it. Sacred mountains were generally a product of Counter-Reformation Catholic penitential culture, and hence we would not expect many in presbyterian Scotland. (Simon Schama, *Landscape and Memory*, 1995, p. 436-42.)

There is a rumour that a Fingalian warrior guarded a spring on the summit of Cruachan, and another that the ancient Picts may have ascended Schiehallion, if indeed that mountain was – as has been claimed – of some crucial significance to the Caledonians. But the general assumption is that outsiders discovered the Scottish mountains, rather than the native inhabitants.

There are almost no accounts of the epoch of pre-mountaineering history in Scotland. One of the few I am aware of is the article by D.B. Horn, 'The Origins of Mountaineering in Scotland', printed in the limited circulation *Scottish Mountaineering Club Journal* (SMCJ) in May 1966, Vol. XXVIII. Horn's essay in itself is to a large extent the recirculation of materials already brought together in the series 'Rise and Progress of Mountaineering in Scotland' in the SMCJ Vol III. (1894), Nos. 15-18, to which he adds further information of his own. It is disappointing that a project begun so promisingly by the SMC a century ago should have, in its hands, advanced little further, especially as the editor of the *Journal* appended to Horn's 1966 work a rider on the need 'to outline the role of the Scottish mountains in the *Gaidhealtachd*' (p. 173).

Horn's work, to which I will frequently return, does a very useful job in collecting gleanings – in the limits of an article he could do no more – from early travellers' tales of explorations and ascents in the Scottish Highlands. Others had often looked at these accounts, but mainly from a literary or social point of view, neglecting the mountaineering angle. We will follow the spoor of many of these travellers later. But when it comes to the activities of the native Highlander, Horn is rather patronising, suggesting that perhaps 'our simple minded forefathers regarded habitual wandering over the high hills as one of the clearest symptoms of a disordered mind' (p. 157), and dismissing the idea of ascents by the Gael before the period of the travellers or tourists.

> I conclude therefore that down to the early eighteenth century the actual summits of most of the Scottish mountains were almost as unknown to the majority of Highlanders as they are in the main to their twentieth century descendants. (p. 158)

A more popular and accessible account of some of the early mountain explorations was given in Campbell Steven's *The Story of Scotland's Hills* (1975) – though this has been for many years out of print. Steven acknowledged his debt to Horn, making 'particular grateful mention' of his article. Steven fleshes out many of Horn's references, often giving extracts from early journals of travel, and adds some accounts from his own investigations, being a little more willing to accept the possibility of early ascents by Highlanders: 'Is it really too far fetched to think that even in those days hills could be climbed simply for the sake of enjoyment?' (p. 65).

Steven's work is a pioneering one, but he himself admits its flaws, saying, 'No doubt it is presumptuous to call this the story of Scotland's hills...' (p. 11). The work is possibly overambitious, attempting to tell the story of the mountains from the earliest days until after World War II, and dealing with skiing, meteorology, mineralogy and a few more things besides. This of necessity makes it a trifle journalistic, sources are not always located, claims not always properly investigated, and his chapters on the pre-history of mountaineering do not venture far into uncharted territory, mainly adding details and colour to Horn's article. I will attempt to delve into the pre-history of Scottish mountaineering in a more thorough, comprehensive and scholarly – yet still accessible – way than Horn or Steven were able, or wished to – while recognising their achievements.

I will try and demonstrate that there were several fairly conclusive ascents of Scottish mountains before the early eighteenth century, many by Gaels, and that the pre-history of Scottish mountaineering should have as its scope roughly the years 1550 to 1850, not 1700 to 1850. These ascents I will deal with in the Magical

Mystery Tour of the text proper, but there are also the ones that got away, and I would like to devote the rest of this introduction to treating of the circumstantial evidence that the Highlanders did know their hills, and that the proverb *Anail a' Ghaidheal, air a' mhullach* – the breathing space of the Gael is on the summit – may not be simple hyperbole.

Today the population centres in the Highlands are mainly the coastline and the arterial glens, leaving much of the mountainous area as uninhabited wilderness. This is not an eternal fact of geography, but a social fact, resulting from an historical process. Starting a quarter of a millennium ago, and proceeding with fits and starts, the Highlander abandoned the area we now know as wilderness, and the population moved out, partly by choice, seeking a better life. More importantly, as conditions were imposed which made traditional life intolerable, the inhabitants left through encouraged or forced migration. Before that, many wilderness areas were either inhabited and cultivated, or even when they were not, were used as areas of passage for men in time of war or animals in times of peace, or were used for hunting when the fruits of the earth were more clan patrimony than the privatised property of the landowner, or for transhumance, when cattle were driven to the *airidhean* or sheep to the summer pastures.

This incontrovertible fact of social history is buttressed by the truth that, from Pont's early journeys in the 1580s which we shall look at, to those of the Ordnance Survey a quarter of a millennium later, the map-makers found the places in the mountains named. With few exceptions, virtually every place name on the OS maps was given to the cartographers by local people. And not just townships, lochs and the names of mountain peaks, but passes, knolls, cliffs and an astonishing variety of other physical features. Pick up any of the original six inch to the mile OS Maps, or *in absentia* even a 1:25,000 OS Leisure Map, and look at the detail of the colours, the physical features, even the quality of the pasturage, mentioned on the mountains, and it is beyond belief that the Gaels before the clearance period were unfamiliar with their hills. (There is a notable exception to all this. The Cuillin of Skye had a poverty of nomenclature which reflected the poverty of the soil and the hills' difficulty of access. I shall return to this in the main text.)

Let us take one mountain at random as an example of familiarity, that of Mullach Coire Mhic Fhearchair in Wester Ross, one of the remotest in Scotland. The Gaels had a multitude of colours for describing hills. Mullach has a Corrie *Ghuirm*, blue, and one *Odhar*, dun-coloured, possibly named after the vegetation. There is also one described as *Fhraoich*, heathery, and one whose lack of vegetation gives it the name *nan Clach*, of the stones. High between the Mullach and its neighbour, Beinn Tarsuinn (the hill going the other way, at right angles) is the Bealach *Odhar*, the dun-coloured pass. Not a gap, or notch – for which there are other Gaelic names – but a pass, used for access to the country behind Mullach. The outlier to the south of the Mullach is Meall *Garbh*, the rough hill – how known unless traversed? The hill itself takes its name from its main corrie, *Coire Mhic Fhearchair*, the corrie of Farquar's son, presumeably the same man who has an eponymous corrie on Beinn Eighe not far away. Farquar MacIntaggart was awarded the Earldom of Ross in the thirteenth century for his exploits against the Norsemen. Farquar's son, William, was rewarded with lordship of Skye in 1266, and was almost certainly the person after whom the mountain was named, at a time when Gaelic nomenclature would have been replacing Norse influences. ('The Clan Period', Jean Munro, in *The Ross and Cromarty Book*, 1966, p. 128-9) Now, Farquar's son may not have climbed the Mullach, though he must have been associated with some deeds upon it. The nomenclatural evidence shows every part of this fine, remote hill was known to the local inhabitants. Faced with the cartographic evidence, only the wilful can deny that the Highlander knew his hills.

It might be argued that the Gael might have had reason to visit corries and passes – economic reasons – but no reason to ascend actual summits. I would dispute this. Summits could be of use not only as lookout points in time of war, but also as vantage points for hunting, or searching for lost livestock. There is a *Suidheachan Finn* on the aforementioned Beinn Tarsuinn; we may doubt whether Fingal himself actually sat there, but somebody did, somebody identified the mound in the hollow at that great height as a mythical resting place of the warrior. The seat lies not all that far below 3,000 ft, and from it, it is an easy stroll to the summit, in case Fingal had wanted a better view. (J.H. Dixon, *Gairloch*, 1886, p. 4.) Drummond's *Scottish Hill and Mountain Names* takes the reader through the fascinating story of the usage of colour, of the human anatomy, of the various animals' names and other ways the Gael had of identifying his local peaks, and rather than plagiarise, I would recommend that the reader consult this work, to corroborate the idea that the Highlander was *intimately* familiar with his or her hills.

Drummond also lists many hills which were given character names. Now, many of these related to Fingalian legends, or to witches and devils, and therefore cannot be taken as representing real mountain ascents. But there is a *prima facie* case for arguing that some of the mountains named after people were so-named because those bearing that name actually climbed them, though the person and the incident may be lost in the mists of time. Those for which we have some more than hypothetical evidence will be featured in the main body of this work, but there are others. *Carn an Fhidhleir* lies south of the main Cairngorm massif; did a fiddler play a tune on its summit? *Sgurr Dhonuill* stands near Ballachulish; is Donald an unsung and forgotten pioneer of Scottish mountaineering? Who was the stonemason who gave *Beinn a' Chlachair*, far from any quarry, its name, and what Petrie gave neighbouring *Creag Pitridh* its title? We do not know, and possibly never will, but it is surely an arrogant attitude which assumes that the Gael did not love his hills enough to find his breathing space on the actual summit. Why else name a mountain, Hill of Delight, *Beinn Eibheinn*, or *Carn a' Choire Boidheach*, Hill of the Beautiful Corrie? And occasionally, oral tradition confirms this hypothesis. In this book you will meet the Gaelic mountaineers *Cailean Gorach, Fionnladh Dubh* and *Donnachadh Ban* – who *definitely* ascended the tops centuries ago.

This work then, will try to assess the available evidence as to early explorations and ascents in the Highlands, putting them in their social and historical contexts and attempting to redress the balance a little in favour of the native Highlander, who had carried out much activity before his homeland was discovered by the *Sassunnaich* (English and Lowland Scots), many of whom even in the period of early tourism relied heavily on often unnamed Gaels as guides. From being the master in his lands, he had become a servant, and our journey from the middle of the sixteenth century to the high Victorian period will of necessity reflect these changes in Highland society in the period before the mountaineers.

After some thought, I adopted a geographical format for the book, dividing the Highlands into four manageable areas: Central Highlands, Cairngorms, West Highlands and Islands. This does pose problems of organisation, and occasionally I breach my boundaries. But the alternative method of a biographical-chronological approach posed greater problems, of dealing with the history of attempts/ ascents on a particular mountain in several disconnected sequences. Though it means we meet some of our travellers in different geographical locations, the format adopted keeps the focus where it should be: on the mountains themselves.

This book has been some years in the formulation and conception, three years in the researching and a full year in the writing. I am conscious that in many ways it is a preliminary work, and hope to open up a dialogue with my readers to correct any errors or omissions the book may contain, in order to progress towards a more complete knowledge of its subject matter. After all, I have located possible first ascents of (roughly) a mere one-third of the Scottish peaks over 3,000 ft. Further investigation, particularly of estate papers, may reveal more, though my own in the *Forfeit Estate Papers*, ed. A.H. Millar (1906), uncovered none. My feeling is that many other peaks not mentioned here had their summits trodden before the frenzied rounds of bagging by Hugh Munro and Archibald Robertson in the last two decades of the nineteenth century. However, despite its exploratory nature, I am confident that the reader will find the journey through the pre-history of Scottish mountaineering in the pages which follow, interesting, informative and instructive.

In all quotations and sources I have retained the original orthography; it should be remembered that English – still less Gaelic and Scots – spelling was not standardised in much of our period.

Ian Mitchell
November 1998

CHAPTER I

Summitteers in the Central Highlands

THIS EXTENSIVE AREA, lying to the east of the Great Glen and to the south of the Cairngorms, borders the Central Lowlands for a great distance along the Highland fault line. It was fairly intensively travelled and sketched by the cartographer Timothy Pont in the late sixteenth century. Of Pont's life little is known; more indeed is known of his father, who was a leading figure in the Scottish Reformation, helping draw up the Kirk's *Book of Discipline*. Pont was born in the early 1560s, and graduated from St Andrews University in 1583. He was minister in Dunnet, Caithness, for a decade or so till about 1610/11, and died possibly four years afterwards. Apart from the fact that he subscribed to the Plantation of Ulster with Scots Protestants, buying 2,000 acres of land for 400 pounds Scots, we know little more of him. (*Fasti Ecclesiae Scoticanae*, Vol 7 p. 119.) The recently established Project Pont, based on the Map Library of the National Library of Scotland, may help to shed more light on Pont. Even the motivations for his cartographic journeys, which probably occupied him in field work from 1583 till 1596, are shrouded in mystery, and his maps were never published in his lifetime. A grant of one hundred pounds (English) from Charles 1 ensured that Pont's work eventually found outlet in Blaeu's epochmaking *Atlas* of 1654, published in Amsterdam. Robert Gordon of Straloch, who was involved with the work, wrote in his dedication of the Scottish maps to Sir John Scot of Scotstarvit, that:

> He (Pont) travelled on foot through the whole of the Kingdom, as no-one before him had done; he visited all the islands, occupied for the most part by inhabitants hostile and uncivilised, and with a language different from our own; being often stripped as he told me, by fierce robbers, and suffering not seldom, all the hardships of dangerous journeys, nevertheless at no time was he overcome by the difficulties or disheartened. (Qu. in *The Pont Manuscript Maps of Scotland*, Jeffrey C. Stone, 1988, p. 30)

Pont's sketches of the Central Highlands, published in *The Pont Manuscript Maps of Scotland*, show that Pont knew many of the mountains in this area. Not only did he know, but he drew outline sketches of *Bin Lawers, Struik-chron* and *Bin Voirlye, Kraich* (by which name he knew Schiehallion), and *Bin Nevesh*, amongst many others. Pont could not speak Gaelic, so he clearly did not name any mountains, though he must have had a Gaelic guide/interpreter. From the outlines, one can speculate on Pont's position when he drew the hills. Lawers, Schiehallion and Stuic a' Chroin would appear to be sketched from a series of low positions, but the drawing of Nevis, it is tempting to argue, must have been from a high point on the Mamore ridge, rather than from Glen Nevis itself. Pont's sketch shows the summit plateau, the lower Carn Dearg summit, and between them possibly the Allt Coire Eoghain glen. Sgurr a' Mhaim might be a useful place to check on the perspective. However, we do not even know whether Pont's sketches were drawn from a single point, or were composites, so it is difficult to speculate on which, if any, mountains he might or might not have ascended. The absence of documentary evidence also compounds the problem, in relation to possible ascents by Pont.

The Owl of Strone and the Mad Mountaineer

Despite his achievements, it has to be emphasised that much of Pont's knowledge came from local people, here as elsewhere. And we are fortunate to have an extant example of the minutely detailed knowledge of his environment – including that of the mountains – possessed by the Gael, in the form of the poem *Oran na Comhachaig*, The Owl of Strone, which deals with Lochaber and its contiguous areas. I am using an edition of the poem from a course-book for students at Edinburgh University Celtic Department, kindly given me by Ronald Black, and translated by Angus Mackenzie of Inverness. *Domnhall mac Fhionnlaigh nan Dan*, Donald, son of Findlay, of the Lays, was a poet and deer hunter, active in the Lochaber area, whose life roughly spanned the period 1530 to 1600, and a very different man from the scholarly Pont. He was obviously involved in some shady deeds in his youth for, as he says,

Bu lionmhor cogadh's creachadh
Bha 'n Loch Abar anns an uair sin.
(There was much warfare and raiding in Lochaber at that time.)
(*Coursebook*, p. 3)

His poem celebrates the joys of the chase, and complains about the encroachment of debilitating old age, 'wrinkle-faced and shaggy, blear-eyed and dismal...' which keeps him from the hunt. The topographical detail of the poem is extraordinary, showing a knowledge of the territory from Glen Nevis through to Loch Treig and eastwards to Loch Ericht, as well as the lands southwards to Glen Lyon. Possibly a Glencoe MacDonald, Donald was one day taken in Campbell lands by Black Duncan, laird of Glenorchy, but saved his life by the feat of shooting a stag through the eye with his arrow. His impressed captors freed him instantly.

The poem centres round Creag Uanach near Loch Treig, but mentions several mountains by name. *Beinn Nimneis* is Ben Nevis, *Beinn Allair* is Ben Alder, 'the most eminent of bens', and *Lap-Bheinn* is Beinn na Lap near Corrour. The context of the poem shows that he has been on *Sron na Garbh-bheinne*, the northern ridge of Stob Coire Sgriodain, a Munro above Loch Treig, and is familiar with the rivers and slopes of all these hills. There is even a suggestion that he knows that the sea is visible from the summit of Nevis or its neighbour, Carn Dearg. (Op.cit. p.18.) His detailed descriptions of the area show not only his intense knowledge of, but also his intense love of, the landscape, which he describes in glowing terms.

Creag mo chridh-sa Creag Uanach...
A' chreag aighearach urail eunach.
(Joy of my heart, Creag Uanach... A refreshing, joyful, bird-filled crag.)
(*Coursebook*, p. 4)

The writer is also familiar with the high ground, describing *Coire Ratha*, high on the Grey Corries, and several high passes between the mountains, such the *Mam Ban* between Carn Dearg and Sgor Ghaibhre. Most significant of these passes is possibly the *Bealach nan Sgurr* which lies between Sgor Gaibhre and Sgor Choinnich between Lochs Ossian and Ericht. This pass lies at a height of almost 2,700 ft, and from it the ascent of both aforementioned peaks is easy. In the section of the poem bidding farewell to the hills, *Soraidh leis nam Beanntan*, he takes leave of 'both sides of the Bealach an Sgurr' (*da thaobh Bealach nan Sgurr* p. 7), indicating he knew the area intimately. In fact, I would think that the first ascents of Carn Dearg and Sgor Gaibhre, as well as of Stob Coire Sgriodain, should go to *mac Fhonnlaidgh*, as well as possibly Beinn na Lap, Ben Alder and even Ben Nevis/Carn Dearg.

If our hunter did not climb any of these peaks, it was not because he was unable to, or thought them not worthwhile. However, I suspect that the author of *Oran na Comhachaig* stood often on the summits of the hills he mentions. There is a striking similarity between this poem and the works two centuries later of Duncan MacIntyre, in the expression of the love of, and intimacy with, the hills experienced by the Gael. Indeed, the later Glenorchy Bard may well have known the work of *mac Fhionnlaigh*, though it is certain that Lowland Scots did not, nor did they know the territory described in the poem.

Despite Pont's explorations of the Central Highlands, and their proximity to the Lowlands, the area did not really become known to outsiders much earlier than the remoter lands to the north and west; or at least not until pacification in the later eighteenth century, after which the Central Highlands began to experience an influx of tourists. The reason lies in the paradox, explained to the naive Englishman, Francis Osbaldistone, by Baillie Nicol Jarvie in Walter Scott's novel, *Rob Roy*, set in the early eighteenth century, though written a century later. The Central Highlands, explained the wily Baillie, especially on their borderlands, were actually more turbulent, lawless and threatening than the lands further afield. From their territories in this area, the wild Highlanders had the opportunity, not only of plundering each other in clan warfare, but also of raiding the richer agricultural lands of the Lowlands, in *creachan*, where gear, cattle and even women were carried off. The burghers and peasants of the Lowlands, who had long since divested their military obligations to semi-professional armies, were largely helpless before this threat, though the Highlanders earned their neighbours' undying enmity from an early date. In his poem *The Sevin Deidly Synnis* written in the early 1500s, William Dunbar gives vent to the widespread anti-Highlander feeling of that time. Dunbar has the Seven Sins led in pageant by Highlanders 'schouting the correnoch' and 'clattering' in *Ersche*, that is, Irish. (Highlanders were then regarded more as an Irish overflow than Scottish.) Finally they meet their deserved fate:

> The Devill sa devit wes with thair yell
> That in the depest pot of hell
> He smorit thame with smuke.
> (*Poems* ed. J. Kinsley, 1964, p. 53)

This fear and hatred of the Highlander continued to dominate the Lowland borderlands long afterwards. In the fertile country south of Loch Lomond, a full moon was known as *MacFarlan's Lantern*, since it usually heralded a raid by that wild tribe. Further to the east the Macgregors levied the notorious black mail, a tax upon Lowland farmers not to raid their property, coupled with a pledge to recover stolen cattle (often taken by accomplices). Even after the 1715 Rebellion, with the establishment of strategic forts and the initiation of the building of military roads in the Highlands, a traveller visiting the Great Glen could write:

> ...all that mountainous, barren and frightful country which lies to the south is called Loquabre. It is indeed a frightful country full of hideous desert mountains and unpassable, except to the Highlanders who possess the precipices. Here, in spite of the most vigorous pursuit, the Highland robbers, such as the famous Rob Roy..find retreats as none could pretend to follow them, nor could he ever be taken. (Daniel Defoe, *A Tour Through The Whole Island of Great Britain*, 1724-6, 1971 edn. p. 672)

And subsequent to the 45 Rebellion, the sons of Rob Roy were still engaging in depredations, including abduction and forcible marriage on Loch Lomondside. The hanging of one of the pair doubtless encouraged timid tourists to think that it might now be safe to travel. A little further to the east, in Perthshire, things quietened down earlier, but there too the turbulence of the clansmen and the ineffectiveness of the writ of law, had not exactly encouraged tourist-friendly circumstances to prevail, and outsiders to visit. Therefore it is possibly not surprising that the earliest recorded mountaineer in the Central Highlands was a native – of Glen Lyon in Perthshire – rather than an outsider. And possibly fitting too that he was a bandit himself. As well as looking at his mountaineering, we will consider some incidents from the life of *Cailean Gorach*, since they give a perfect picture of a particular epoch in the story of the mountains before the mountaineers.

The four-hundredth anniversary of the death of Colin Campbell of Glenorchy, builder of Meggernie Castle in 1582, falls around 1997 or 98. Colin was a fairly typical laird in those troubled times beyond the Highland frontier, and often found himself on the wrong side of the law. He had originally married a cousin, who died in 1585, and his method of procuring a replacement lacked a certain subtlety, as the Countess of Errol pointed out in a complaint to the Privy Council in 1587:

Colin Campbell of Glenlyon, with convocation of men, bodin in feir of weir, to the number of one hundred... treasonably raised fire at the gates... where through she was constrained, for fear of the fury of the fire... to come forth; at which time the said Colin Campbell and his accomplices put violent hands on the complainer... of intention to have used her according to his filthy appetite or lust. (Quoted in Duncan Campbell, *The Lairds of Glenlyon,* 1886, p. 329)

The timely arrival of help foiled this attempt. Colin failed to appear to defend himself at the Privy Council and was declared an outlaw. But this only served to emphasise the powerlessness of the law. Two sheriff officers who served writs on Colin were given a good dinner at Meggernie, according to Highland hospitality. Then they were bound on biers, as if dead, and carried in a funeral procession to the edge of his lands, with pipers playing laments and women crying the *corranach*. The terrified officers were then dumped in the Allt-a Ghobhlain burn, but otherwise unharmed. Eventually, charges against Colin were dropped due to the influence of the powerful Campbells at James VI's court, 'saving his Highness from daily fasherie'. This experience does not seem to have sobered Colin, for in 1591 we find Lord Ogilvie of Airlie complaining that 'the broken men of the Hielands', including Colin Campbell, had come down into the low country, burning homes and driving off cattle.

Many other tales are told of Colin, but his downfall came when he ambushed and captured a party of Lochaber men who had raided his estates, killing two of his tenants. Fearing that to hand them over to the courts in Edinburgh might mean that private influences would secure them a pardon, Colin strung up thirty-six of the raiders at a place east of Meggernie, subsequently known as *Leachd nan Abrach*, Lochabermen's Brae. The leader of the raiders Colin shot with his own hand. This was a crime so appalling, that – again outlawed – it hardly looked as if even Colin could escape this time.

However, Colin had 'gotten a clout on the heid' in a foray into the Lennox, and – possibly as a stratagem – his son dispossessed him of his estates (avoiding forfeiture) by declaring his father mad, hence *Cailean Gorach*, Mad Colin. He was left at large with his loyal servant Findlay, and that is when, in retirement, *Cailean* took up mountaineering. Some of his behaviour in the latter years of his life leaves us in little doubt as to his insanity.

Map of Breadalbane (c. 1750) William Roy.
Topographical knowledge improved after the 45, as this overview of Breadalbane, with its close attention to detail, shows. River courses and mountain shapes are accurately delineated, including Schiehallion, later climbed and barometrically measured by Roy.
(The British Library)

The master and servant ranged the hills in pursuit of game. One day they had had little luck, then surprised a herd of wild goats at the summit of Stuchd an Lochain (3,144ft) above Meggernie. Colin in a fury drove the herd over the precipice and into the corrie cradling Lochan nan Chat below. Even this did not assuage his anger, and he ordered the loyal Findlay to jump after the goats to his certain death. But Findlay obviously had the mea-sure of his master, and asked for time to say his prayers. While he did so, Colin wandered to the cliff edge. Findlay pounced on him and gave him a taste of his own medicine, threatening to throw the madman over unless he begged mercy and promised not to repeat his behaviour. The madman swore, and was released. The date of this ascent cannot be exactly determined, but it was between Colin's dispossession and his death, i.e. in the 1590s. (Sadly, this does not make him Scotland's First Munroist; for a prior claim, see *West Highland Wanderers*).

Like many other mountaineering companions, who may have occasionally felt justified in throwing each other over a cliff, Colin and Findlay continued their friendship and wanderings till the death of the deposed laird. The last we hear of this fascinating character is a complaint from his own cousin in 1596, regarding *Cailean's* poach-ing and howffing in Mayne-Lorn (Mamlorn forest, the territory of Duncan Campbell of Glenorchy), where we are told the former laird:

> ...biggis sheillis within and aboute the same, and remains the maiste part of the summer season at the said forest, shuiting and slaying in grite nowmer the deir and wylde beastis. (Qu. *The Lairds of Glenlyon*, p. 333)

And in the process of these wanderings, it is likely he climbed more hills, unbeknown to us. Tales such as these about *Cailean Gorach* lived on in the oral traditions of Glen Lyon until well into the nineteenth century. Many are collected in Duncan Campbell's book cited above, the author hearing them from an old man in the 1830s, as well as adding information from the Privy Council records. Some of *Cailean's* madness lived on as well as his tradi-tions; he was the great-grandfather of that Campbell who com-manded at the massacre of Glencoe a century after Colin's death. It was to be many years after the mad Laird of Glenlyon's exploits before we have another record of an ascent of a mountain in the Central Highlands.

Bandits and Baillies

In the seventeenth century the Highlands were integrated a little more into the mainstream of Scottish life. This was because the largely Royalist clansmen intervened repeatedly in the fifty years of now undeclared, now open, warfare between the Stuart monarchs, attempting to impose royal absolutism, and their Presbyterian, Covenanting enemies in the Lowlands, attempting in turn to limit monarchical pretensions. Opening in 1640 with an uprising against Charles I, this struggle ended with the exile and defeat of James II in 1690. An excellent short and accessible account of this complex period is given in *The Covenanters* by D. Stevenson (1988).

The Civil Wars of the seventeenth century brought many visitors to the Central Highlands, but not – as far as I have been able to discover – any summiteers. The military campaigns of the Marquis of Montrose led his Royalist Highland and Irish armies all over the area, inflicting a series of disastrous defeats on his Covenanting foes in the 1640s. In one of these, he force-marched his army partly over the Corrie Yairack Pass, and then towards Inverlochy, where he enjoyed a comprehensive victory over the Campbells; but there is no suggestion that scouts, still less his army, scaled any summits. A decade later the punitive actions of General Monck, Cromwell's commander in Scotland, led him over similar ground against rebel Royalist Cavaliers, but again without any incidental peak-bagging. Perhaps the most epic tale is that of another Royalist, Claverhouse, after the Revolution of 1688-9 overthrew the Stuarts. 'Bonnie Dundee' as he was later called, left Edinburgh and gained the southern Highlands, traversing the Moor of Rannoch before reaching Lochaber, and re-crossing the Central Highlands to engage the forces of William II at Killiecrankie. Victory here was accompanied by his own death and the defeat soon afterwards of the Royalist army at Dunkeld. This journey was the subject of the epic poem in Latin, the *Grameid* by James Philip. Again, there is no reference to the fugitive Claverhouse, or any of his followers, ascending mountains on this trip. The highest point they attained on their journey north was the pass between Stob Choire Claurigh and Sgurr Innse, where their hair and beards froze stiff with ice in 'Regions never before trodden by the foot of man or horse', according to Philip. ('Bonnie Dundee's Six Weeks in Lochaber' by K. Fforde, in *Transactions of the Gaelic Society of Inverness* Vol LVIII, 1994, p. 272.)

The same paucity of ascents is the case for the conflicts of the Jacobite period in the following century, which were really little more than a postscript to the struggles of the preceding period, and which have been cogently explained in summary form by Bruce Lenman in *The Jacobite Cause* (1986). Now the exiled Stuarts tried to regain their throne with foreign, largely French, help and the use of their power base amongst the Highlanders who were still hated by the Lowlanders as 'bare-arsed banditti' in the words of David Hume, the Edinburgh philosopher. Bonnie Prince Charlie has fairly definite claims to a cluster of first ascents west of the Great Glen (pp. 111-118), during the Rebellion of 1745-6, but in the Central Highlands he was confined to the lower slopes, including a period spent dossing rough in Cluny's cage at Ben Alder; and none of the extant records suggest that the fugitive traversed the summit of Ben Alder or any other mountain in the region, although it is possible he passed through the Window below Creag Meagaidh. (W.B. Blaikie, *The Itinerary of Charles Edward Stuart*, 1897.) In fact, it is well into the eighteenth century before we have any record of a mountain other than Stuchd an Lochain being climbed in the Central Highlands. Not unexpectedly, this mountain was Ben Lomond.

Easily accessible, and prominently visible from the populated Clyde valley, the question must be, why did Ben Lomond not attract pedestrians earlier? The answer lies in the fact that it was the haunt of the bandit MacGregor clan, and this fact even appeared on contemporary maps, such as that of H. Moll. His *The Shire of Lenox* (1724) shows 'Rob Roy's Country' and 'The Lomund Hills' as being co-terminus (even if on the wrong side of the loch, putting them in the territory of the hardly less bandit Macfarlans). The death of Rob Roy, followed by the crushing of the 45 Rebellion, and the arrest of the outlaw's sons – leading to the exile of one and the hanging of the other in 1754 – ended this period of lawlessness, and was soon followed by a tourist influx. And the first tourist ascent of Ben Lomond took place only four years after the execution of Robin Oig MacGregor. However, there is some doubt as to whether this ascent, by companions of William Burrell, in 1758 deserves the laurel of the first ascent, as it is given by Horn (p. 163) and Steven (p. 69).

Walter Macfarlan was a native of Loch Lomondside, and chief of that clan of that name. Amongst other literary researches, he tried to collect historical and topographical information on different parts of Scotland. In his *Geographical Collections* Volume 1, published in

1758, there is an entry dated 1724 from Alexander Graham of Duchray, a gentleman living on the southern margins of the loch – in the Buchanan parish, which stretched northwards to Ben Lomond. Graham suggests that the mountain had been climbed, if not by him, at least by some, or others, who reported their ascent:

> In this paroch is the mountain of Ben Lomond, reckon'd the highest in Scotland, off the top of this mountain in a clear day a person will discover not only the Cape of Kintyre... but also some of the mountains of the County of Donegall in Ireland. (*Geographical Collections*, Vol 1 p. 347)

Though Graham may have climbed the mountain, and I feel he talks from experience not from hearsay, nevertheless the first recorded ascent was Burrell's – or as we shall see, his companions'.

William Burrell (1732-96) was a young Englishman and Cambridge graduate, scion of a landed and mercantile family, and later an M.P., who made a tour of Scotland in 1758, the narrative of which survived in the National Library of Scotland (NLS 2911), and was published while I worked on this book. Burrell travelled with a companion, John Symonds, and two servants, William Beal and John Swan, as we know from his entry in the records at Inveraray when he was granted freedom of the burgh on 2nd September 1758. Burrell had come to view gardens and gentlemen's seats, and did not like mountains, talking of the 'disagreeable mountainous country' between Taymouth and Blair castle. Glen Kinglas was 'horrid, barbarous and disagreeable'. Nevertheless, Burrell left a detailed account of his ascent of the Ben, or rather of the ascent by his trio of companions.

> On the opposite side [of Loch Lomond] stands a mountain of the same name of a prodigious height overshadowing all the neighbouring rocks. The way to it is very irksome and in some places so steep that we were obliged to crawl on hands and knees. From the beginning of the ascent to the summit is five English miles. In several parts we sunk up to our knees in mire. We were fortunate enough to have a fine day and from the top, on one side we could see Edinburgh and Sterling castles at 40 miles distance... About two miles from our landing place we experienced the hospitality of the laird of Blairvochy, who, though a poor farmer and labouring at his harvest, left his work to entertain us with the best fare his cot afforded. It consisted of sour milk and goats' whey... which... we received with greater pleasure..than all the dainties of a palace...

[The laird also] furnished me with a little horse that carried me up to the steep part of the hill (where I was obliged to dismount)... When I got within 100 yards of the top, I had the misfortune to be seized with a dizziness which prevented my quixotism being carried to so great a height as that of my friends, who feasted very heartily on the summit whilst I was descending with the utmost caution or, rather, creeping down on all fours... (*Sir William Burrell's Northern Tour, 1758*, ed. J.G. Dunbar, 1997, pp. 80-2)

Burrell's ascent soon became *de rigueur* for English visitors to Scotland to repeat; Thomas Russel in 1771, and Sir John Stoddart in 1799 both did so and wrote of their experiences. That the Chevalier de Latocnaye was not the first foreigner to climb the hill in 1797 is shown by the comment in Charles Ross's *Travellers Guide to Loch Lomond* (1792) – one of the first Scottish guide books – five years prior to the Frenchman's ascent – that 'In the months of July, August and September, the summit of Ben Lomond is frequently visited by strangers from every quarter of the island, as well as by foreigners' (p. 70). Ross described the route from the south, but noted that the mountain could be climbed 'in perfect safety' from the north, though it was 'steep and rugged'. Many of these ascents were unremarkable, but one which is of historical interest is that of Colonel Hawker in November 1812, which involves the first recorded account of step cutting on ice in Scotland:

To get to the most elevated point of the shoulder we found impossible, as the last fifty yards was a solid sheet of ice, and indeed for the last half mile we travelled in perfect misery and imminent danger. We were literally obliged to take knives and to cut footsteps in the frozen snow, and of course, obliged to crawl all the way on our hands, knees and toes, all of which were benumbed with cold; and were repeatedly in danger of slipping in places where one false step would have been certain destruction... We had some very providential escapes, and on our getting down... my guide told us that, 'had we slipped nothing would have stopped us'. (*The Diary of Colonel Peter Hawker*, 1802-53, 1971 edn. p. 59)

Hawker tells us that it was common for ladies to ascend in a party, and take a piper, for dancing on the summit. Hawker (1786-1853), was from a military family and had fought in the Napoleonic wars; he was mainly interested in slaughtering game, and climbed no more hills in Scotland.

Ben Lomond was soon a honeypot. The paintings of the mountain in 1834 by John Knox, the Glasgow landscape painter, show several tourists on the summit admiring the view – possibly a dozen or so. One of the most interesting ascents of the mountain, one that was *sui generis*, had taken place shortly before, in 1831. It was an election year, the last election before the Reform Bill of 1832 swept away some of the worst excesses of the corrupt British parliamentary system. Glasgow, Dumbarton, Renfrew and Rutherglen chose an M.P. between them, selected by commissioners chosen by the town council of each burgh. One of the candidates was Joseph Dixon, son of the Provost of Dumbarton. Doubtful Rutherglen councillors' wives were showered with gifts by Dixon, and then his father invited fourteen of them to enjoy his hospitality:

> Provost Dixon entertained them lavishly. They were taken up Loch Lomond to Rowardennan, whence they climbed Ben Lomond. Frequent halts were made on the mountain-side to quench their thirst. The summit was reached after great difficulty and many halts for stimulants. A council meeting was then held. A council meeting on Ben Lomond! An incident without parallel! The Rutherglen men renewed their vows of fidelity to Joseph Dixon in flowing bowls of the best champagne. (*On Foot Through Clydesdale*, Iain C. Lees, 1932, p. 5)

Dixon won the election, but was charged with corruption by his opponent. He was admonished on the grounds of a reversal of the Biblical dictum that the sins of the fathers be visited on the children, for in the Judge's view the son could not be held responsible for the actions of his father. And Ben Lomond, from being an inaccessible nest of bandits had, in less than a century, become... an easy day out for a baillie. Bandits... baillies, *plus ça change*...

The Glenorchy Bard

Walter Scott is often held uniquely responsible for the change in perception of the Highlands, with the publication of his historical novels of Jacobitism and his accounts of trips made to the Trossachs and Skye. But it is clear that Scott's writings merely summed up a process that was already underway amongst existing travellers. Scott's books were not the cause of that change. In the career of Duncan Ban MacIntyre, Gaelic poet and mountaineer, the process of the romanticisation of the previously barbaric Highlander is encapsulated. And Duncan was a celebrity long before Scott published *Waverley* in 1815.

Unlike many of the surveyors, geologists, astronomers and others who recorded ascents of the Scottish hills before the mountaineers, the Glenorchy Bard speaks more directly to his modern counterpart, for he saw the mountains as a place for healthy exercise and the appreciation of natural beauty, secondary to any utilitarian or ulterior purpose.

Donnachadh Ban nan Oran, fair-haired Duncan of the Songs is often called the Glenorchy Bard. He was born near, though not in, that glen in 1724, at a place called *Druimliaghart* by Loch Tulla, Argyllshire – now marked by a memorial cairn. He was a crofter's son and married *Mairi Bhan Og*, the daughter of the local innkeeper, living at a place which is now the Inveroran Hotel. He was thrust out of this obscure life and into poetry by the events of the 45.

Duncan's clan was the MacIntyres, or the *Clann an t-saoir*, the race of the carpenters. But like many others in the area, they gradually fell under the influence of the Campbells, especially that of the Earl of Breadalbane, second only in degree to the Dukes of Argyll themselves. When the Argyll Militia was being raised in 45 to oppose the Chevalier, *Donnachadh* was persuaded by pressure from Breadalbane, and a sum of 300 merks (about 17 pounds) from a certain Fletcher – who wanted to avoid military service – to enlist in the latter's stead. Equipped with Fletcher's sword, Duncan finally met up with the Jacobite host at the battle of Falkirk in 1746.

Duncan seems to have been an unaggressive fellow, unenthusiastic about a military calling. And at this time his sympathies appear to have been Jacobite. (He wrote a poem in support of Charlie which was suppressed until the 1848 edition of his works!) At Falkirk, with many others, he departed the field in haste, leaving Fletcher's sword behind, in the face of the Jacobite charge. However, the experience prompted Duncan to compose poetry, and he produced the first of his works, *Blar na h-Eaglaise Brice*, the Battle of Falkirk.

Because of the lost sword, Fletcher refused to pay Duncan the 300 merks, and in his poem the bard cursed the useless sword, which had rusted and would not cut. Taking this as an insult to his own bravery, Fletcher struck Duncan, saying *'Dean oran air sin, a'ghille!'* (Make a song on that, my lad). But Breadalbane made Fletcher pay up, and also installed Duncan as his forester, or gamekeeper, on

Beinn Dorain near Glen Orchy, and on Creag Mhor nearby. For the next 20 years Duncan lived the fairly relaxed life of a forester in Auch Glen (where the ruins of his house remain) below Beinn Dorain – and later in Glen Etive below Buachaille Etive Mor, working for another of the ubiquitous Campbell gentry.

Duncan's duties involved servicing the hunt, but much of the time he simply wandered the hills for pleasure, socialised and composed his poems, the best of which date from this central period in his life. An example of his lifestyle is given by the following anecdote. One day he was lying in bed composing a poem, when he instructed his wife as follows, 'A Mhairi Bhan Og... bi falbh a mach agus cuir tugha air an tigh, tha snigh a tighinn a stigh' (roughly: Fair Mhairi, get out and repair the roof, it is leaking). What a life, what a woman!

Any residual Jacobitism the bard may have had disappeared after Culloden, and anyway, the easy-going Duncan knew which side his bread was buttered on. Thus he began to produce poems which would please his Campbell employers: poems in praise of the ruling dynasty such as Oran do'n Righ (Song to the King) or the powerful Lament for Colin of Glenure (Cumha Chailean Ghleann Iubhair), which concerned the assassination of the so-called Red Fox in 1752 by an unknown Jacobite. A fine lament, there is little doubt of Duncan's sympathy for the victim and hatred for the assassin. The bard praised those who – like Glenure – he felt were lenient in their treatment of the defeated Jacobites, and protested against legislation banning the bagpipe, Highland dress (which he always wore himself) and the Gaelic language, 'Bu mhor am beud gu'm basaicheadh' (Great pity that it should die). Duncan further wrote in praise of the beauty of his wife (he doesn't mention her thatching skills). When someone pointed out that the real article hardly matched up to the praise, he replied, 'Chanfhaca tusa i leis na suilean agamsa' (You have not seen her with my eyes).

Many mountaineers may feel a similar puzzlement in relation to the Glenorchy Bard's other great love, the mountain he sang of in his most famous poem Moladh Beinn Dorain (In Praise of Beinn Dorain). He describes it as follows:

An t-urram thar gach beinn
Aig Beinn-dorain,
De na chunnaic mi fo 'n ghrein,
'S i bu bhoidhche leam.

(Praise over every mountain to Beinn Dorain/ It is the most beautiful mountain I have seen under the sun.) Later in the poem Donnachadh claims it the most beautiful in all of Europe (*Songs of Duncan MacIntyre*, George Calder, 1912, p. 161)

Beinn Dorain is a fine hill, surely. But Duncan spent many years in Glen Etive, under the Buachaille, which would have few rivals in the eyes of today's mountaineers for the crown of beauty. Few would also deny the supreme beauty of Glen Etive, compared to Auch Glen which is a pretty dreich place. Certainly later in life, when in Edinburgh, Duncan did extemporise thus:

Is truagh nach robh mi 'm Buachaill Eitidh
Gu h-aird na sleisde anns an t-sneachd ann...
(I would love to be on the Buachaille, thigh-deep in snow...)

However, this hill did not seem to rate with the poet anywhere near Beinn Dorain. Was it just familiarity breeding contempt, or did even the Bard share the eighteenth-century view of beauty, which would have seen the shapely, rounded form of the Auch mountain as more pleasing than the shattered, dramatic visage of the Glencoe hill?

Moladh Beinn Dorain was, according to Derek Thomson *(An Introduction to Gaelic Poetry,* 1974 p. 187), written sometime between 1750 and 1765, and is the Bard's longest and greatest poem. It is written in the structure of the classical *piobaireachd*, with an *urlar*, or ground, followed by a *siubhal,* or swift movement, with a *crunluadh* finale. The greatness of the poem is not in dispute; but for the mountaineering historian the question must be: did the Glenorchy Bard climb to the summit? Can he claim a First Ascent?

Reading the poem, it contains a fantastic amount of detail about the flora and fauna of the mountain, as well as a host of names of spots the poet had visited, many very high on the mountain. This list includes places not on any OS map, even the original surveys, names whose location is lost, such as *Larach na Feinne, Doire Chro* and *Croabh na h-ainnis*. The poem talks of the finest view in Europe being had *'Air farruin na beinne'*, which, according to Dwelly's *Dictionary,* translates as either on the pinnacle of the mountain, or on the gap between the mountains – enough to drive a researcher to drink! In my opinion, it is extremely unlikely the Bard did not tread the summit ridge of the mountain he immortalised, for work or pleasure, and only the churlish would deny him the mantle of the first ascender of Beinn Dorain. Indeed, another poem, *Coire a' Cheathaich* (Coire of the Mist) describes that corrie, which lies high on Creag Mhor, so that I feel inclined to award Duncan the first ascent of that hill also, which was on his beat. The man who wrote '*S riomhach cota na Creige Moire*' – Lovely is the coat of Creag Mhor – had surely been there to see it.

Duncan at this time knew almost no English, though he picked up some later in Edinburgh. His lack of English did not trouble him; apparently someone once told him he was studying a newspaper upside down, to which Duncan replied with magisterial disdain, 'To a scholar it does not matter which way up you hold the paper'. The Bard was also illiterate in Gaelic, though he could recite his own verses, all 7,000 of them, by heart. His first volume of poems was published in 1768 to great acclaim, but brought little money. Like many other Highlanders he gravitated to the Lowlands for economic security. In the later 1760s he joined the Edinburgh City Guard, in which he served, apart from a brief period in the Army, until 1806. The easy life of the City Guard, where his wife was a cook, suited him, as doubtless did the fact that the Guard was composed almost entirely of ageing Highlanders who did not take their duties of policing Auld Reekie too seriously, preferring to consume Mairi's illicit whisky with her husband instead.

While in Edinburgh Duncan continued to compose songs and poems, but few would claim that overall they have the quality of his earlier verse. He continued also to visit the Highlands, and composed laments on the changes he saw coming, particularly the clearance of the glens for sheep and the displacement of the people, and 'our land put out of cultivation'. He savages the sheep economy in his poem, *Oran nan Balgairean* (Song to the Foxes):

> Mo bheannachd aig na balgairean
> A chionn bhi sealg nan caorach.
> (My praise on the foxes, for they take the sheep.)
> (Calder, p. 371)

But there is one great poem of his later years which mountaineers would probably prefer over *Beinn Dorain*. This is the Last Farewell to the Bens (*Cead Deireannach nam Beann*), composed when he was an old man in 1802. (Calder, pp. 407-13.) In the poem the Bard matches the magic and beauty of the mountains against the knowledge of physical decline, and this gives the poem, in my opinion, an intellectual muscle that is lacking in his other verse. The mountains may be eternal, but we are not. He begins by telling us that *'Bha mi 'n de 'm Beinn Dorain'* (Yesterday I was on Beinn Dorain). Though we know that 'yesterday' in the poem was 19th September 1802, Duncan still does not say if he ascended to the summit on this last occasion – though I would like to think he did, 'gazing over the mountains and glens that he knew'. He talks of the beauty and health-giving qualities of the mountains:

> Chuidich e gu fas mi
> 'S e rinn domh slaint is fallaineachd.
> (They helped me grow in health and strength.)

But the people have gone from the glens, the world is teeming with sheep. The poet's eyes are failing, his teeth are rotting, and *'O'n chaill mi trian na h-analach'* (I've lost a third of my breathing ability). He knows that this is his last farewell, he will see the mountains no more. Every mountaineer who reads this poem, aware of his own mortality in the face of the hills, knows that *Donnachadh Ban* was not simply a splendid poet and a fine human being, but a fellow mountaineer. A man who would understand without hesitation why we pursue our – to so many – pointless activity. A man who saw the mountains with our eyes.

Donnachadh died in 1812 and is buried in Greyfriar's Kirkyard in Edinburgh. A modest man, he was once asked if it were he who had made Beinn Dorain. 'No', he replied, 'God made Beinn Dorain, but I praised it.' Let us praise him, whose name is forever linked with that mountain.

The Jacobite Cleansers... and the Tourists

There was a Jacobite/Hanoverian connection to the career of Duncan MacIntyre, and in this his story was not untypical of the period. Many of the mountain explorers of the eighteenth century were soldiers, surveyors or engineers in the anti-Jacobite 'cleansing' which, in addition to making the Highlands a safe place for women and Whigs, added greatly to the knowledge of the region, and prepared the way for the pleasure-seeking traveller. However, not many of these cleansers saw the romantic side of the Highlands.

The Hanoverian connection is especially marked in the case of Ben Nevis, which was already suspected by many in the eighteenth century of being Britain's highest mountain, though Macdhui in the Cairngorms also had its devotees. In 1811 the Rev. Keith conducted barometric experiments, which appeared to establish the superiority of the Lochaber mountain over its nearest rival, but these were disputed, and it was not until further measurements were made by Colonel Winzer of the Ordnance Survey on Ben Nevis and Macdhui in 1846 and 1847 respectively that Nevis was finally awarded the laurel. Winzer stated, 'Ben Nevis has the advantage by at least 100 feet of height'. (*Account of the Observations and Calculations of the Principal Triangulation*, 1858, p. 555), We are fortunate in this case of having a splendid biography of the Ben, written by Ken Crocket, *Ben Nevis* (1986). This book, on the history and pre-history of mountaineering on the mountain, also looks at geology, flora and fauna, and social history. It is a model work, and it is rather to be regretted that it is the only real contribution to the subject from the Scottish Mountaineering Club.

The Ben was early known, being marked as *Bin Nevesh* on Pont's sketches, and in Blaeu's publication of maps by Gordon of Straloch based on Pont, in 1654. An initial reference to the possibility of the mountain being ascended occurs in a letter of the Jacobite agent, Drummond of Balhaldy, to the Jacobite chief Lochiel, about 1737, where Drummond describes the summit as being covered with perpetual snow. But the first recorded attempt on the mountain had taken place several years before this date, by some of Drummond and Lochiel's Hanoverian enemies.

Edward Burt was the name, or pseudonym, of a man who was General Wade's agent and surveyor in the Highlands. As well as building roads, Wade collected intelligence information, and Burt was probably involved in that work. Though cartographic representations of the mountains and lochs of the Highlands were still vague and inaccurate, mental intelligence maps showed greater sophistication. In the Map Library of the British Library (K. Top 48.12) is a *Description of the Highlands of Scotland*, (1731), after C. Lemprière, produced for Wade. It is rough-and-ready geographically, but shows the location of all the main clans, the military force at their disposal and their Jacobite or Hanoverian inclinations. The Rebellion of 1745 replicated in almost every detail the allegiances of this map, so Burt and his like had 'done good'. Burt wrote a series of letters to a

London friend in 1725-6, which were published in 1754 under the title, *Letters from a Gentleman in the North of Scotland*, just before the author's death in 1755. Like his fellow countryman and intelligence agent, Defoe – whom he probably knew – Burt was no mountain-lover, describing the mountains as 'monstrous Excrescences' (p. 36) and their summits as consisting of 'huge naked Rocks... producing the disagreeable Appearance of a scabbed Head.' In particular, he disliked the hills when the heather was in bloom, which in his view produced nothing but monotony. The height of the mountain aroused his professional interest as a surveyor, and he quoted with support previous estimates of the height of 'that Part of the Summit only which appears to View' as being 'found to be three-Quarters of a Mile of perpendicular Height' (p. 34). Three quarters of a mile is just under 4,000 ft, and given that the real summit, as Burt points out, is higher than the visible summit, this was a pretty good estimation.

Despite his mountainphobia, Burt nevertheless left us an account of an attempt on Nevis by some of the garrison at Fort William – possibly as a warning to others to discourage further assaults. Burt's disapproval of the officers' fancy for their 'wild expedition' shows through, as does his lack of interest in the fact that they saw 'nothing' but the tops of other mountains. The attempt is undated, but must have lain between 1715 and 1725-6, and might have been related to Burt directly by those involved.

> Some English Officers took it in their Fancy to go to the Top, but could not attain it for Bogs and huge perpendicular Rocks; and when they got as high as they could go, they found a vast Change in the Quality of the Air, saw nothing but the Tops of other Mountains, and altogether a Prospect of one tremendous Heath, with here and there some Spots of Crags of Snow. This Wild Expedition..took them up a whole Summer's day, from Five in the Morning. This is according to their own relation. But they were fortunate in an Article of the greatest Importance to them, i.e., that the Mountain happened to be free from Clouds while they were on it, which is a Thing not common in that dabbled (*moist*, IM) part of the Island, the Western Hills; – I say, if those condensed Vapours had passed while they were at any considerable Height, and had continued, there would have been no means left for them to find their Way down, and they must have perished with Cold, Wet, and Hunger. (*Letters*... Vol II, 1974 edn. p. 34-5)

Where did the officers get to? By the description of 'huge per-pendicular Rocks', one is tempted to think they passed into Coire Leis: plenty of 'Bogs' there too. They also ascended high enough to see the tops of other mountains; could they have attained the col between Carn Mor Dearg and Ben Nevis itself, whence they would have seen summits a-plenty?

Nevis did not have to wait overlong for its first ascent, and again there is an anti-Jacobite aspect. After the Rebellion, many estates of leading Jacobites were forfeit to the Crown, and Commissioners appointed to run them; which they did with much more efficiency than their previous owners had done. One of the tasks the Commissioners set themselves was ascertaining the mineralogical and agricultural potential of the estates. A letter of 1769 from John Hope, Professor of Botany in the University of Edinburgh, mentions one of those acting for the Commissioners:

> Mr James Robertson is an eleve of mine, and has been employed by the commissioners of the annexed estates to make a botanical survey of the distant parts of Scotland. (Letter to W. Watson, *Phil. Trans Royal Soc.*, 1769 No. 59, p. 242)

Presumably Robertson had been a student at Edinburgh before taking up his field work, though little is known of him; Crocket says he later emigrated and found work with the East India Company. Robertson is a great believer in progress, and constantly comment-ing on opportunities for economic improvement in the Highlands, while criticising the superstitions and laziness of the inhabitants. After his explorations of the Cairngorms (see pp. 75-6), Robertson crossed from Badenoch to the area of the Great Glen, where he muses upon the utility of constructing a canal, 'An expense that may be termed trifling when compared with the unspeakable advantage of the effect' (NLS 2508, p.130). He also climbed Ben Nevis for the first recorded time on 19th August, 1771, noting briefly:

> I ascended Ben Nevis which is reckoned the highest mountain in Britain. A third part of the hill towards the top is entirely naked, resembling a heap of stones thrown together confusedly. The sum-mit far overtops the surrounding hills. (NLS 2508, p. 131-2)

That is all Robertson had to say about his achievement. He was a Whig, and a bit of a Prig as well, so it is refreshing to find him commenting at much greater length on a Highland wedding he was invited to, where copious amounts of whisky were consumed by all, including Robertson, whose tongue is loosened enough to comment on the attractions of the bride who was, 'a buxom, blithe widow of thirty'. Indeed he was, while critical of their uncivilised ways, always willing to celebrate 'the hospitality of the Highlander, a quality in which they are outdone by no people on earth' (p. 88).

Leaving Fort William, Robertson travelled over Rannoch Moor, which 'had the appearance of a forsaken waste', before visiting John Stuart, the minister at Killin. With Stuart he climbed 'Craig callich' on Tarmachan, and a hill called 'Corrivan Drivach, between Meggernie & Ranach' (p. 142), in pursuit of botanical samples, which they found in abundance. But there is a paucity of detail in Robertson's Breadalbane wanderings to credit him with any definite ascents of a first nature. Interestingly, many of the botanical treasures which Robertson found in profusion on the slopes of Tarmachan are 'on the verge of extinction' according to the NTS magazine *Heritage Scotland* (Vol 14, 1997, No. 4 p. 16), due to centuries of poor land use, especially the grazing of sheep.

Three years after Robertson, another agent for the Commissioners, John Williams, ascended Ben Nevis to see if there were any mineral reserves of exploitable value on it. He was able to report that there were not, and gave the first geological account of the mountain, mentioning that it rose from a base of 'elegant red granite'. He also estimated its perpendicular height at about a mile, making it well over 5,000 ft in his view. A party led by Lieutenant Walker, stationed at Fort William, repeated the ascent in military fashion in 1787, with grappling irons and rum, and found thirty small cairns on the summit, indicating theirs was not the first ascent since Williams'. Though there would still be a garrison at Fort William for many years, the Jacobite threat was long extinct by 1787.

The same year of 1787 saw probably the first pure tourist ascent of Nevis, by a Thomas Wilkinson from Westmoreland, where he did most of his walking, and where he was a friend of Wordsworth. Wilkinson was accompanying John Pemberton the Quaker on a tour of Scotland, and had already climbed Ben Lomond in 1 hour and 38 minutes, though he had not managed Cruachan. Nevis impressed Wilkinson as 'sublimely dreadful' and 'hung with terrors' on its north side (*Tours to the British Mountains*, 1824, p. 63). The poet John Keats ascended the mountain in 1818 with the help of a guide and whisky, and wrote a poem at the summit. Though not a great work, this poem is interesting in that it shows the beginning of the usage of the mountain environment as a metaphor for mental states:

All my eye doth meet
Is mist and Crag – not only on this height
But in the world of thought and mental might...
(Qu. in Crocket, Op. Cit. p. 9)

By Keats' time Ben Nevis had become, with Ben Lomond, the hill most visitors sought to climb, and a regular tourist industry had built up in the town of Fort William. One aspect of this was the appearance of guides, both two-legged and written. Peter and George Anderson were the authors of a *Guide to the Highlands and Islands of Scotland*, which appeared in 1827. It informed the reader that:

The ascent of Ben Nevis usually occupies three hours and a half from the base of the mountain, and the descent rather more than half that time. (1834 edn. p. 268)

However, more useful was the information that the traveller should pay no more than seven or eight shillings for a guide in Fort William (an enormous sum of money for a local peasant), and that he or she should take plentiful spirits with them, to 'qualify' the hill water! Carrying spirits and hiring a guide seemed to be commonplace on Nevis at this time. But not all guides were reliable, as John MacCulloch found. In his *Highlands and Western Islands of Scotland* (1824) he describes how, arriving at the summit he and his guide were caught by a snowstorm (on 20th August!), and the guide offered to return his fee, if MacCulloch could lead them off the mountain, which he did by the use of a compass bearing. MacCulloch mentions that his guide's 'kilt was thoroughly cooled' by the experience, but does not say whether 'the poor animal' as he described his guide, forfeited his fee.

One of the more interesting accounts of the ascent of Nevis was of an early one, or possibly a series of ascents, by the Rev. Alex Fraser, minister of Kilmallie, the parish which contains the mountain. A description of Nevis is the largest single item in the clergyman's contribution to the *Statistical Account,* which he submitted in 1792 (Vol XVII, pp 122-6). The man of the cloth describes the ascent by roughly the present tourist route, and at every stage in the process of ascent gives a detailed account of what can be seen. This indicates that he had probably climbed the mountain several times, to obtain such views, and also his wide knowledge of the neighbouring mountains, amongst which he names the Paps of Jura, Cuillin hills, Ben Cruachan, Ben Lawers, and Ben Wyvis. He had read John Williams' book, which described the geology of the mountain of which Fraser was immensely proud, commenting:

> Could one pass a night in October on the summit of Benevis, it is probable that he would discover the heavenly bodies in greater splendour, than upon Mount Blanc itself. The latter it is true is much higher, but the former is in a colder climate, and consequently, when fair, in a less shaded sky (p. 125)

The good Reverend would doubtless have been delighted by the establishment a century later of the Nevis Observatory. The reference to Mont Blanc is in all probability because the acute clergyman was aware of the French mountain's fame, following the first ascent by Balmat and Paccard in 1786, showing an early internationalisation of mountain culture. Fraser ends his account of the mountain with a delightful juxtaposition of the sacred and profane, the spirit and the flesh, variations of which we have all felt on Ben Nevis and other hills.

> The traveller, who is so callous, as to behold all this, and not feel the greatness and majesty of the ALMIGHTY ARCHITECT impressed upon his heart, must indeed be strangely devoid of sense, of taste, of sentiment... Few can perform a journey to the top of Benevis... without feeling, in their limbs, the effects of the fatigue, for a day or two after (p. 126)

Scientific Studies

We have lingered long on Ben Nevis. Let us proceed to other peaks, and look at some more ascents, arising from the most varied of motives. One of the strangest of these was to measure the density of the earth... The Astronomer Royal, Nevil Maskeleyne, acted upon the proposal of the Royal Society to conduct experiments on Schiehallion in 1774, the mountain being chosen for its accessibility and distance from other mountains which would simplify calculations. Many years later Maskeleyne was to talk rather ungraciously of his trip to Scotland as follows:

My going to Scotland was not a matter of choice, but of necessity. The Royal Society...made a point with me to go there to take the direction of the experiment, which I did, not without reluctance, nor from any wish to depart from my own observatory to live on a barren mountain, but purely to serve the Society and the public, for which I received no gratuity, and had only my expenses paid for me. (*Nevil Maskeleye, the seaman's astronomer*, D. Howse, 1989, Qu. p. 138-9)

Maskeleyne spent four months on the mountain, working firstly at a bothy-observatory on the south side of the mountain, then at one on the northern slopes. From these he observed the gravitational attraction of the mountain on plumb lines, and according to the memorial plaque at the foot of the mountain, this 'became the first determination of Newton's Universal Gravitational Constant'. The whole expedition cost the Royal Society £597 16s, and was a great success. In his calculations of his expenses, the Astronomer did not include the cost of the farewell party, which was quite an event by all accounts. A certain Duncan Robertson, who was a cook and cleaner, was sent to Kinloch Rannoch for supplies of whisky, and supplied lively fiddle music at the farewell shindig. However, as will happen, the hut caught fire and the fiddle was destroyed. Maskeleyne told the fiddler, 'Never mind, Duncan, when I get back to London, I will seek you out a new fiddle and send it to you', and he was as good as his word, sending him a Stradivarius. Duncan subsequently composed an air, *A' Bhan Lunnainneach Bhuidhe*, the Yellow London Lady, in honour of the new instrument. However, in his paper to the august Royal Society the next year, 1775, Maskeleyne summarised his scientific findings – but did not mention the fiddle. It is not clear if Maskeleyne himself climbed Schiehallion, though Horn states that the scientist's assistants erected cairns on the summit ridge (Op. Cit. p. 169). What we do know, however, is that amongst the many visitors Maskeleyne entertained on the mountain during his residency, at least one did ascend to the summit, there making observations of his own.

William Roy was born in 1726, the son of a factor in Lanarkshire. Though in his lifetime he was most famous as an antiquarian of Roman Britain, Roy has a vital role in the evolution of Scottish cartography. Cumberland had been aware of how poor the maps of Scotland were in his campaign of 1745-6, and ordered a Military Survey to be carried out of Scotland on the crushing of the Rebellion. From 1747-55 General Roy was in charge of this survey, which covered all of mainland Scotland, his draughtsman being the artist Paul Sandby. Though they were still quite primitive, Roy's maps were an improvement on what had gone before, especially as regards communications and settlement patterns; he was characteristically modest in his own estimation of his work as 'rather... a magnificent military sketch, than a very accurate map'. (Roy, quoted in Y. O'Donoghue, *William Roy 1726-90*, 1977, p. 16.) There were no lines of latitude or longitude on Roy's maps (though Gordon had them a century earlier on his), and there were no heights given of the mountains, with hachures providing a crude forerunner of contour lines – the latter still a century away. The illustration showing Schiehallion, a mountain he was later intimately connected with, gives a good example of his map craft. Despite the limitations of his work, today Roy is rightly regarded as the pioneer of the Ordnance Survey. His maps were not published in his lifetime, though a large-scale one was printed in his *Military Antiquities of the Romans in North Britain* (1793), and Aaron Arrowsmith published maps based on Roy's work in 1807. (See R.A. Skelton, 'The Military Survey of Scotland 1747-1755' in *Scottish Geographical Magazine* 1967, Vol 83.) Roy's motives were as he explained, military ones:

> The rise and progress of the rebellion which broke out in the Highlands of Scotland in 1745... convinced Government... that a country so very inaccessible by nature, should be thoroughly explored and laid open... (Qu. Skelton, p. 5)

Although many more hills are named than in Gordon's maps of the previous century, it is debatable whether Roy ascended any mountains on his Survey, indeed it was done with such speed that he would have had little time. If Roy did ascend a ben or two while making his cartographic contributions to opening up the Highlands, he left no record of such ascents. My own inquiries in relation to the British Museum Map Library, Public Records Office, Ordnance Survey archives and the records of Roy's regiment, the Royal Engineers, all located nothing in Roy's hand relating to his period in Scotland on the Military Survey. Skelton (Loc. Cit.) mentions that the logs and field books of the surveyors who went with Roy have also been lost. Moreover, Skelton also records that the map-maker Arrowsmith, interviewing some of Roy's associates half a century later, was told that the surveyors had followed river and burn courses, mapping ground detail, and estimating other features such as mountains by eye – which might suggest that few of the larger hills were climbed.

Roy was, however, interested in estimating heights by barometric methods, though his work in this area was carried on much later than that for the Military Survey, i.e. from 1771-76. In 1777 Roy submitted a rather long-winded paper with a long title to the *Philosophical Transactions of the Royal Society*. It was called 'Experiments and Observations made in Britain in order to obtain a Rule for measuring heights with the barometer' (PTRS 1777, LXVII, Pt. II). In it he comments on his visit to Maskeleyne, and his ascent of Schiehallion:

> In 1774, when the Astronomer Royal was carrying on the Society's experiments for ascertaining the attraction of Schihallion, I found, from my own geometrical operations... the western summit of the mountain to be 1,183 feet above the South observatory (Loc. Cit. p. 721).

He gives an estimated height for the hill of 3,281 ft (3,547 actual). Roy had climbed Snowdon and Tinto, but it is very difficult to state exactly which Scottish mountains other than Schiehallion he climbed – and which were climbed by junior officers under his command, or civilian co-workers. It is clear from Roy's own account that the Table of Barometrical Observations he gives on p. 785 of his article, is a compilation of those made by other people.

> To the British observations a table is annexed, containing the barometrical computations of altitudes not yet determined geometrically. In the chief part of these the inferior barometer stood at Belmont Castle, the seat of the Lord Privy-Seal for Scotland, by whose directions the corresponding observations were made. The table likewise comprehends Mr. Bank's observations in 1772 for the height of the South-pap of Jura, above Freeport [*sic*] in the island of Isla... *(Experiments and Observations... p. 762)*

However, if he did not actually take part in them, Roy is responsible for the first recorded ascents of, and barometric measurements of, Ben Lawers on 17th September 1776, and Ben Gloe (*sic*) five days previously. That more than one party was involved in these ascents and measurements is almost certain from the fact that the 17th September also saw an ascent, though not the first, of Ben More in Perthshire, and computation of its height, as well as of

Lawers. Ascending both peaks would be beyond a single party in one day. I think 'party of Gen. Roy' would be an acceptable form of words for the recording of these original ascents, of which no details, bar the dates and computed heights in the Table appended to Roy's article, remain.

When Roy's party ascended Lawers, they would undoubtedly have passed the extensive shieling systems whose ruins today are scattered over the mountain, and which then would have been in constant usage for transhumance. The sheer extent of the hut system on this mountain makes it scarcely credible that locals did not ascend some if not all of the tops on the Lawers range, for work or play when 'at the shieling'. Many Lawers shielings are particularly high; those below Lochan nan Cat, for example, are well over 2,000 ft, whence it is an easy walk to the summits.

It is interesting that Maskeleyne does not come across as a mountain-lover. He went to Schiehallion reluctantly, and was glad to get back to London. Neither is there much praise of nature amongst Roy's scientific pre-occupations. Though change in perception was occurring, mountains were still seen as hostile, to be tamed if possible. This is exemplified by a canvas of Ben Lawers, painted shortly before Roy and Maskeleyne were in Breadalbane. It was painted in 1741 for the Duke of Hamilton by R. Norie (1711-76), one of Scotland's first professional painters, who aimed to 'raise the standard of Scottish painting'. The painting, which is in Holyrood House, certainly raised the standard of Scottish mountains. What is most remarkable is not that Lawers ends up looking like the Matterhorn, rather than a big lump, but that the foreground is occupied by an Italianate composition of nymphs, shepherdesses and classical ruins with exotic foreign trees. *This* is how most people liked their mountains in the mid-eighteenth century, and how they tried to see them. This work by Norie is probably the first actual representation of Scottish mountains in painting. As has been stated,

> The mountains of Scotland were never painted before the middle of the eighteenth century. Where possible, they were avoided. (*The Discovery of Scotland; The Appreciation of Scottish Scenery through Two Centuries of Painting*, James Holloway and Lindsay Errington, 1978, p. 3)

Previous artists, such as the Dutchman John Slezer, whose *Theatrum Scotiae* appeared in the later seventeenth century, had avoided the Highlands altogether, outlining only the hills behind

Dunkeld in one drawing. The mountains were not painted because no one wanted to look at them, regarding them, as did John Clerk of Penicuik the Grampians, as 'nothing but a barbarous tracts of mountains... (with nothing)... to entertain our views as in other places southward.' The appearance of Norie's works, with those of later artists like David Allan, who put mountains in as backdrops to his paintings, indicate that taste was changing.

It would still take a later, Romantic eye to see anything beautiful about Ben Lawers on a dreich Scottish day, unless it were to be the sight of rare flowers in the eye of a botanist.

John Hope, Professor of Botany at Edinburgh, had been partly responsible for organising the journeys of James Robertson, already mentioned. Hope was also responsible for introducing John Stuart to the botanist Lightfoot, which meeting had a big impact on Scottish mountain exploration. The latter (1735-88) was an Anglican curate and chaplain to the Dowager Duchess of Portland, as well as an eminent botanist, who published his two-volume *Flora Scotica* in 1777. The former (1743-1821) was a Presbyterian minister, who wrote the contribution on Luss to the *Old Statistical Account*. This shows his interests by including, along with the economic and historical materials, a table of all the animals, birds, reptiles and fish found in the parish. Stuart also translated the Old Testament into Gaelic (*Fasti*, Vol 3, p.360).

Lightfoot had been with Pennant (see p. 155) on his trip to Scotland in 1772, studying Scottish flora, and he made several journeys in the ensuing years with Stuart, to further his knowledge. As he himself acknowledged in the preface to his work:

> To the Rev. Mr. Stuart, late of Killin in Breadalbane, now of Luss, in the county of Dumbarton, I am indebted for every assistance... The young gentleman, a most accurate observer of Nature's works and critically versed in the Erse language... I had the good fortune to share as a fellow traveller and companion... (*Flora Scotica*. Vol I. p. XII-XIII)

They travelled widely, including visits to the islands of Rum and Skye, but their most favoured locations appear to have been Breadalbane, which Stuart knew intimately, the area around Loch Broom in Wester Ross, and the Glenelg peninsula in Inverness-shire. These men were botanists first and foremost, and it would be wise to exercise caution in attributing ascents to them, on the basis of their simply being in an area. They talk of bunting, hares and ptarmigans occupying 'the highest summits', but this does not prove they were there, as hearsay would suffice for this intelligence. Neither does the recorded occurrence of Dwarf Honeysuckle, '...on the sides of highland mountains... in Athol, about Loch Rannoch, on Ben-Mor and Chialleach in Breadalbane, and in Ross-Shire on the mountains about Loch Broom...' (*Flora* Vol 1, p.119) prove they were anywhere near the tops. However, a close examination of the thousand-page volumes of Lightfoot's work does prove that he ascended many summits, and that Stuart ascended many more and reported his findings to Lightfoot. What follows should be of especial interest to gardeners.

The Trailing Thyme-leaved Azalea was found:

> Upon dry barren ground near the summits of the highland mountains in many places, as on Ben-Mor in Breadalbane, Ben Crochan in Argyleshire, Ben-na-scree and other high mountains about Loch Urn in Invernesshire... (Vol 1, p. 140)

Leaving Ben More (which had been climbed), we have (possibly) the first recorded ascent of Cruachan (*Crochan*), and a possible ascent of Ben Sgriol. The case for the latter is strengthened by a later find, of the Trifid Rush, which Lightfoot records.

> I have found... upon the summits of the highland mountains to the South of Little Loch Broom in Rosshire, and on Ben-na-scree, above Arnesdal on the side of Loch Urn in Invernesshire (Vol 1, p. 184)

What the mountains to the south of Little Loch Broom are, we do not know, but he asserts he climbed 'about two-thirds of the way up' (p. 199) to get Alpine Willow Herb, and that 'almost at the summits' (p. 201) he found Bilberry.

But we have strayed from the Central Highlands; let us return there. *Dryas Octopetala*, the Mountain Aven, is given a location or two by Lightfoot before he mentions that, 'It has likewise been found by my oft-mention'd friend, Mr. Stuart, upon the top of Carndearg, one of the lower heads of Ben-sguilert, a high mountain in Glen Creran...' (Vol 1, p. 275). The Alpine Cudweed occurs 'upon the tops of highland mountains... as... upon Mal-ghyrdy...' (Vol 1, p. 471), while 'Upon the top of Mal-ghyrdy' (Vol 1, p. 1100) Mr Stuart found Two-flowered Rush. Further, regarding Saffron Lichen, 'We are indebted to Mr Stuart for the discovery of this rare Lichen, who found it upon a rock near the top of Benteskeney in Breadalbane'

(Vol 1, p.856). Finally, the Alpine Soft Thistle can be found, 'near the top of Ben cruipen, in Breadalbane... (and) upon Ben-achalader and Ben-dotha in Glenorchy...' (Vol 1, p. 448). What can we make of all this?

Stuart and Lightfoot have, I think, a cast-iron claim to Ben Sgriol, though the mountains south of Little Loch Broom cannot, with any degree of certainty, be identified as An Teallach. Stuart has a reasonable claim to Ben Sgulaird, and definitely climbed Meall Ghaordaidh and Benteskeney, which I believe is Beinn Heasgarnich. Beinn Achaladair and Ben Dothaidh are possible, though not – from the evidence – definite, lacking the 'at the top' or 'near the summit' riders. However, there is one astonishing ascent, undertaken by Stuart without Lightfoot. In describing Alpine Hawkweed, Lightfoot mentions that it is to be found:

> In dry soil near the summits of the highland mountains... (and) near the top of Bedan-nam-bian, the highest mountain in Glenco, being according to the observations of the ingenious Mr. Stuart, 3,150 feet above the level of the sea... (Vol 1, p. 435).

'Near' is not the top, and methods of estimating height from the base of a hill existed at this time, but doubts are dispelled when we move on to Lightfoot waxing eloquent about the location of *Anthericum calyculatum*, which can be spotted:

> About Corry-na-beich, a rocky bason in the ascent of Bedan-nam-bian, the highest mountain in Glenco, which according to Mr. Stuart's observations, is 3,150 feet above the level of the sea (Vol II, p. 1,120).

Stuart's measurements may be wildly out, underestimating the hill by more than 500 feet, but the use of the word 'ascent' by Lightfoot indicates that Stuart climbed Bidean – and by the route of Corrie nam Beith, no easy stroll – for botanical purposes, and to estimate its height – probably barometrically. And it must have been Bidean that Stuart climbed; no eye could confuse any of the outlying peaks of the massif as being higher, with the exception of Stob Coire nan Lochan, which would have been an equally impressive achievement in the 1770s. It was to be half a century before MacCulloch's ascent of An Teallach (pp. 128-130) would equal Stuart's of Bidean.

Exploits of a Bagger

As with Roy, there is an OS connection with John MacCulloch (1773-1835), who probably deserves the title of Scotland's first peak bagger, and was the self-proclaimed hero of the snowstorm on Ben Nevis already mentioned. MacCulloch was born in Guernsey, but his father was of Gallovidian stock, and early holidays were spent in Scotland. He studied medicine at Edinburgh University, as so many from south of the border did then, and remained in Scotland a while, becoming a friend of Sir Walter Scott. After a period working in the south he was appointed by the Board of Ordnance to conduct experiments in Scotland, and determine on which mountains Maskeleyne's experiments might be repeated. Shortly afterwards he obtained the post of geologist to the Trigonometrical Survey, and made yearly scientific trips to Scotland from 1811 until 1821, being later commissioned to produce a geological map of Scotland. But his main mountaineering interest lies in his four volume *Highlands and Western Islands of Scotland*, published in 1824. This is part guide/gazetteer, and part account of his mountaineering feats, of which he was – some might say, inordinately – proud. In a canny marketing move, he addressed the book to the Abbotsford Wizard. (For MacCulloch's life and work, see *Dictionary of National Biography*, Vol XII pp. 461-3.)

MacCulloch claimed, 'I have ascended almost every principal mountain in Scotland', and by that he meant what were regarded as the notable peaks, the ones worth bagging, rather than claiming to be a pre-Munro Munroist. Many of his ascents were not firsts, as for example that of Ben Nevis. He followed the well-worn tourist trek up Ben Lomond, ('many a time I have sat on its topmost stone'), and he ascended Ben More in Perthshire, ('the ascent is so easy as to permit riding to the top'). The latter was not a first ascent, the hill having been climbed by an anonymous party of astronomers as far back as 1769, to observe the transit of Venus. (G. Fennel Robson *Scenery of the Grampian Mountains,* 1814, Illust. 17, Ben More). The geologist also repeated Roy's ascent of Schiehallion, and other hills. However, in the Central Highlands as elsewhere in Scotland, MacCulloch added several new peaks to his tally of touristic repeats.

MacCulloch made the first recorded ascent of Ben Chonzie, in Perthshire. He gives little information on it, or on his more impressive ascent of Ben Vorlich above Arrochar, apart from saying that:

There is a fine view also... from the summit of Ben Vorlich, an elevation not much inferior to that of Ben Lomond itself. (*Highlands*... Vol 1 p. 220)

MacCulloch also 'wandered (the) recesses' of the Perthshire Ben Vorlich, but does not mention climbing it. And he is irritatingly coy about his – quite impressive – pioneering ascent of Beinn a' Bheithir above Ballachulish, which must have been a little taxing logistically.

The ascent of Ben-na-vear, on the south side of the ferry, is not difficult, though long, as it is a lofty mountain. (Op. Cit. p. 314)

MacCulloch gives peaks, but not dates; all we can say is that these ascents took place between 1811 and the early 1820s. One mountain MacCulloch viewed as a plum, as had many others, was Ben Cruachan, and he is usually awarded the first recorded ascent. This mountain attracted notice early, and it is one of the first Scottish hills to be mentioned in any written source by name. In John Barbour's *The Bruce*, an epic poem on the Wars of Independence written in the late fourteenth century, the author describes King Robert's passage of the mountain, (though neither here, nor in the King's other wanderings, e.g. in the Grampians, is there a suggestion that he ascended the summits):

On athyr halff ye montane was
Swa combrows hey and stay,
Yat it was hard to pas yat way;
Crechinben hecht yat montane
I trow nocht yat in all Bretane
Ane heyar hill may fundyne be.
(*The Bruce* Vol 11, p. 240 ed. M. McDiarmid and J. Stevenson, 1980)

MacCulloch makes up for his previous reticence by the verbosity with which he describes his ascent of Ben Cruachan, or rather the gastronomic circumstances preceding it. Note that, as with his contemporaries, it was the view that was most important for MacCulloch – very few pioneers give details as to their actual route. However, the geologist's breakfast occupies more space than his day on the hill, and we include, with his ascent of Cruachan, his account of Highland inns before the mountaineers – though some might say they had hardly improved a century and a half later.

The ascent of Cruachan is tedious, but not difficult; and, from its position no less than its altitude, it presents some of the finest and most extensive mountain views in Scotland... From the bold, rugged precipices of its sharp and rugged summit, which is literally a point, we look down its red and furrowed sides into the upper part of Loch Etive... (*Highlands*... Vol 1 p. 267)

There follows an account of the view, and a comparison of those from Lawers and Lomond, which I will spare the reader, then MacCulloch gets his teeth into his subject:

The morning is fine, it is seven o'clock, and you are in a hurry to depart for the top of Cruachan which you know will occupy you for nine or ten hours... You order (your breakfast) immediately... having ordered it the previous night, to be ready at six, having ordered it again when you got up an hour before. After ringing, stamping and knocking three times, up comes a bare-footed woman... 'Aye', she says, 'it is breakfast you was wanting'... All this time the sun is shining temptingly bright on the summit of Cruachan, as it may not shine again for six months, and another period of patience is passed... (Op. Cit. p. 268-9)

A tea-pot 'never washed since it issued from the furnace' eventually arrives, with a tea-canister 'holding a mixture of black dust'. Meanwhile, the fire goes out. MacCulloch is temporarily cheered by 'a delicious herring, hot from the fire', though there is no cutlery to eat it with. But normal service is resumed with damp sugar and curdled milk. The traveller asks for bread for the umpteenth time, to be greeted with a surprised, 'Is it bread you was wanting?' Finally 'a musty damp loaf' arrives, and butter 'pulled out of a pot by her fingers' to eat the bread with.

You depart for the top of Cruachan, and arrive just with a cloud that remains there the whole day, and will probably remain till you come this way again. (Op. Cit. p. 270)

Though often credited with the pioneering ascent of Cruachan, it is doubtful if MacCulloch was the first to gain its summit. Even if we say there is no proof that Stuart and Lightfoot gained the very highest eminence of the hill, there is a reliable report that someone had done so before the disgruntled breakfaster.

Painting the Mental Picture

There were many other tourist guides beginning to appear around the time MacCulloch produced his, which – in my opinion – is the best of the bunch. Works like these, along with improving maps and road and steamer communications, meant that the Highlands, especially the Central Highlands, were becoming much better known. Guides, such as that of the Anderson brothers already mentioned, were very different from the earlier personal peregrination type of account, and aimed at a much wider audience. We have, for example, *The Scottish Tourist's Companion*, or *Guide to the Steam and Canal Boats* (anon. 1823), describing the mountain views from the deck on the west coast and Caledonian Canal. We also have the *Scottish Tourist* (1825), by W. Rhind which went through several editions. This was especially notable for having the first Table of 'Mountains in Scotland' (p. 398) – though some of these, such as Ailsa Craig and Calton Hill might raise an eyebrow by their inclusion. Facial hair might be further displaced by some of the heights suggested, though many are quite close to the mark. Mealfourvonie almost gains half again of its real size to become a peak of 3,060 ft, while one of Scotland's top heights is... Rona, in Orkney, at 3,944 ft! Meanwhile the *Buchael Etive* in Glencoe just manages to attain 2,500 ft, and Macdhui towers over Nevis by almost 50 feet. This period also saw *The Scottish Tourist's Land Pocket Guide* (1838), a miniature (6 by 4 inch) re-cycling of Rhind and MacCulloch for the weight-conscious pedestrian. Also in circulation was the delightful *Lakes [sic] of Scotland*, published in 1834 by Joseph Swann, with the publisher's own engravings of paintings by John Fleming of the various lochs, and their attendant mountains, such as Ben Alder (Loch Ericht) and Creag Meagaidh (Loch Laggan). This book had a text by John Leighton, describing the ascents of the easier hills in the Central Highlands, such as Lawers, Lomond, Schiehallion and Ben Vorlich, with their timings. Of all these guides, perhaps that by the Anderson brothers most repays closer attention, and here the reader will pardon, I hope, my straying a little from the Central Highlands.

The brothers were based in Inverness, and appear to have been involved in good works of a charitable and improving nature; the book is dedicated to the Highland Agricultural Society. They were well read, and the book is a solid historical and geological gazetteer, with some considerable mountain interest. We have already quoted their view of the time and cost ascending Nevis should take. They tell us that Cairngorm itself is easy but that none of the passes through those mountains should be attempted without a guide. They inform us that Ben Ledi is 'upwards of 3,000 ft' – a common error at that time, and mention that, 'Near the top, towards the end of the last century, an iron ring was discovered, attached by a staple to the rock' (p. 411) – though as we shall see, this antiquity was actually located on Stuic a' Chroin. Further indications that knowledge of the mountains, though improving, was not perfect is given in their view that on Skye 'the mountains are a great deal higher' (p. 472) than those of Glencoe, and that on Mam Sodhail 'is the largest known glacier... in Scotland' (p. 542). But there is one comment by the brothers which none could disagree with, concerning the bane of many people before the mountaineers, and since, and the need for prophylactic measures:

> ...the tourist should make use of this thin veil to protect himself from the myriads of mosquitoes, or midges, which infest the central and western coasts of Sutherland... to strangers the pain inflicted by these little creatures is at first quite excruciating. *(Guide to the Highlands and Islands of Scotland, p. 599)*

As well as gaining information from guidebooks, further information on the increasing knowledge of Scottish mountains can be got by comparing the two versions of the *Statistical Account*, produced at an interval of roughly half a century. For the Central Highlands in particular, the difference is little short of astonishing.

From the commonly named *Old Statistical Account*, we have already cited the Rev. Fraser's impressive account of Ben Nevis. There is also the oft-quoted description by James Robertson, the minister of Callander, concerning Druidical rites on Ben Ledi in pagan times, when the natives would gather at the summer solstice to worship, in an area cleared on stones piled into a central cairn.

> By reason of the altitude of Benledi, and of its beautiful conical figure, the people of the adjacent county... assembled annually at the top, about the time of the summer solstice... to worship the Deity. (OSA Vol XII, p. 143)

The same source also gives the correct account of the ring-in-the-stone, misplaced by the Anderson brothers:

> Stuic-a Chroin, the Peak of the Rutting. There has lately been dis-

covered here an iron ring, fixed by a staple to the rock. This ring is said to be very old, and corroded with rust and the lapse of time... (OSA Vol XII, p. 144)

Vulcanist geologists, advocates of the formation of the earth's surface by volcanic upheavals, claimed this proved that the summit of the mountain had been at sea level, and raised – arguing that the ring had been for tying up boats. The canny Callander minister, however, gives his opinion that it was simply a place for poachers or herdsmen to tether their dogs or animals, and to these unknown bucolics must go the honour of the first ascent of one of the Central Highlands' most impressive peaks, sometime before 1790.

This apart, one of the few entries of any real utility in the OSA, is by the Rev. Joseph MacIntyre, of Glenorchy and Inishail, dated 1792-3. He mentions an Ossianic legend that a Fingalian warrior guarded a spring on the summit of Cruachan, adding '...by the measurements of the late Colonel Watson, with the quadrant, its perpendicular height is said to be 1,130 yards above the level of the sea. (OSA Vol VIII, p. 116.) MacIntyre further mentions the mountains of *Beindoran* and *Beinlaoi* in his parish. *Cruachan Bean* is also familiar to the Rev. Ludovick Grant, minister of Ardchattan and Muckairn parish as 'one of the highest mountains in Scotland...', and he continues interestingly,

...the summit is divided into two parts... The North point is regarded the highest, *and commands a very noble and most extensive prospect.* The sea-pink grows upon it, and *sea-shells have been found on the summit...* (OSA Vol VIII p. 2). [My emphases. I.M.]

From this, and supposing that the word of a Scottish clergyman cannot be doubted, it would appear that Cruachan had been climbed at least twenty years before the ascent by MacCulloch, already discussed. If not by the Rev. Ludovick Grant of Ardchattan and Muckairn himself, possibly by the late Colonel Watson, who had measured the height of the hill? Or by Stuart and Lightfoot in the 1770s, who had dropped in with some curious seashells to show the Ardchattan cleric? Be that as it may, odd gleanings apart, these are the sum total of useful accounts of mountains in the Central Highlands in the OSA When we come to its often Cinderella of a sequel, the *New Statistical Account*, the detail is much fuller. The NSA is less consulted because by the 1840s so many other sources for social history exist; less useful for historians than its predecessor, it is more interesting to mountaineers; it appeared at a time when tourism had expanded considerably compared with the 1790s.

Taking Fortingall parish first, in place of a couple of mountains known to his predecessor, the Rev. Robert MacDonald gives us a table of thirteen local mountains, complete with their estimated heights, though he qualifies that 'perfect accuracy is not to be expected'.

1.	Sich-caillin (as ascertained)	3,564	8. Sgur-chairie	3,400
2.	Beinn-gharbhlagian	3,044	9. Garbh-mheall	3,280
3.	Beinn-udlamain	3,520	10. Meal-Bhuide	3,480
4.	Sgur-ghaibhre	3,140	11. Meal Ghaordie	3,480
5.	Carn-dearg	3,140	12. Beinn-chreachinn	3,860
6.	Cruach-confines of Argyl	2,790	13. Beinn-Sheasgarnic	3,890
7.	Carn-a-mairce -Glen Lyon	3,390		
	(NSA Vol x p. 529.)			

In addition, MacDonald gives us an account of *Sith-chaillinn* (Schiehallion) itself, and makes mention of Makeleyne's experiments upon it. And mountains beyond his parish such as the *Buachaille Eitibh* in Glencoe are known to him (NSA Vol x, pp. 528-9).

The Glenurchay and Inishail parochial incumbent was now a Rev. Duncan Maclean, who also 'kens his bens'. Where his predecessor could name three, Maclean was also aware of *Beinabhuiridh, Bein Macmonaidh*, and *Stob an daimh*, as well as *Beinachleidh*. He was further familiar with the mountain poetry of the Glenorchy Bard, and wrote,

> Bein dourain, or the mountain of the otters – a mountain dear to the Highland muse, and rendered immortal by the most distinguished of our late Highland bards, the pre-eminently poetical, though illiterate, Duncan Ban M'Intyre. (NSA Vol VII, p. 83)

But there is no doubt as to his favourite mountain, mixing its praise with a lament:

> Benlaoidh is unquestionably the loftiest mountain in the parish (Ben cruachan being situate in the parish of Ardchattan), and though now denuded and shorn of the woods which even at a comparatively recent period clothed and adorned its sides, it is one of the most elegant of mountains in a district in which it is no easy matter to adjust the competing claims... (Op. Cit. p. 84)

And as for the minister of Ardchattan, he is obviously so proud of his mountains that his entry in the NSA (Vol VII, pp. 470-2) is in danger of becoming a guide-book. Not only does he list and praise the mountains, but he gives a description of every-one worthy of note, including the first I have found of the Buachailles of Glencoe, though Etive Mor had been mentioned by the Glenorchy Bard in the previous century. The Rev. Hugh Fraser's efforts must be rewarded by an extract of his comments,

> *Mountains* – Ben Cruachan. This is the highest mountain in the county of Argyle. It is said to tower to a height of 3669 feet. Its base describes a circumference of more than twenty miles... it terminates in two conical summits, which command a panorama of surpassing magnificence. (NSA Op. Cit. p. 270)

The minister then describes *Ben-cochail,* and *Ben-starive,* which surprisingly he estimates at only about 2,500 ft, as well as *Ben-nan-aighean* and *Ben chaorach*, in terms of their pasturage for sheep, as well as availability of rock crystals; the mountains were becoming familiar, the mental gaps were being filled in. Fraser continues, awe-struck:

> We now come to the two most striking of all the masses in this wilderness of mountains, to which the significant names of Bua-chail Etive, or 'the keepers of Etive' has been given... they seem to frown in solemn sullenness on the puny mortals who venture to encroach on the solitudes over which they have for ages so patient-ly kept watch... Neither of them is supposed to be less than 3000 feet in height. (Op. Cit. p. 471)

Next comes *Ben-veedan*, the peak of the deer skins, ie, Bidean nam Bian to us, of which the writer says, 'It is a stupendous mass; so much so, indeed, that, by the inhabitants, it is alleged to be not inferior in elevation to Ben-cruachan.' (Op. Cit. p. 472.) For once local patriotism erred on the side of caution; Bidean is the higher of the two mountains. The minister is also familiar with *Ben-auley* and *Ben-scoullard*. Like many others, he comments on the 'reckless destruction' of the native woodlands, in this case for iron-smelting, and the denudation of the landscape taking place in Glenkinglas and Glenetive. The degradation of the Highland landscape is not only knowable through hindsight; contemporaries commented on, and often criticised, the process at the time.

Tickers and Timers

None of these reverend clergymen writing in the NSA make any personal claims for ascents, but given the increasing knowledge of and access to the Central Highlands, it is to be expected that unconquered peaks would soon fall like dominoes. It was becoming fashionable to list one's bagged bens in travel accounts, to compose tables of mountains, to give timings for ascents, and it is not fanciful to assert that such rationality was a reflection of the rise of industrial capitalism at this period, and its values of accumulation and the economics of time. One of the most active of tickers was another clergyman, the Rev. Thomas Grierson, whose *Autumnal Rambles Among the Scottish Mountains* appeared in 1850. Grierson was born in 1790, a son of the manse, and himself became minister of Kirkbean and Kirkgunzeon at Criffel's foot in Galloway. Presented by the Duke of Buccleuch, he was an ardent advocate of lay patronage and did not join the Free Kirk in 1843. He wrote the *New Statistical Account* for the parish of Kirkbean, and was a keen curler, writing poems on the sport, as well as a sturdy walker. He died in 1854, having witnessed his book having a great success; the third edition appeared in 1856. In the introduction to this work (3rd edn. 1856), Grierson gives a list of his bag to date, 'so far as I recollect'. Grierson was an embryonic 'Further', having climbed the 3,000ft peaks of Snowdon, Skiddaw, Helvellyn and Sca Fell outside Scotland. As well as many other Southern Upland hills, he had ascended the Merrick, which Gallovidian patriotism caused him to erroneously estimate at over 3,000 ft. But here is his list in as far as it concerns our present purposes:

> ... I have been on the tops of Ben Aulder, Ben a-Hallader, Ben Molloch, Ben Oudleman Garraval, Carey, Craig Caillach near Killin, and no less than five times on the top of Schihallion; twice on top of Ben Lawers; on Ben More, Ben Voirlich at Loch Earne, Ben Ledi, Ben Venu, Ben Chochan, Ben-y-Vracky, Faragon twice... Ben-y-gloe... I have also been on the tops of Cairngorm Bel-rinnes, Creag Phadrig, Ben Wyvis, Ben Nevis, Ben Cruachan, Duniquaigh, Ben Lomond twice... (pp. 10-11)

The orthography is pretty inexact, as one might expect from a man whose attitude to Gaelic was that it was a barbarous language and should be suppressed (p. 222), and that the Highlander was 'profoundly ignorant and bigoted' (p.58), but the following are fairly definite first (recorded) ascents (leaving aside those falling below 3,000 ft):

Ben Oudelman(Udlamain)
Ben-a Hallader (Beinn Achaladair)
Ben Voirlich (Loch Earn Ben Vorlich)
Ben Chochan (Beinn a Chreachain?)
and most notably, Ben Aulder

– despite the visits of the Pretender and later MacCulloch to Cluny's cave, there is no suggestion they beat Grierson to the summit.

My calculations give MacCulloch twelve Munros, and Grierson fourteen, making the Gallovidian the biggest bagger at the half-way stage in the nineteenth century. It is all the more infuriating that Grierson's book gives little account of these expeditions, but instead covers much later wanderings in Arran, the Borders and the Cairngorms. He tells us (p. 13-14) he made a trip to Perthshire in 1811, when his 'corporeal energies were at their height' (p. 10). As he was 21 in 1811, we can assume that most of his explorations and ascents took place in the second decade of the century. One incident is amusing to the modern reader, who erroneously thinks he has located a skeleton in the minister's cupboard.

> This huge mountain, Ben-a-Hallader, is rarely visited. The approach to it from Brae Lyon or Loch Tulla may be practicable enough; but let no man try it from the Moor of Rannoch... On my return from Ben-a-Hallader... after crossing and re-crossing the horrible Moor of Rannoch... I verily believe that the dose I got from a good woman at a shieling would have finished me... (*Autumnal Rambles*, p. 17)

However, the dose in question was an excessive amount of milk, against which Grierson cautions the traveller.

Robert Christison was a friend of Grierson, and himself a strong pedestrian. A busy academic, he was the Queen's Physican in Scotland and held the chair of Materia Medica at Edinburgh. His *Life* (1885), was edited by his two sons, based partly on his own *Autobiography* (*c*. 1880). In this are details of large-scale excursions he had in his youth. In 1816 he climbed Ben Lomond, walked through the Trossachs and then Glen Tilt, and in the following year did Ben Nevis, where he had an escapade. Glissading down a slow slope, he lost control, and only stopped by throwing out his arms and legs to increase friction. 'Had I not, what then?', he asks. Indeed. He des-

cribes the snow as 'névé' showing the internationalisation of mountain vocabulary by 1880. In 1826, in an unparalleled heatwave, he
climbed Ben Lawers.

> Here Turner, though fresh from the Alps, where he had several
> times ascended much greater heights without inconvenience, began
> to suffer so severely from the *mal de montagnes*, that we had to
> pause for a few seconds every twenty or thirty steps... (*Life,* Vol 1,
> p. 358 – again, notice the vocabulary.)

Christison continued to climb, using his summer home at Ballachulish as a base, till late in life. At 78 he climbed the Loch Earn Ben
Vorlich in 2 hours and 40 minutes, and indeed Christison was modern is his obsession with timekeeping on his ascents; Ben Donich in
1854, for example, took him 2 hours 54 minutes. Christison climbed
Ben Im, of which there is a charming drawing from his own hand in
his *Life* (Vol 11. p. 392), and also, from internal evidence (Vol 1 p.
109), appears to have trodden the summit of *Ben Arnan* (Narnain).
Though it is doubtful that, by this period, these summits had not had
tourist ascents, these are the first which I have been able to trace of
Ime and Narnain, and merit his inclusion in this survey.

The neighbouring Cobbler, or Ben Arthur, or properly *Ben Gho-
blach*, through not 3,000 ft, is so magnificent a mountain as to
require some historical details to be given concerning its ascents. The
legend of its having to be climbed by subsequent chiefs of the Clan
Campbell, to prove their right to come into their Kingdom, appears
to have no historical validity. There are two claims to a probable first
ascent, both appearing in works published in the same year, 1824.
The first is in the book by MacCulloch, already referred to, his
Highlands and Islands..., and the other is from Thomas Wilkinson,
an English tourist, in his *Tours to the British Mountains*. Mac-
Culloch's ascent is undated, but lies between 1811 and 1821, while
that of Wilkinson had taken place much earlier, in 1787 – the year
he climbed Ben Nevis, one of its earliest ascents. But, irrespective of
dates, the internal evidence of their respective accounts is fairly conclusive in awarding the laurels. Wilkinson writes of his attempt on
the mountain, which he remarks looks much less like a cobbler at
work than a monk in a cowl:

> I felt a wish to visit the reputed Cobbler. I inquired of the people
> about Arroquar, but found none that had been there, except an old
> man now almost blind... It rained, and a cloud covered the object

of my wishes... I set off and reached the top of the mountain in about two hours. I rested and the mists... finally departed. It was now an entertaining but awful scene. At the two corners of the mountain rise two perpendicular rocks, perhaps between fifty and a hundred yards high; several lesser rocks appear along the heights between, among which arises something of a connecting wall... (which) might be for hindering sheep... (*Tours to the British Mountains*, 1824, p. 42-3)

Leaving aside any prior claims by the old, blind man and the anonymous dyke-builders, Wilkinson would not appear to have gained the summit of the Cobbler, though compensated by sublime feelings 'I do not remember having known before.' He seems to have climbed the south peak and possibly the north peak, these being at the 'corners' of the mountain. There is no indication he ascended the 'lesser rocks' between them, which he – not alone – considered as lower. In fact, it is the *central peak* of the Cobbler, not one of the pair on either 'corner', which is the highest of the three, and the most difficult.

MacCulloch on the other hand, specifically mentions that he ascended the Central Peak, and sat 'with one foot in Loch Long and the other in Glencroe', and therefore was the first, if not the last, to sit on the Cobbler's Last. On a fine day he determined to climb this 'extraordinary object'.

It is well worth ascending; and, as far as the foot of this extra-ordinary object, the ascent is not difficult... Thus clambering... I reached the summit of the ridge, and found myself astride on this rocky saddle... I was surprised to find the summit so acute and so narrow... (*Highlands*...Vol 1. p. 253, 255)

Looking at the Glen of Weeping

Ways of seeing the mountains had changed for ever by the mid-nineteenth century. What had been regarded as a hostile and ugly region, full of bandits and rebels, had become a land for tourists, where romance, trains and hotels awaited. What had been a jumbled mass of hideous mountains without any form, had settled into an ordered topography of bens and glens. And more interestingly, what had looked like near-vertical, unbroken precipices, had become recast as mountains whose easier declivities could be separated off from their more difficult by the inner and outer eye.

If we look at Turner's painting of Glencoe (1833), it is probably a reflection of both the fear inspired by the glen's mountains amongst early travellers, and also the inability of their eyes at that time to separate the wheat from the chaff, the avenues of possible ascent from those barred to the pedestrian. How other can we explain, that of all the mountains in Scotland, nay, Britain, Glencoe's were deemed the most difficult by almost all visitors, including some who had been to Skye? The ascent to the summit of Bidean nam Bian in the 1770s by Stuart we must see as the astonishing exception which proves the rule. Was the additional horror produced by knowledge of the massacre in 1692 partly responsible for the awe which even experienced pedestrians felt in Glencoe?

Grierson visited Skye in later life and considered the Cuillin do-able, though he didn't, being in his late 50s. At around the same time he traversed Glencoe, commenting, '...the mountains here... shoot out in the most singular forms... The summits of some of them seem wholly inaccessible' (*Autumnal Rambles...* p. 65). Didn't people see Lagangarbh Corrie on the Buachaille, or that the Aonach Eagach could be attained easily at its western end from Carnach village? Or, as Erchie Boomer once said to a party on Buachaille Etive Mor's Rannoch Wall, 'There's an easy wye roon the back'? The answer must be, no they didn't, they did not 'see' the mountains as we do; the eye for a 'line' is not innate, but a social construction. And Grierson's comment could be echoed in that of countless visitors to the Glen of Weeping.

Duncan MacIntrye had, according to one of his poems already quoted, wandered on the Buachaille, waist-deep in snow; or at least, down in the comfort of Auld Reekie, wished he were doing so. There are precious few accounts of others (Stuart aside) leaving the security of the road, and attempting Glencoe's hills, for another century. Sir John Stoddart, an English friend of Walter Scott, visited Scotland in 1799. He was a romantic admirer of Wordsworth and the Lakeland poets, and quite a Scotophile, defending even the Scots tongue against its southron detractors. He did Ben Lomond without a guide, and described feeling 'the most sublime sensations' which 'will never be blotted from my memory', on the summit. (*Remarks on Local Scenery and Manners in Scotland,* 1801, Vol 1, p. 236, 7.) His desire to bag Ben Nevis was foiled by the weather, and he moved to Glencoe where he was mightily impressed, 'In no other part of Britain have I ever seen mountain summits so wholly consisting of bare crags, as here' Vol 11 (p. 29). He gives us his motives for, and account of, an attempt to reach Ossian's Cave on Bidean nan Bian, an attempt which failed:

> There is a degree of juvenile ambition, sharpened by curiosity, which often prompts one to scale these seemingly inaccessible clifts.(sic). About the middle of the glen, at a great height, in the face of a mountain, is a yawning chasm, of between two and three hundred feet... I could not learn with certainty, that any person had ever explored it... I ascended alone, with the hope of getting a nearer view of the crags, by which it is formed. After some hours of painful and persevering toil, I climbed beyond the height, to which sheep go in search of food, and was on the highest border of vegetation; all beyond was bare rock; but, alas! the cave was still some hundred feet above me; and I reaped nothing, but the satisfaction of viewing this wonderful glen... (Op. Cit. p. 31)

Stoddart might have been consoled by knowing that it was only in 1868 that the first ascent to Ossian's cave took place, by a local shepherd, Nicol Marquis.

However, when the Anderson brothers visited Glencoe, they found that local people were more familiar with the mountains than Stoddart had thought. After giving us the usual hyperbole about the 'wonderful and terrific' scene of 'gloomy precipices', filling the viewer with 'awe', and before giving a quick tour round the events of the massacre of 1692, the brothers describe Aonach Eagach, whose name was apparently not known to them. From this, it is quite clear that the summit ridge of this range, if not the actual peaks at its extremities, were familiar to local foxhunters. And if the latter could do the difficult central sections of the ridge, there is no reason why Meall Dearg and Sgorr nam Fiannaidh would be out of bounds to them in pursuit of Reynard.

> The mountains on the north side of the glen terminate so sharply as, at one particular spot, ...to resemble exactly the roof of a house. To surmount this critical obstacle, requires no little nerve and resolution, for the only way to advance is to sit astride, and crawl cautiously alongst (sic) the narrow ridge; yet many foxhunters do not hesitate to perform this trying adventure, burdened with both dog and gun. Nor is this the whole of the exploit; for a little further on they have to leap a height of about ten feet from the top of the precipice, to where the slope becomes so gentle as to make this practicable by care and dexterity. (*Guide to the Highlands*... p. 416)

In footnote, this is the first instance of the use of the *à cheval* technique in Scotland, (or of a dog (*à chien*?) – shades of Hamish Brown – on a mountain top), which I have found. Suggestions as to the section of the ridge described by the Andersons would probably be as many as suggesters, but it lies clearly on the central, difficult section of the traverse. An impressive feat.

However, Glencoe's reputation delayed its development as a centre for pedestrian tourism until the very end of the pre-mountaineering period, when the Buachaille was ascended by John Stuart Blackie in 1867. Blackie was born in 1809 of good bourgeois stock, in Glasgow, though he had the fortune to move as a boy to that sound centre of learning, Aberdeen, where he attended school and university. After intellectual and physical wanderings on the continent, he obtained the Latin Chair at Aberdeen in 1839, thirteen years later being appointed to that of Greek in Edinburgh. He was an eccentric, energetic, and amiable man, of many interests. His entry in the DNB describes him as having 'genial eccentricities', 'boundless good-humour' and 'a rich fund of Scottish prejudices' (Vol XXII p. 206). He was a Hellenophile, and also a great lover of Highland culture. He saw the Highlanders (somehow) as the modern Ancient Greeks, and endowed a Chair of Celtic at Edinburgh University, which was offered to Alexander Nicolson, who turned it down. He was a Liberal, defender of parliamentary reform and causes like Italian unification, but no democrat; he polemicised against the Chartists' demands for universal suffrage. On the other hand, he campaigned actively for the land rights of the Highlanders during the Crofters' War of the 1880s, and visited Skye during the agitation. He taught himself Gaelic, and made one of the many translations of Duncan MacIntyre's *Beinn Dorain*. (See his own *Notes of a Life*, 1869, as well as his entry in the DNB.)

Blackie early became acquainted with the Highlands, through holidays which he continued all his life. Latterly, he spent every summer at a house near Oban. His *Altavona* (1882) is an account, through dialogues between imaginary characters, of the history and problems of the Highlands; prolix and fanciful, it does not appeal to modern taste. In the introduction to the work, Blackie comments, 'Having resided for nearly twenty years in the Highlands... not a foot of ground is mentioned which I have not travelled over' (p. VII, IX). But to say one has been everywhere in general, does not say where one has been in particular, and it is likely that many pioneering ascents and explorations by Blackie are forever lost to us. Even of his ascent of the Buachaille, where we have the date, we have almost nothing else.

Incurable addicts to convoluted Victorian prose can benefit from studying Blackie's letters to his wife, which A.S. Walker thought, in 1909, were worth collecting. We should be grateful at any rate for the following:

FAIREST BEING – I am regularly out on the moors from 9 till 7... I mounted the steep, apparently unapproachable, Buchail Etive with grand success and very little fatigue... (Blackie to Elizabeth Blackie, Ballachulish Sept. 18th 1867.) (*The Letters of John Stuart Blackie to his Wife*, p. 169)

And that is it – apart from a subsequent letter, which she received first:

FAIREST BEING – ... I called at Ft. William on MacLaren the banker, who received me with great kindness and gave me some valuable information. I had got an introduction to him from Cambell of Monzie. He had got a letter from the gamekeeper at King's House, requesting him to prosecute me for climbing Buchail More!... It would be splendid fun, no doubt. (Blackie to Elizabeth Blackie, Kinloch Aylort, Sept. 21st 1867. Op. Cit. p. 164)

Though Blackie was not prosecuted, the incident is significant in that it is one of the early occasions of the Empire striking back, of landlords, aware of the commercial gain from deer-hunting, beginning to attempt to restrict access to the mountains. The Scotch Trespass Act of 1865 had imposed a fine of twenty shillings or fourteen days' imprisonment on anyone lighting unauthorised fires or camping on private land; the reason it fell into desuetude is that almost everyone who followed Blackie, followed his example and ignored the law, making it unenforceable. This process of trying to close off land, affected not only mountaineers, but also the inhabitants of the Highlands and Islands, as we shall see subsequently in this study, when we look at Kintail.

Blackie wandered at will and at random, he belonged to no club, and had no specialist gear. He was a pedestrian, rather than a mountaineer. The spread of ideas, equipment and practises from continental mountaineering would mean that he was to be one of the last such. The day of the 'Alpenstockist' was at hand, the person, equipped with ice axe, rope, the os maps, having at least a passing knowledge of Alpinist techniques, was just over the horizon in 1867, in the Central Highlands and elsewhere. Compare Horatio McCulloch's painting of Glencoe, done three years before Blackie climbed the Buachaille, with Turner's; the mountains are all in place, recognisable: impressive, but not 'wholly inaccessible'. McCulloch sees the mountains – notwithstanding a certain visual hyperbole – as we do, not as they were seen before the mountaineers, though old men in Glen Lyon might still tell tales of *Cailean Gorach* round the fire at night.

And for the mountain tourist, the Highland transport infrastructure was more developed at this time than many recognise. The German poet and novelist, Theodor Fontane, made a tour in Scotland in 1858, published under the title *Beyond the Tweed*. Fontane left Oban one morning, sailed in the steamer to Kintyre, took a coach across the peninsula, then took another steamer to Dumbarton, and finally a train to Loch Lomond, with still time left for an evening sail on the loch in the steamer *Rob Roy*, after booking into his hotel.

In an astonishingly short time after pacification, the Highlands came to be seen not as a threat, but as a romantic and magnetic area. Painters such as Nasmyth and later Raeburn used Highland scenes and figures as subjects for their wealthy clientele, while Mac-Pherson's Ossianic productions were a great success in polite Augustan society. Now that the clan system was broken, Enlightenment philosophers like Adam Fergusson could re-assure their readers that it had just been the Scottish stage in the transition from barbarism to civil society, in his *Essay in the History of Civil Society*. Highland dress, the bagpipes, Gaelic, all ineffectively banned after the 45 had, a quarter of a century later, become quite chic. And in the Victorian period this trend in romanticisation become full-blown, and eventually, on Deeside, achieved the stamp of Royal Approval. 'The Highlands' were being invented. (See 'The Historical Creation of the Scottish Highlands', C. Withers, in *The Manufacture of Scottish History*, ed. Donnachie and Whatley 1992, for a fuller development of these themes.) One of the profoundest revolutions in history in 'ways of seeing' with regard to the natural world, had taken place. Savagery had become Sublime.

CHAPTER 2

The Cairngorms before the Climbers

SINCE TACITUS GAVE THE NAME Mons Graupius to the place where Agricola defeated the Picts in AD 84, the term Grampian mountains has been applied to the central mountain chain of Scotland. The Gaelic name, *Monadh Ruadh*, Red Mountains, to distinguish them from the *Monadh Liath,* Grey Mountains west of Speyside, has never had more than local and academic usage. However, from the early nineteenth century the term Cairngorms – applied especially to the Braemar Highlands – rivalled and gradually supplanted Grampians in common usage. Colonel Thornton, in his *Sporting Tour* (1804), refers to 'Aurora peeping over the immense Cairngorms'. This semantic conflict has been summed up in the classic Scottish Mountaineering Club Guide, *The Cairngorms*, by William Alexander.

> Strangely enough, however, the term 'Grampian', though well recognised in maps and though enjoying a certain literary usage, has never passed into popular favour... On the other hand, the term 'The Cairngorms', taken originally from a single mountain... is now being more and more widely used as descriptive of the whole region. (Op. Cit. Third edn. 1950, p. 2)

I will use the name of the mountain Cairngorm for the range itself, although I will not be restricting myself in this section only to the Braemar Highlands, but will also look at the adjacent Monadh Liath and Atholl districts.

Cartographers, Miners, Tinkers...

The north-east boasts some of the earliest known hill ascents in Scotland. Mons Graupius itself (according to P. Marren, *Grampian Battlefields*, 1990, p. 18), almost certainly Bennachie and over 1,700 ft, was the scene of a Pictish or proto-Pictish fort before the Romans came, and the spectacular fortification on Tap o Noth further west approaches nearer to 2,000 ft. (*Early Grampian; a guide to the archaeology*, I. Ralston and I. Shepherd, 1979, p. 23). A millennium later, Malcolm Canmore, King of Scotland, on a visit to the Forest of Mar, watched a hill race on Creag Choinnich (1,764 ft), and in awarding a prize to the victor, is supposed to have begun the tradition of Highland Games. (*Royal Valley*, Fenton Wyness, 1968, p. 87.)

This area of the Highlands appears to have become known to outsiders earlier than lands to the west or even than the Central Highlands. The region is penetrated by three long and fairly accessible river glens: the Dee, the Don and the Spey. Additionally the Grampian chain, or the Mounth, as it was anciently known, separates two Lowland areas; that of central Scotland and that of the north-east Lowlands, from Elgin to Aberdeen. From earliest times it has been traversed by a series of highways, the Mounth Roads. The tale of these roads, and the surprising amount of usage they met, is told in Robert Smith's *Grampian Ways* (1980). Such constant trafficking to and from undoubtedly spread knowledge of the region beyond its boundaries.

The extent to which the Braemar Highlands was reasonably *terra cognita* is shown in Robert Gordon's 'Notes for a Description of the Two Shires of Aberdeen and Banff', written in the 1650s and published in 1748 in Walter MacFarlan's *Geographical Collections*, Vol 11. Gordon was a geographer, and laird of Straloch. After the death of Timothy Pont – the cartographer originally appointed to the task – Gordon was chosen by Charles 1 to help complete the Scottish maps for Blaeu's *Atlas*, eventually published in Amsterdam in 1654. Though started at the turn of the century, Pont's death, and then Gordon's involvement in the Civil Wars between Royalists and Covenanters – where he attempted to act as a moderating intermediary – greatly delayed the work. Armed bands were roaming the region, and several military engagements took place on the borders of the upland area, where the Highland clansmen generally favoured the Royalists and fought with Montrose's forces (for details see *Legends of the Braes o Mar*, John Grant, 1876).

According to Jeffrey Stone, Gordon made almost no revisions to Pont's maps in the majority of cases, yet those of the north-east were extensively revised, indicating that Gordon had travelled widely in his own back yard, and possibly was the main contributor to the maps in question; and the *Atlas* names Gordon, not Pont, as the author of the Aberdeen and Banffshire map (*The Pont Manuscript Maps of Scotland*, 1988, p. 9). The knowledge Gordon gained in his cartographic work is demonstrated in the 'Notes...'

The Dee, cleaving the Grampians from its source to its mouth... has its source not far from the range of low hills called Scairsach, which separate Braemar from Badenoch, at the base of the lofty mountain called Ben-Vroden... At Innerey... seven miles from its source, it meets its first cultivation. (*Geographical Collections,* Vol 11, W Macfarlan, 1906, p. 283)

Here Gordon uses the traditional term Grampians. He also allows us to see that population was still quite thinly spread, due to the 'aridity of the land'. The inhabitants Gordon describes as 'vigorous, shrewd and frugal' – a more sympathetic portrayal than normal at that time of Highlanders by Lowlanders. Later, settlement was to spread several miles westward of Inverey to the Chest o Dee, where Farquharson of Invercauld's map of 1703 shows townships at Dalvorar and Dubrach (*Mar Lodge Estate; An Archaeological Survey,* RCAHMS (1995) p. 6). But most interestingly, in Gordon we do not have a man used to scaling the tops; how otherwise can we account for *Scairsach* (An Sgarsoch) being described as 'low', while *Ben-Vroden* (Beinn Bhrotain) gets the appellation 'lofty'? The former is 3,300 ft, while the latter is 3,795 ft, a height difference hardly meriting the semantic one. Clearly the eye of the geographer was not used to judging heights, a common failing in early travellers.

Gordon had some Gaelic, telling us for example that *crag* means mountain and *Kennacoil* is 'a name that signifies the *head of the wood*'. But he clearly did not name the hills, and neither did Pont. The fact that so many of the hills were named, with titles recognisable to the modern mountaineer, indicates that the process of name-giving had been going on for a long time. If we look at *Aberdonia & Banfia*, as published by Blaeu, the following are the names then in current use, with their modern equivalents, aside from An Sgarsoch (Hill of Rough Stones) and Beinn Bhrotain (Mountain of the Mastiff) already mentioned:

Carn-Gorum M.	= Cairn Gorm	Blue Hill
Bin Neur	= Beinn Uarn (Glen Ey)	Hills of Hell (poss.)
Month Kein	= Mount Keen	Smooth Hill
Bini-Bourd M.	= Beinn a'Bhuird	Table Mountain
Ben Chichues	= Lochnagar	

(Its original name was Hill of the Breasts.)

Surprisingly, Alexander (Loc. Cit. p. 23) says *Ben Chichues* is 'impossible to identify'. Surprising because the Cairngorm Club had already published an article on the etymology of Lochnagar. 'The

Benchinnans', by the Rev. J.G. Michie (*Cairngorm Club Journal* Vol
11 pp. 33-5), traces the evolution from *Ben Cichean* (Hill of the
Breasts), to *Binchichins* (1678) and *Benchinnans* (1831). *Chichues* is
clearly a simple error in transliteration, which Alexander should
have known.

The Mountains of Bin-Avin are placed by Gordon beside *Loch
Avin*, or misplaced if Ben Avon itself is meant. In the place of Ben
Avon is a mysterious *Bad-Renald M.*, which I am unable to identify.
This mountain re-appears in Moll's map of 1724, before disappear-
ing into a cartographic black hole. (Moll largely copied Gordon, and
added a few of his own errors, e.g. *Bin Chombie* replaces Ben
Chichues, and the entire western Cairngorms disappear under *Bini
Wrode*!) To the south-west of Cairngorm is found the *Corintrack
M.*, according to Gordon. From its position, I venture this is an
extremely corrupt form of Cairn Toul (Corin=Cairn). Anyone using
Gordon's map would have found it a very useful guide to the district;
however, few probably did use it. Blaeu's *Atlas* was for the Library
not the outdoors. Farquharson's map additionally identifies *Carn-
balg*, (Hill of the Bags) which is our Cairnwell, as well as *Cairntoul*
(Hill of the Barn). But those who wandered the glens and bens relied
mainly on mental maps.

It is impossible to doubt that the summits of the Cairngorm
mountains were visited by hunters and poachers long before the
period of the pre-history of Scottish mountaineering; though there
are no mountains in this area definitely named after legendary figures which might give us a clue to their eponymous possible first
ascenders. An exception might be thought to be *Carn an t-Sagairt*,
the Hill of the Priest. But this priest, Patrick by name, did not climb
the hill, though the nearby Loch Phadruig is also named after him.
At a time of severe frost, Patrick prayed at Loch Callater by a holy
well for a thaw, and rain clouds gathered over the summit of the
mountain to the east, and water trickled from the frozen well. There
are claims that Ben Macdhui was named after a Macduff, but in my
view that is a black pig in a poke, as the name could as easily be the
Gaelic for a wild boar.

There is a *Ciste Mhearad* on Cairngorm; the kist or coffin is
supposed to mark the spot of an unhappy maiden of legend. But
if the story is more than apocryphal, she did not make the summit,
failing by several hundred feet. Further west on the Sgorans ridge,
just below the summit of Creag Dhubh is the Argyll Stone, where

the leader of the Clan Campbell is supposed to have halted before preceding with his clan army to the Battle of Glenlivet in 1594 in an attempt to chastise the 'Popish' Gordon family. At 2,760 ft, this is one of the highest recorded points reached to that date – and as we have seen, it was another Campbell, *Cailean Gorach*, who was to be among the first Munroists at roughly the same time.

More likely first ascenders were the Cairngorm miners, who – often with their families – from the mid-eighteenth century ascended the mountains in search of 'pellucid stones', i.e. the semi-precious Cairngorm stones – hexagonal quartz crystals of great beauty. In the early nineteenth century Farquharson of Invercauld was drawing two hundred pounds a year in rent from such mining, and occasional single crystals could fetch that sum. Though much mining would simply have been searching rock-falls in gullies, in some areas the ground was trenched to a depth of several feet. Ben Avon was a favourite area for the search, and at the Meikle Eas burn on its southern slopes are the remains of mining works which were active about 1800. At an altitude of 2,800 ft, these works employed about 30 miners, but were not the highest habitation on the mountain:

> By the burn side, above the 'miners' hut' there is a 'Poachers' Cave', capable of sheltering about half a dozen people. (A.I. McConnochie, 'The Eastern Cairngorms' in CCJ Vol 1 p. 245)

Can we believe that none of these miners and poachers went the few extra feet to the summit of Ben Avon? The summit of the hill, at 3,843 ft, now supports the name *Leabaidh an Daimh Bhuide*, bed of the yellow stag, however McConnochie names it after local tradition as the *Clach an t-Saighdeir*, the tor or stone of the soldier. Who was the *saighdear*? A deserter turned poacher, an ex-serviceman turned miner, or a myth of local folklore – we will probably never know. Other possibilities suggest themselves. *Carn Cloich-mhuillin*, just breaching 3,000 ft, is an outlier of Beinn Bhrotain. The former name signifies peak of the mill-stones; were they quarried on the hill, or selected from the massive stone detritus on its summit? Speculation would be fascinating, but most likely fruitless.

However, we *do* have a fairly certain account of a local ascent, prior to the travellers and tourists. An Sgarsoch, the hill of the sharp stones, is reputed in both Atholl and Mar folklore as having been the location in former times of a horse and cattle market, and several stone piles are pointed out on the summit as relics of those fairs. A remote area, it may have been a convenient place for dealing in goods many of which were contraband, near the junction of the three counties of Perth, Aberdeen and Inverness. So we can award multiple repeat ascents of An Sgarsoch to tinkers, cattle thieves, rustlers and the odd honest merchant.

There are other fairly reliable accounts of early mountain ascents in this area. The reivers from the west earned themselves the name of the Cleansers, because they cleared out everything moveable on their raids into the eastern Grampians region. In 1591 the Campbells raided Glenisla and 'murthorit all the inhabitants' before they 'took much spulzie, a grit nowmor of nolt, schiep etc.'. In 1644 the tables were turned, when a party of Campbells returning from their raid on Glen Isla and Glen Shee, were themselves attacked near the Cairnwell, which gave its name to the ensuing battle. Things were going well for the Campbells till a local archer, the *Cam-Ruadh* (the one-eyed, red-haired man), despatched his arrows with telling effect, and the reivers fled leaving their spoils behind. The *Cam-Ruadh* himself did not escape unscathed. When he got home his wife informed him, '*Chaim Ruadh, Chaim Ruadh! tha saighead na do thoine!*' (Cam Ruadh, there is an arrow in your arse!), before pulling it out and serving his supper. They don't make women like that any more! (*Legends of the Braes o Mar*, John Grant, p. 88.) For mountain historians, the important part of this story is that the reivers crossed to Gleann Beag from Glen Isla, over *Creag Leacach* – possibly just south of the summit ridge – before being engaged on the slopes of *Meall Odhar*, itself over 3,000 ft. It is therefore just possible that, apart from 38 Campbells whose widows would cry the *corranach*, a couple of tops may also have fallen that day, and even Creag Leacach itself.

Towards the end of the seventeenth century occurred another probable first ascent in the southern Cairngorm area. Ian Mackeracher, or Farquarson, or *Lonavey*, meaning greedy for deer – *lonach fiadh* – was a freebooter in the region surrounding Beinn a' Ghloe and Carn an Righ. He had had his arrow-hand cut off for poaching, but taught himself to be an expert one-handed shot with the gun. Though partly tolerated by the Earl of Athole who showed him off in marksmanship contests, he was eventually captured and died in Perth prison. There he expressed as follows his despair at his confinement, on seeing a bird fly past from out his prison window,

Had I my gun, from Carn Righ's height
I'd break your wing and stop your flight.

He told fellow prisoners that his gun was hidden in a cave high on that mountain, though *Lonavey* never left prison to retrieve it. The tale of gun on Carn an Righ lived on in local folklore. It was found in the 1870s, in a cave high on the hill its owner must surely have climbed many times. (*The Romance of Poaching in the Highlands*, W. McCombie Smith, 1904, pp.30-8)

And there are other ascents, or misses near enough to be considered as such. Of Beinn a' Bhuird, A. Inkson McConnochie writes,

> A little to the north of the South Top is a circle of stones which has puzzled not a few. This circle is known as 'Lamont's Seat'... it is on the Duke of Fife's side of Beinn a Bhuird, and it was used as a lookout post by 'watchers' in the Mar Forest. (CCJ Vol 1, p. 250)

The Duke of Fife acquired Mar Forest in 1735; we could speculate that Lamont (a common local name) ascended Beinn a' Bhuird sometime afterwards; but did he do so before its first recorded ascent (infra)? Heat, rather than light, would be the subject of such speculation, so we pass on.

For in general, credit must go to those who can provide names and dates for their claims to be given a place amongst the pantheon of early mountaineers in the Cairngorms as elsewhere. And we are not without accounts from the surprising number of visitors who, for the most varied of reasons, wandered the Cairngorms and visited their tops, in the period before mountaineering for pleasure pure and simple became a common pastime in the middle of the Victorian era.

After the Tinkers, A Taylor

Though hardly the first English tourist or traveller in Scotland, John Taylor, a bargeman on the Thames whose literary ambitions earned him the title the Water Poet, would appear to have been the first to scale the heights. In the fashion of the time, Taylor undertook an unlikely journey as a bet; he stated his intention to tour Scotland without a coin in his pocket, and neither to beg nor borrow. Hence the title of his eventually published account, *The Pennyles* [sic] *Pilgrimage*.

Taylor's motive, apart from winning his bet, was to increase his standing at court. In 1603, James 1, or Jamie the Saxt as he was known at home – had become King of England. Scotland and Scots were unpopular in London, and James and his hangers-on were seen as fleecing the southern kingdom. Writing a favourable account of Scotland would not do Taylor any harm, with a King who already thought highly of him. Ben Jonson, who executed a trip to Scotland in the same year of 1618 observed caustically that James felt there were not 'any verses in England (equal) to the Sculler's.' Taylor, for a bargeman, appears to have been well-connected. He organised a water pageant for the King in 1613, during which he met the Earl of Mar, who invited him to come to Scotland.

Taylor seems to have been a gregarious, easy-going fellow, and there is no doubt that he enjoyed his three months in Scotland. On his return to London in October 1618, he published at his own expense an account of his travels, which appears to have been successful. It gives us a fascinating account of the Cairngorm Highlands at this time.

The early part of the bargeman's journey in Lowland Scotland is little from the ordinary. Things change, however, when he gets to Brechin, or *Breekin* as he calls it. With typical traveller's hyperbole, he describes what then happened:

> Then I tooke another guide, which brought me such strange wayes over mountains and rockes, that I thinke my horse never went the like... I did go through a countrey called Glaneske... where the way was rocky and not above a yard broad in some places, so fearfull and horrid it was to looke downe into the bottome, for if either horse or man had slippt, he had fallen(without recovery) a good mile downeright; but I thanke God, at night I came to... an Irish house, the folkes not being able to speak scarce any English, but I supped and went to bed, where I had not laine long, but I was enforced to rise; I was so stung with Irish muskataes, a creature that hath six legs, and lives like a monster altogether upon mans flesh...

> The next day I travelled over an exceeding high mountaine, called mount Skeene, where I found the valley very warm before I went up; but when I came to the top of it, my teeth beganne to dance in my head with cold, like virginals jacks; and withall, a most familiar mist embraced me round, that I could not see thrice my length any way: withall, it yeelded so friendly a deaw, that it did moysten thorow all my clothes; where the old proverbe of a Scottish miste

was verified, in wetting me to the skinne... the way is so uneven, and full of bogges, quagmires, and long heath, that a dogge with three legs will out-runne a horse with foure... ('Pennyless Pilgrimage' from *Early Travellers in Scotland*, ed. P. Hume-Brown, 1891, p. 119-20)

Scotland was generous to Taylor almost four centuries ago; he travelled for three months, without spending his penny. However, to confirm him with the accolade as the first to ascend Mount Keen, we may need to be as generous again today. The old Mounth road had been travelled by many before Taylor, across the shoulder of Mount Keen. It passes about 600 feet below the summit. True, Taylor says he got to the top. But even though grammar (like spelling) was less rigorous in Taylor's day, the 'top' might appear to refer to the valley, not the previously-mentioned 'mountaine'. However, if we assume that our honest bargee meant the mountain 'top', how could he have known he was there when visibility was so bad – less than twenty feet, in his own estimation? Yet the man spoke well of Scotland and its inhabitants – an unusual occurrence at this time, even if his motives were self interested. So let us repeat our former generosity and award the Water Poet the first ascent of Mount Keen – though not of a Scottish 3,000ft mountain. At least that belongs to a Scotsman.

Taylor's adventures were far from their end after crossing Mount Keen. He arrives at the *Brea of Marr* where he observes:

There I saw mount Benawne, with a furr'd mist upon his snowie head instead of a nightcap: for you must understand that the oldest man alive never saw but the snow was on the top of divers of these hills, both in summer, as well as in winter. (p. 120)

Whatever this may make us think about global warming, or the veracity of Taylor or his informants, it shows that the name of Ben Avon was known in 1618. This makes it all the more surprising that Gordon of Straloch does not appear to have discovered it for Blaeu's *Atlas*. Ben Avon and Mount Keen are the only 'mountaines' mentioned by Taylor.

And he mentions much else of interest; that the Highlanders' stockings and jerkins are 'made of a warm stuffe of divers colours which they call Tartane', compleating their garb 'with a pleade about their shoulders' and adding that 'as for breeches, many of them, nor their forefathers, never wore any'. He also remarks that all ranks were similarly dressed, from lords to peasants, 'as if Licurgus had been there, and made lawes of equality' – in preparation for a hunting party.

Led by the Earl of Mar, this party lasted twelve days and resulted in a vast slaughter of bestial fish and fowl, which amazed Taylor. He mentions seeing wolves, still extant, and that he feasted on 'caperkellies' – both would be extinct in a century. The hunting party, 1,500 strong, stayed in turf bothies built for the hunt, which utilised the Irish greyhound, and appears still largely to have used the bow and arrow. The hunt ended up in Badenoch, at Ruthven, after heading westward from the Braes o Mar; the Geldie or the Lairig Ghru was probably the route.

Accompanying the feasting were huge fires 'of firre-wood as high as a may-pole'. To an England already experiencing a timber shortage, Taylor feels obliged to state:

> For I dare affirme, (the Earl of Mar) hath as many (firre-trees) growing there as would serve for masts (from this time to the end of the worlde) for all the shippes, carackes, hoyes, galleyes, boates, drumlers, barkes and water-crafts, that are now, or can be in the worlde these fourty yeeres.

It is unlikely that a visitor would feel today that the Braemar Highlands supported much tree cover, and thus we can take Taylor's opinion as evidence for the existence, at that date, of a much larger remnant of the ancient forest of Caledon. In 1730 the York Building Co. felled Abernethy forest, and in the 1780s a Hull merchant cut down that of Glenmore. The 'Muckle Spate', or Great Flood, of 1829 uprooted many more of the Scots pines, before sheep and deer did the rest.

On the hunting trip, Taylor resided in 'Lonquards', rough hunting lodges made of turf and stone. One of these was probably *Boandun Geoldie*, marked on Farquarson's map already mentioned. This massive structure, too big for a shieling, probably served as a 'lonquard', and was occupied against poachers in 1727; its outline still exists. (Grid Ref. NN 923 868.)

After evading the lust of a deaf and dumb Scottish wench on his return to Breekin, Taylor headed south, well pleased with his journey, the Scots, and it must be said, with himself. He wrote in 'The Epilogue' to his tale that he had failed to do the country full justice.

I vow to God, I have done Scotland wrong,
And, justly, 'gainst me it may bring an action,

I have not given't that right which doth belong,
For which I am halfe guilty of detraction...

A Slaughterhouse Tour

Taylor was a maverick, and it was to be many years before his example of visiting, and revelling in the scenery of, the Scottish Highlands was to become common for his countrymen. One such was a Colonel Thomas Thornton, who in his *Sporting Tour* 1804, expressed what was to become a common viewpoint, i.e. that the pleasures of England were tame and domestic as the Anglo-Scot Byron later put it. Thornton wrote:

> South Britons may talk of their beautiful, highly finished land-scapes... but from their small, pitiful extent they soon grow flat and loose their effect. Here the case differs: for the immense extent of these views, and the reflection of the sun, presenting various tints, each differing from another, though all beautiful, give this country every advantage and a decided superiority... (*Sporting Tour...* 1896 edn. p. 179)

Thornton was born in Yorkshire in 1757 of a father who had served the Hanoverians at Falkirk and Culloden. He gained a love of Scotland in his teens from time at Glasgow College. A gentleman of ample fortune, he sold his estate in 1805 for nigh on quarter of a million pounds, retiring to France. He could jump his own height, and was able to walk four miles in half an hour.

As one of the idle rich in an increasingly wealthy Britain, Thornton undertook his grand tours. Others collected culture in Italy and Greece, he collected game. He has left us an account of a *Sporting Tour in France* in 1802, which appeared before the more renowned Scottish *Sporting Tour*, published in 1804. However, the Scottish trip had actually taken place much earlier, in the year 1786 in all probability. Thornton's aim, like other 'sportsmen', was to slaughter as many animals, birds and fish as he possibly could; yet he saw himself as an animal lover and recommended his readers to 'cultivate a sympathising disposition towards the brute creation' – a contradiction impossible to reconcile for a modern reader. He took as a companion and illustrator George Garrard, a sporting artist, whose drawings accompany the book. He also took a sloop, the *Falcon*, which deposited every conceivable luxury for him at convenient coastal supply points. The published work was slated by Walter Scott as 'a long, minute and prolix account of every grouse or black cock which had the honour to fall by the gun of our literary sportsman', in the 1805 *Edinburgh Review*, but it is relieved by passages of social and mountaineering interest.

Though mainly interested in his 'bag', Thornton was not averse to 'bagging' the odd hill, and he has credit for more than one first ascent. On August 6, he set out on an expedition 'up the vale of the Fishie' (Feshie), and 'at ten o'clock we were at the foot of the mountain, the heat intense, the mercury standing at 84 Fahrenheit' (p. 99). Thornton does not name the mountain, but authorities such as Horn (SMCJ XXVIII, p. 162) and Steven, *The Story of Scotland's Hills* (p. 72), credit him with the ascent of Sgoran Dubh. I believe the internal evidence of Thornton's account points to his climbing Sgor Gaoith, to the south – which is actually the highest point, and the present Munro.

Firstly, Thornton mentions some of his party descending from the mountain to *Glen Ennoch* (Einich) and the loch at its head. It is doubtful these gentlemen could have descended the crags of Sgoran Dubh's buttresses to the glen, whereas from Sgor Gaoith, the Allt Fuaran Diotach gives a much easier access to Loch Einich. Secondly, Thornton mentions waiting for his companions at a 'charming spring'. Below Sgor Gaoith is the *Fuaran Diotach*, the Dinner-Time Spring. Either the ghillies knew of this spot, or we can speculate that it was named after the celebration lunch which followed the ascent and the day's bag of game. However, the evidence points to Thornton's party having climbed Sgor Gaoith, not Sgoran Dubh to the north. Here is his account:

> A severe labour we had to ascend this mountain, as steep as the side of a house; rocky, sometimes boggy: whilst frequently large stones... would give way, and whirl down the precipice... At twelve o'clock we got up to the first snow, and, before one, we thought we were near the mouth of Glen Ennoch, and then depositing our champaign, lime, shrub, porter etc. in one of the large snow drifts, beneath an arch, from which ran a charming spring, we agreed to dine there.
>
> Having rested a few minutes, the gentlemen left their horses to the care of the servants... (and) kept moving forward, according to my directions (until) they at last arrived at the top. It is impossible to describe the astonishment of the whole party when they perceived

themselves on the brink of that frightful precipice, which separated them from the lake below! They remained motionless a considerable time, equally struck with admiration and horror... Let the
reader figure to himself a mountain at least eighteen thousand feet
above him, and a steep precipice of thirteen thousand below,
encompassed with conical and angular rocks; then let him imagine
men and horses, scrambling over huge masses of stone, which,
though of immense size, are frequently loose... and the very idea
will be enough to make him shudder. Yet the eye, having dwelt
awhile on these frightful, naked piles, is soon relieved... from the
scene beneath, where the lake, like a sheet of glass, reflects on its
bosom all the objects around... bordered by soft, sandy banks...
and a single bothie – the temporary residence of the lonely herdsman... (p. 100-1)

It is interesting that, despite the heat of the high summer, there
was still snow on the ridge, in August. In that month, too, the cattle
were still at the summer shieling at the head of Loch Einich, where
the herdsman's bothy was the forerunner of a series of shelters which
stood there till around 1950. A certain John of Corrour (*Coire
Odhar*) who was born in the bothy, left a sum to ensure that there
would always be meal in it for the traveller. Thornton's account of
the climb is over-blown, yet seeing the cliffs around Loch Einich
would have staggered travellers in his day. The account of the ascent
from the west, little more than a stroll, is his main exaggeration.
Main, but not only. Thornton makes Sgor Gaoith higher than
Everest, at a time when the heights of many mountains had been
estimated by the military road-makers and others. It would be nice
to excuse our Sassenach by claiming a misplaced digit; but he does
not write the hill's height as a combination of 18,000 and 13,000
feet, which could be a printer's error, but as 'eighteen thousand' and
'thirteen thousand'. Possibly the potent mixture of excitement, heat
and champagne had affected his judgement.

Thornton comments that he had so much enjoyed his day at
Glen Einich, especially the summit views, that he resolved on a
repeat foray, in the region of Loch Laggan. On August 23rd he set
out with a couple of companions and 'a herdsman who knew these
mountains', in order to hunt mountain hares, which they did with
falcons. The mountains Thornton describes leave us in no doubt that
he was on the Creag Meagaidh range, the 'dreadfully high mountains which almost overhang Aberarder' can be no other. The fact
that in his hunting he tried several *corrys*, which he defines as

'amphitheatres of rocks', strongly suggests that his trek of fifteen miles round trip, included the main summit itself, since the outlying peaks are smoother. The Colonel describes his panorama at one point:

> As we proceeded, we met with several charming scenes, and got a view of the almost unpassable road over the Coriarich [Corriegearrag, or Corrieyairick, to the north of Meagaidh]; also discerned, at a distance Ben Nevis, and other hills, whose names are not known, and whose northern sides are covered with quantities of snow-drifts. (p. 129)

This was a view he could certainly have had from the plateau of Creag Meagaidh, though hardly from its eastern outliers. Thornton mentions that the day was planned to end thus: '...we meant in the evening to come by Corgarderer (Coire Ardair), said to have a lake at the foot of it... full of trout'. He also states that the return to Aberarder at the end of the day was four miles. This allows us, with reasonable confidence, to describe his route as having done a circuit of the range, starting in the morning around Carn Liath, and proceeding towards Meagaidh itself, descending by Coire Ardair, and returning to Aberarder. Thorton got two brace of mountain hares, animals which favour the high summits, such as Meagaidh's plateau, commenting that 'on the top it blew a hurricane' – indicating he had been there.

Thus the first ascent of this mountain, which has been credited to Colonel Colby of the Ordnance Survey, must, I feel, go to his countryman and fellow military man, Colonel Thornton. Here is his description of the descent towards Aberarder, almost certainly by Coire Ardair:

> The mist came on about six o'clock... Surely, such a descent was hardly ever passed by man. I repeatedly thought I should have broken my neck; nor did I get down the first mile in less than an hour and forty minutes, the loose stones falling almost every step I took...
>
> I narrowly escaped breaking my legs, or a more fatal accident; for, leaping on a stone... my feet slipped in such a manner, that... I hurt myself very much... my feet, though, from experience I had ordered the strongest bear-soles to my shoes, were severely cut... (p. 130)

Thornton mentions in astonishment that 'The herdsman, without shoes, walked unhurt, with his horny feet... over the angular rocks...' (Loc. Cit.). Morally one feels that the unnamed ghillie deserves the credit of this first ascent, and one can hardly avoid the suspicion that he had probably already covered the ground Thornton describes many times, to harden his feet to a level which so impressed the Yorshire sportsman.

Jacobites and Hanoverians

Just two years before Thornton's *Sporting Tour*, the estates forfeit by the Jacobites after his father's military tour in 1745-46, had been returned to their owners. While in government hands, attempts had been made to increase the productivity of and revenue from the estates, and this entailed mineralogical and topographical surveys. Before his conquest of Nevis detailed above, James Robertson had visited the Cairngorm area on behalf of the Annexed, or Forfeit, Estates Commission, whose 'Commissioner Clerk' he refers to in his notes (NLS 2508).

From Perth Robertson penetrated Glen Clova, and thence traversed a mountain he writes as *Mare*, which is Mayar, covered in snow in early June. He adds that: 'From the top of the Mare I saw nothing but towering hills called Bennyhigh or Benchichin' (p. 19) – the latter being the older form of Lochnagar's name. Of this he says, after coming to the Spittal of Glenmuick:

> ...on the hill called Lochnagan a variety of crystal is found. This is the highest mountain here, and it is the only one on which, for some time, I have observed the rocks formed into inacessible precipices. (p. 23)

So, did he climb it, or was he simply 'on' it?

Braemar he does not like. The castle is 'a pitiful old building' with only 15 soldiers and the population are Erse-speaking Papists, which appalls the Whig Robertson. Neither is he impressed by their industry:

> Indeed Agriculture here is neither understood nor encouraged... cattle being the chief object of attention... Poor, ignorant, unskillful... the inhabitants have sunk into a state of abject idleness... veneration for old customs... impells the highlander, like all savages, to oppose all innovation... (pp. 45, 48)

Heading northwards for Grantown, Robertson completed the first recorded ascent of Ben Avon, including a side trip to Loch Avon itself upstream. He repeats the opinion of Taylor (cited earlier) that the summit is never free of snow, and his detailed description of the summit leaves no doubt as to his ascent:

> June 10th. Leaving Braemar I proceeded to Gavilrig in Glen Avin. In my way I crossed the top of Ben Avin, the highest hill in the shires of Aberdeen, Bamff and Murray... Ben Avin itself is a prodigious mass, not less, in my opinion than three miles broad and six miles long, steep on all sides, but in some places presenting horrid precipices altogether inacessible. The top is flat like a large piece of gravel. On this flat top a number of natural pyramids have arisen, some of them above 30 feet high. (p. 32-3, 34)

There is some confusion both as to Robertson's subsequent route, and as to the mountains he climbed. He moved to Speyside and comments that 'I traversed the mountains which lie South from Invereich.' (p. 72). This could be the Sgorans range, ascended three years later by Thornton, but could well be any other of a number of hills. Thence he traversed the Monadliath from Badenoch, 'crossing the mountains that lie at the head of the water of the Findhorn' (p. 81). These had snow on top, and on the summit of one he was caught in a horrendous thunderstorm which led to his showing advanced navigation skills. 'Having fixed my route by the Map and Compass, I advanced towards Strathdearn.' (Loc. Cit.). Clearly Robertson ascended a Monadliath summit on his 1771 tour, but the evidence is too scanty to determine which one. Half a century later occurred the first recorded ascent of a top in this rather undistinguished range of hills.

In order to avoid loading this work too heavily with biographical details of our actors when first they come on the mountain stage, I will survey the life and times of Colonel Thomas Colby of the Ordnance Survey, when we deal later with his much more important exploits in the West Highlands. Colby and his OS party including Major Dawson visited the Meagaidh area in 1819, and according to Horn (Op. Cit. p. 161), 'on the third day Creag Meagaidh was apparently climbed'. In fact, his party climbed not Meagaidh but *Bui-Annoch*, which as A'Bhuinneach is the name of the ridge on which Carn Liath stands, the outlier of the higher peak. Dawson estimated the peak at over 4,000ft and, a visitor to the Alps, he regarded the view to Ben Nevis from its summit as the equal of any he had seen

(*A Memoir of the Life of Major-General Colby*, J.E. Portlock, 1869, p. 141.) But the previous day, 24 July 1819, the party did have a first ascent in the Monadh Liath, reaching, as retailed by Major Dawson, after crossing:

> a rough tract of boggy country... the summit of Cairn Derig, a mountain about 3,500 feet high... and having built a large pile of stones upon it... (proceeded) thence again across country to Garviemore... (Op. Cit. p. 140)

Though summits to the south of the Cairngorms, such as Ben Lomond, became early an easy day for a lady in an increasingly liberated world for upper-class women, the first female with a Cairngorm peak to her credit would appear to be Mrs Sarah Murray. This redoubtable woman lost her maiden name – Maese – through marriage to a Scotsman. She was an enthusiast of all things Caledonian, and at the age of 52 in 1796 she made a two-thousand

Thomas Colby
(artist unknown)
A fine study of the Ordnance Survey man, showing possibly a less severe countenance than one might have expected.
(Ordnance Survey, Southampton).

mile-journey through the country, which resulted in her guide *A Companion and Useful Guide to the Beauties of Scotland* (1799). She visited Skye, Mull and the Central/Southern Highlands, only skirting the Cairngorms via Speyside. However, she returned in 1801, and in the third edition of her *Guide*, published nine years later, she gives the first first-hand account of the ascent of Cairngorm. Mrs Murray rode to the summit, while her four male companions walked. They had a good day with fine views and refreshed themselves near the summit at 'a well of the finest spring water I ever tasted, and it is also the coldest I ever touched'. Mrs Murray was clearly pleased with her ascent, commenting, 'To ride up Cairngorm is an arduous task, and to walk down it a very fatiguing one.' (Third edn. 1810 pp. 335, 6)

Mrs Murray is sometimes credited as making the first ascent of Cairngorm on record (see CCJ Vol 1 MacConnochie p. 375) –

however she had been beaten to it by about 50 years, according to local legend cited in the Rev. W. Forsyth's *In the Shadow of Cairngorm* (1900). James McIntyre had fought with the Jacobites in the 1745 Rebellion. He reputedly saved the colours of his regiment after Culloden, and according to Forsyth:

> [The standard] was brought from Culloden by its brave bearer, James McIntyre, commonly called *Fear ban Bheaglan*, and cherished by him long as a precious relic. Once every year, on the anniversary of the raising of the Prince's standard at Glenfinnan, he used to take it to the top of Cairngorm, and there unfurl it with much pride. He wished, he said, to give it fresh air. (p. 184)

No doubt James was a brave man, but to carry out such an act would have cost him his life in the aftermath of Culloden. Braemar and Speyside had been Jacobite strongholds in 1689, 1715 and in the 45 itself. In the years after 1746, on the fringes of the Cairngorms, ex-Jacobites and bandits were in a state of semi-war with the occupying Redcoats and the irregular militia, composed mainly of Hanoverian Campbells, and still known locally as Cleansers. The carrying of arms or wearing of tartan – still more the displaying of Jacobite colours, most of which had been burnt by the hangman – were offences punishable by prison – or worse. Thus I think we could, with a degree of safety, place McIntyre's first ascent in the 1750s at the earliest.

An account of the Braemar Highlands at this time, is given in the author's 'Pacification in the Braes o Mar and the Murder of Sergeant Davies', *West Highland Free Press* (14.2.1997). Davies was billeted at Dubrach near the hamlet of Inverey. On his way out hunting one day in 1749 he met a couple of locals, armed and wearing tartan, and Davies challenged them. They killed him, and were later tried and acquitted, despite their guilt, for lack of evidence. Sergeant Davies' body was found on the summit of Cristie Hill in Glen Ey, which is well over 2,500ft, and a distant outlier of the present Munro, Carn Bhac. Clearly Davies hunted high, and it is not impossible that he had traversed Carn Bhac on that fateful day.

Ministers and their Munros

A calmer age followed the 45: an age of rationality and science, of economic progress, of Enlightenment. An age with a mania for collating and measuring, of statistical accounts, and surveys and enumerations – such as the first census in 1801. Ministers of the Kirk of Scotland were heavily involved in such 'improvement', and their contributions to the *Old* and *New Statistical Accounts* of the parishes of Upper Deeside make fascinating reading, showing us the changes taking place between 1783 and 1842. Although Gaelic was generally spoken on both occasions, almost all local inhabitants could speak English at the latter date, compared with only a majority at the former. (For a fuller account of this issue, see 'Aberdeenshire Gaelic' by A. Watson and R.D. Clement in *Transactions of the Gaelic Society of Inverness* Vol LII, 1983, pp. 373-404.) Braemar had a bank – opened in 1815 – and daily coach and post communication with Aberdeen by the time of the NSA Population was declining, from 2,251 in the parish of Crathie and Braemar at the time of the OSA, to 1,712 by the time of the NSA Interestingly, while Catholics made up over one third of the total population in 1783 (and were in a slight majority over Protestants in Braemar itself), they made up just over one fifth of the inhabitants in 1842. (Figures calculated from O & NSA). Missionary activity – supported by Royal Bounty and the SPCK (Society for the Propagation of Christian Knowledge) – as well as depopulation, halved the Catholic population in less than half a century.

Other forms of improvement certainly gladdened the heart of the writer of the NSA which bring anguish to the modern reader. He laments the lapsing of a 'conservation' scheme, ie conservation of sheep, game and poultry, whereby a premium was paid by the landlords for the destruction of 'vermin'. We are told the scheme was a great success for 10 years:

> ...during that period there were killed 634 foxes, 44 wildcats, 57 polecats, 70 eagles, 2,520 hawks and kites, 1,347 ravens and hooded crows... (NSA Vol XIV, p. 475. 1982 edn.)

The minister of the Kirk of Scotland at Leith Hall and Kinkell appears from his entry in the *Fasti Ecclesiae Scoticanae* to have led an eventful life, and the said Rev. Dr. George Skene Keith, certainly shared – as did many clergymen – in the improving passions of the time. He wrote on religious and constitutional matters, on the improvements of weights and measures and – nice work – '...at the request of a Committee he made experiments in distilling for which Parliament voted him five hundred pounds' (*Fasti*, Vol 4, p. 365, 1923) – six times his annual salary! He was an 'active and bustling' minister, and – canny Scot – cultivated his own glebe scientifically.

Keith was also responsible to Sir John Sinclair, President of the Board of Agriculture (who had earlier been the architect of the *Old Statistical Account*, to which Keith had also contributed as Kinkell minister), for drawing up in 1811, the *General View of the Agriculture of Aberdeenshire*. Rather like the earlier government-commissioned surveys of the Forfeited Estates, this was intended to present recommendations for the improvement of agricultural practises and output. Here we will limit ourselves to Keith's observations on, and activities in, the Marr (so-spelled) division of the county, where are found its mountains. This involved Keith in a series of arduous journeys at a time when the minister, born in 1752, was almost 60 years old.

Keith observes that the main economic activity at that time was the mining of Cairngorm stones, then at its height. He suggests that the miners be obliged to construct enclosures from their mining waste, and that these be limed and sown with grass for sheep-fodder. He also suggests that drainage could convert moorland to pasture. But he is forced to admit:

It must be acknowledged however, that in this Alpine district, there is a great proportion of the surface that produces neither grass, nor corn, nor wood of any kind. (p. 589)

But it is Keith's experiences as a mountaineer, rather than as an agricultural improver, which really interest us. As part of the mania for measurement of the epoch, Keith wished to ascertain the heights of various mountains. He undertook a journey in the summer of 1810, an outline of which is printed as an Appendix to his *General View...*, and entitled *'Short Account of Two Journies, Undertaken with a view to ascertain the Elevation of the principal Mountains in the Division of Marr'* – a short account, but a long title! Equipping himself with a barometer and a spirit level, he set off.

On 14th July he and his companions ascended Lochnagar (by then so-called) and measured its height at almost exactly 3,800 ft. They remained three hours there, dining and admiring the views, till the weather changed, and they descended in thick fog.

Our descent was accompanied by a number of awkward tumbles, and one of the gentlemen was rolled nearly 100 feet; but no accident happened to any of us, except the loss of my spirit level. After 12 hours absence, we returned... completely drenched with rain... (p. 643)

Robert Gordon *Aberdonia et Banfia* (ex.) (1654) from Blaue's *Atlas*
Gordon's map, based largely on his own explorations, shows that many mountains we
know today, including Cairngorm and Beinn a' Bhuird, were familiar in his time. It also
shows settlement patterns, e.g. *Inner-Ey*, and extant tree cover.
(Ian Mitchell)

Two days later he completed the first recorded ascent of *Ben-a-bourd* (Beinn a' Bhuird), 'an immense mass, without beauty or fertility, extending about three miles in length, and almost flat on top', computing its elevation at 3,940 ft. Ben Avon he found to be more interesting, on account of its varied surface of tors, but that mountain had already been ascended by James Robertson. This dual ascent passed without mishap.

On the 17th July the party visited the newly-built Marr [*sic*] Lodge. After inspecting the Linn o Dee, they passed 'a little above the Doubrach (which is the highest arable, or inhabited land in the county)'. Somewhat south of the present Corrour Bothy they came upon a 'shealing' belonging to some Badenoch shepherds, 'the only human habitation' in this region. The party were doubtful as to their route, when – near the summit of the Lairig Ghru at an elevation of roughly 2,000 ft – they met a man from Badenoch, carrying provisions to the sheiling, who directed them; indicating the possibility that theirs was not the first, only the first recorded, ascent. For on that day Keith and his companions climbed Braeriach, and then for good measure, added Cairn Toul. This is such an epic, told in the understated prose of the early nineteenth century, that we would do any reader a disservice by extensively editing it. Here is Keith's account:

> At 2 o'clock P.M. we set out to climb the mountain, still keeping in sight of the river... It was in flood at this time, from the melting of the snow, and the late rains; and, what was most remarkable, an arch of snow covered the narrow glen from which it tumbled over rocks... and then we had to climb among huge rocks, varying from one to ten tuns, and to catch hold of the stones or fragments which projected, while we ascended in an angle of 70 or 80 degrees. A little before 4 o'clock we got to the top of the mountain which... I knew to be Breriach, or the speckled mountain... We sat down, completely exhausted, and drank of the highest well... We mixed some good whisky with the water, and recruited our strength. Then we poured, as a libation, into the fountain, a little of the excellent whisky... After resting half an hour, we ascended to the top of Breriach, at 5. P.M., and found it to be 4,280 feet above the level of the sea. Then we descended amidst a thick fog, which suddenly overwhelmed us, and attempted next to get to the top of Cairntoul... which we found to be only 5 feet higher than Breriach... On this summit the rain poured out in such torrents, and the wind battered us so much, that two gentlemen holding

umbrellas over my head, could not protect me while I marked the height of the barometer in my journal...

Unfortunately we had no pocket compass, and afraid of falling over the huge rocks of Poten Duon (Devil's Point, I.M.), which are nearly 1,600 feet high, we turned too much to the right hand and completely lost our way... It was 9 o'clock at night before we found that a small river, whose course we happily followed, was the Guisachan... And it was half an hour past 9, when we arrived... at the shieling which we had passed at noon. We were now completely exhausted with hunger and exertion; and the shepherds had neither ale, milk, whisky nor any thing, except... bannocks baken of oatmeal, and nearly two inches thick... these bannocks appeared to me the best l had ever tasted, while the stream of the Dee allayed out thirst. Our horses joined us at 10 o'clock and we arrived at Allanaquoich, about half an hour past 1 next morning... after nearly 19 hours of fatigue.
(General View... p. 644-5)

After re-ascending Lochnagar to check his original measurements, and then bagging Mount Keen and calculating its height on the way home, Keith finished his first journey back in Aberdeen on the 22nd July, thus accounting for the most significant week's work to that date in the history of Scottish mountaineering.

After some tedious efforts, Keith finally obtained the use of an improved barometer, and departed again, arriving at Mar Lodge on the 14th September, in time for breakfast. Then his group set off and retraversed, in better weather, the Cairn Toul/Braeriach plateau, correcting the errors in their earlier measurements, before descending to Aviemore. On Speyside he was lent a compass by the Duke of Gordon, who also recommended a fox-hunting guide, John Gordon, for the ascent of Macdhui. Setting out at 5a.m., Keith, Gordon and his party climbed Braeriach again (his third ascent), descended 2,200 ft to the Lairig Ghru and re-ascended almost 2,300 ft to the top of *MacDouie* (so spelled by Keith), where they dined on the summit, but dethroned it from the highest in the land, by comparing its barometric measurements with those just taken by a party (including his son) Keith had sent off beforehand to Ben Nevis, to measure that mountain. A sad day for the Cairngorms indeed! Local resentment was soon expressed, partly with a plan to build up Macdhui to the required height to regain its position, partly by a dog-in-the-manger attitude expressed by the Rev. Archibald Henderson, minister of

Crathie and Braemar in 1842, who claimed, in the *New Statistical Account*:

> According to the last geometrical survey by order of the Government, this mountain (Ben Macdhui) was found to be 20 feet higher than Ben Nevis, which was beforehand considered to be the highest in Britain. (Op. Cit. p. 647)

Proceeding from Macdhui in what he described as a 'most delightful day', Keith and his companions arrived at the summit of Cairn Gorm where the measuring continued. From its summit could be seen Ben Nevis, which Keith had enthroned as the highest mountain in the British Isles, and to the north, Caithness. After a dram by Huntly's Well below Cairngorm, they descended to Glenmore. What a pity Keith did not re-visit the Cairn Toul summit on that 21st September; then he would have held the honour of being the first to have done all the 4,000 ft mountains in the Cairngorms in one day. But still, three is excellent going, especially without proper maps and modern equipment, and Keith must have been a man of remarkable strength to have achieved what he did. As he himself noted in his *Account*, '...I must remark, that the man must have good stamina, who would regain health by measuring mountains' (p. 648). Scottish mountaineering has its fathers – the Raeburns and Naismiths of the later nineteenth century. If it is ever looking for grandfathers, I suggest that Keith be given pride of place.

Romantic Deeside

Certainly, Keith's published account was consulted by several other travellers, and his heights of the main Cairngorm peaks were soon quoted as authoritative. Soon after Keith's journeys, an English landscape painter, George Fennel Robson, made extensive tours of the Highlands, inspired by the current vogue for the poetry of Walter Scott, whose works he carried with him as he travelled romantically dressed as a shepherd. In 1814 appeared his *Scenery of the Grampian Mountains*, with forty outlines of mountain landscape from Lochaber to the Braes of Mar. This was such a success, that five years later he produced a second edition, where the original etchings in black and white were aquatinted. Though romantically exaggerated, Robson's paintings give us the fullest visual picture to that date of the Cairngorm mountains.

William MacGillivray (artist unknown).
The dour character of the naturalist, with a hint of his vulnerability also,
is captured in the portrait.

Ben Lomond

North-West View. John Knox's somewhat exaggerated, romanticised view of the Ben (c. 1834) does show what a tourist attraction it had become, with several groups of visitors on the mountain in addition to the obligatory locals in Highland dress.

(Glasgow Museums: Art Gallery & Museum, Kelvingrove)

Briariach and Carn Toul

from Scenery of the Grampian Mountains (1819 ed.) by George Fennell Robson. The view is towards where the Corrour bothy would later be built; the de rigeur shepherd is standing on the col at c. 850m between Macdhiu and Carn a' Mhaim. This is clearly where Robson stood when painting – raising the possibility that he climbed the latter mountain.

(Aberdeen University Library)

Ben-Y-Bourd

from Scenery of the Grampian Mountains (1819 ed.) by George Fennell Robson. Notable in the illustration of Beinn a' Bourd is the military bridge at Invercauld, a picturesque feature, and the heavy tree cover in the area, now depleted. Robson originally produced line drawings of his tour for a list of subscribers in 1814, shortly after Keith climbed these hills for the first time. The success of his drawings led Robson to produce water-colour versions five years later. His draughtsman-like eye shows the mountains in accurate detail.

(Aberdeen University Library)

The Cuillins from Ord

(c. 1854) by Horatio McCulloch. Often criticised as 'leathery' due to his predilection for shades of brown, McCulloch here instead gives us a dazzling play of light and cloud against the blue-black of the Cuillin. Again, one could stand where the dog is, and identify most of the peaks today, so accurate is McCulloch. On the right is Blaven, soon to be climbed by Nichol and Swinburne.

(Glasgow Museums: Art Gallery & Museum, Kelvingrove)

Battle of Glenshiel

(1719) by Peter Tillemans. That Tillemans was not at Glenshiel is not credible, so recognisable are the mountains – especially Sgurr na Ciste Duibhe on the right – and accurate the details of the evolution of the conflict. General Wightman is rampant on horse in the central foreground, while half way up the Ciste Duibhe is Rob Roy and band.

(National Galleries of Scotland)

Loch Maree (1866)

Horatio McCulloch. This painting looks over much of the territory of Thomson's map, and the scene is virtually unchanged today, except for the thatched cottages by the loch. Beinn Airigh Charr, which had an early ascent occupies the centre ground, but to the left are visible A' Mhaighdean and Ruadh Stac Mhor, not even on the map till the OS men arrived.

(Glasgow Museums: Art Gallery & Museum, Kelvingrove)

Loch Coruisq near Loch Scavaig (1811)

by William Daniell. Like Robson, Daniell met the demand for picturesque mountain scenes, but unlike Robson he did so in comfort, from a boat. Coruisq may be exaggerated but it is recognisable. The still unclimbed – and also unnamed – Sgurr a' Ghreadaidh is central, with Sgurr a' Mhadaidh on the right in similar virginal state. And those are not fishermen, but about two dozen holidaymakers, tourists, on the loch, on a day-trip from Elgol.

(The Mitchell Library)

Robson (1788-1833) made a number of visits to Scotland, and he specialised in mountain scenery, being admitted to the Society of Painters in Watercolours in 1813. The critic, Ruskin, whose writings did so much to remould appreciation of the mountain landscape, thought highly of Robson. Of his works he said, 'They are serious and quiet in the highest degree, (and) certain qualities of atmosphere and texture in them have never been equalled.' (*Works*, III, 1903, p. 193.) Robson was a strong walker, and travelled on foot from Blair Atholl to Speyside, via Glen Tilt and the Lairig Ghru. He mentions that on top of *Carn-an-Gour*, the highest peak of *Ben-Y-Gloe*, 'has been erected a cairn... which is visible at a remote distance' (*Illust.* XXVII). It is possible this was erected by the party of General Roy sent out in 1776 to barometrically estimate the height of the mountain. Although his main interest was in drawing the mountains – which generally look best from the glens – Robson did climb at least one of the hills, recording the first repeat of Keith's ascent of Braeriach. Robson additionally gives such a detailed account of the summit of Beinn a' Bhuird, that it seems likely he was there also (Illust. XXXIII). Robson quotes the altitude of Braeriach as 4,200 ft on the authority of Keith, and comments:

> ...neither difficulty nor danger should deter the tourist, who has reached the foot of Brairiach, from visiting the summit... let him approach, with cautious steps, the brink of the precipice... (Gloss to Illust. XXXVII Brairiach and Carn Toul, from the head of Glen Dee)

The *de rigeur* shepherd in the painting is standing on the col at well over 2,600 ft. between Macdhui and Carn a' Mhaim. Robson had clearly stood at that point, raising the possibility that he climbed Carn a' Mhaim, an easy walk from the col.

An interesting point from Robson's account, is his use of the word 'tourist', already generally used for the Highland traveller. Although many still had ulterior motives for roaming the bens and glens, such as earning a living from his paintings in Robson's case, it is clear that there were those prepared to do so just for the pleasure involved. One pleasure Robson clearly enjoyed was meeting the local people, of whom he had a high opinion. 'The inhabitants of these miserable hovels are in general much better informed, and seem endowed with quicker capacities, than the peasantry of England.' (*Illust.* XXXVIII.)

The emergence of Deeside as a tourist centre, with the attendant publication of guide-books, owed much of course, to the taking up of residence on Balmoral by Queen Victoria. So much has been written – most of it ephemeral – about the emergence of Royal Deeside that the reader will forgive me if I skim over the Queen's exploits. At any rate, as well as the large outpouring of works on Queen Victoria and Deeside, her own journals of her voyages are readily available. Her book is valuable, readable and conveys interesting information as to customs and local life. The redoubtable Queen repeated many of the now-obligatory tourist ascents from 1848-61, including Lochnagar, Beinn a' Bhuird, Macdhui, and in 1861 on her 'Last Expedition', made a clean sweep of the Tolmount Munros! Her visitors at the Castle included the Liberal Prime Minister Gladstone, who is reputed by many writers to have walked from Balmoral to the summit of Macdhui and back in a day – though his letters show he drove to Derry Lodge. But none of those of Queen Victoria's were pioneering trips, and with all due respect to the lady, it was a bit like painting with numbers, given the large retinue of retainers who accompanied 'expeditions'.

However, even the present writer, despite his unshakeable republicanism, has to give credit where it is due. It seems doubtful that hers was the first, but in 1841 when Queen Victoria climbed the mountain above Forest Lodge in Glen Tilt on 21st September 1844, it is the first recorded ascent that I have been able to discover of Carn a' Chlamain. And she even walked a bit of the way, as is clear from her account.

So we set off and wound round and round the hill, which had the most picturesque effect imaginable...

We stopped at the top of Ghrianan, whence you look down an immense height. It is here that the eagles sometimes sit.. We then went nearly to the top of Cairn Chlamain,... Albert going off to get a 'quiet shot'... and Lady Canning, Lord Glenlyon and I went up quite to the top, which is deep in moss... The view was quite beautiful, nothing but mountains all around us... My pony was brought up for me, and we then descended...

(*Leaves from the Journal of our Life in the Highlands*, 1868, p. 38-9)

Though the local ghillies were doubtless familiar with the mountain, the possibility that they had never trod the mossy summit, allows us to award the first, known, female first ascent of a Scottish mountain to Queen Victoria – and Lady Canning. Lord Glenlyon we designate as the 'token male' (and possible descendant of *Caillean Gorach*). Queen Victoria's main contribution to our knowledge of the Cairngorms at this period comes not so much, however, from her own book, but from the funds she provided for the posthumous publication of the writings of the naturalist William MacGillivray, whose *Natural History of Deeside* appeared in 1855. A wonderful book, a book beyond compare, a classic, whose unavailability in print is a disgrace to Scotland's cultural and scientific history, which should be remedied.

The Naturalist

As a young boy in Aberdeen, I was taken to the Natural History Museum at the university, where the image of a giant red crab was forever imprinted on my mind. I later discovered the museum was the creation of the Professor of Natural History in the 1840s, William MacGillivray. It is only recently that MacGillivray's contributions to natural history have been recognised – at least in his own country – due to the publication of Dr Robert Ralph's *William MacGillivray* (1993). But as we shall relate, the naturalist was a mountain pioneer of distinction also.

MacGillivray is doubly unusual as a Scientific Gael – not an area in which their talents usually found outlet – and as an Aberdonian Gael – since 'the toon' is the least Highland of the Scottish cities. For there he was born illegitimate in 1796, the son of a Highlander who abandoned him at three, and a mother, a local woman he never knew. He was sent to an uncle's in Harris, where he remained until returning to University in Aberdeen, where he studied medicine, natural science and zoology. He did various laboratory work, and then curatorial duties in Edinburgh, before finally achieving a post commensurate with his talents and achievements, the Chair at Aberdeen, which he held from 1841 until his death.

His career was held back partly because, an outspoken man, he made many enemies and few friends, especially amongst the academic 'cabinet naturalists' he despised, saying, 'The naturalist must not shut himself up in his study when the wintry winds blow over the blasted heath.' In fact, his irascible personality is very similar to that of Burton, another dour Aberdonian, whom we shall consider subsequently.

MacGillivray made most of his field investigations on his own, and his solitariness and the unhappy circumstances of his early life made him liable to fits of melancholy and self-doubt; fits which he took refuge from in innumerable workaholic projects. As well as organising museums and writing numerous scientific textbooks, MacGillivray produced, with the renowned naturalist Audubon, the *History of British Birds* in 1837. Though mainly famous due to Audubon's splendid illustrations, the bulk of the scientific work was MacGillivray's. In the book, birds are classed for the first time according to anatomical structure, and Charles Darwin, in his *Origin of Species*, paid tribute to 'the accurate MacGillivray'. Though MacGillivray met Darwin, and himself was beginning to doubt creationist immutability of species, the naturalist died before Darwin's *magnum opus* was published. For, worn out by over-work at his lectures, publications, and field trips, and with the burden of having fathered 13 children, MacGillivray died at the early age of 56 in 1852.

MacGillivray was not the kind of naturalist who worked from stuffed specimens, or corpses brought to his study. He firmly believed in getting his boots muddy and made several remarkable journeys in pursuit of his passion for natural history As a student in 1819 he walked from Aberdeen to London to view the collections in the British Museum, crossing the Grampian mountains on his way south, annotating, classifying, observing – a round walk of over 1,000 miles! In a rare human touch on this trip he records, 'I have not seen a beautiful girl since I left Aberdeen'. But his failure to learn the local dialect – despite spending half his life in the city – caused him problems with the fair sex. He records his inability to communicate with a local serving maid, 'Because I did not speak Scotch'.

MacGillivray kept up his Harris connections, and in 1820 he married an island woman, Marion MacAskill. Three years previously, he had thought nothing of walking from Aberdeen to the west coast, crossing the Cairngorms and walking along Loch Maree on the way, to catch the Harris boat at Poolewe. At the age of eleven he had walked to Aberdeen from Harris to begin his education. He must have been a man of astounding stamina, often sleeping rough, drinking only water, and carrying few provisions. In one of his *Journals*, he describes jumping over the Linn o Dee – which he describes as 'trifling' – and later arriving at a hamlet a couple of miles to the west. MacGillivray writes:

...I entered a house to enquire concerning the source of the river... The good man of the house who appeared to be a shepherd asked if I was hungry, and after I had answered that I was not, ordered his wife to give me some bread for the hills, which she did. (Ralph *Journal* No. 3 of MacGillivray, p. 2)

This hamlet was probably Tomnamoine or Tonnagaoithe, on the north side of the river. Our starving scholar had already experienced hospitality on the facing bank of the Dee, when returning in 1816 from a trip 'across the mountains from Blair in Athol'. Infuriatingly, he says nothing else other than that he explored the source of the river 'of equal size' to the Dee which joins it three or four miles above the Linn. This is the Geldie, which rises in An Sgarsoch, and MacGillivray could well have climbed it:

Came to Dubrach-tenanted by a person named MacHardy, who, expressing his concern at my having been out all night, treated me to a glass of whisky and some bread and milk. (*A Memorial Tribute to William MacGillivray* ed. W. MacGillivray, 1901, p. 145)

Dubrach was the original home of Peter Grant, at the time of MacGillivray's journey, the **still surviving** oldest participant in the 45 Rebellion! And though no longer occupying Dubrach as an outpost, the Redcoats were still – till 1831 – in occupation of Braemar Castle. MacGillivray could not speak 'Scotch', i.e. Doric, but – despite some weird orthography and eccentric suggestions for place and other names (e.g. '*uisge-beath* is not water of life, but water of birch'), it is clear that he had enough Gaelic to converse with the inhabitants of the Braes o Mar, still overwhelmingly Gaelic-speaking at this time. And this would have opened all doors for him. Magical times to be out on the hills...

It is to his expedition *Journals* that we owe our knowledge of MacGillivray's mountaineering, and on the 1817 residence on Harris he first recorded an ascent of a mountain, his native Clisham (p. 162). For although it is tempting to speculate that he climbed hills *en route* from Aberdeen to Harris, through Wester Ross and alongside Loch Maree, no evidence is available. That first ascent of the Clisham we will deal with in its proper geographical context, for there is enough material relating to MacGillivray's exploits in the Cairngorms, to satisfy us in this present division of our work.

Despite having no proper maps, and despite an appalling lack of equipment, for in his student days he carried no compass, no barometer – and it is clear on several occasions *no watch* – MacGillivray in the course of three decades would appear to have climbed most of the Cairngorm summits. In 1819 he repeated Keith's ascent of Beinn a' Bhuird made earlier in the decade, but was in ignorance of the name of the mountain he had climbed until a local informed him the next day! Unlike Keith, MacGillivray was impressed by Beinn a' Bhuird, especially the summit prospect:

> The scene which presented here I considered at the time as the most noble without exception which I had ever seen. On all sides... mountains appeared behind mountains with the rocks, ridges and vallies. A solemn stillness reigned over the whole. (Ralph, *Journal* No. 2 p. 18)

MacGillivray can possibly be forgiven for not knowing much about the topography of the area. The best of a bad bunch of maps at this date was probably the *County Atlas of Scotland* (1855) by W. and A.K. Johnstone, which hardly showed any more named peaks than Gordon had done a couple of centuries before. There are no contour lines, only rough hachures, no heights given, and a river is shown flowing between the south and north top of Beinn a' Bhuird. To the further north is an unbroken chain of mountains, running east-west from Ben Avon to Ben Macdhui, by pure coincidence coinciding with the Aberdeenshire county boundary! The map would have been a hindrance, rather than a help, to navigation. Not till the 1870s would mountaineering proper be launched in the wake of the publication of the Ordnance Survey maps of the Highlands.

MacGillivray further ascended Mount Keen, whose alpines disappointed him, though he thought the view fine. Lochnagar he ascended innumerable times, and it would appear to have been his favourite mountain. In 1850, he and his party made the first descent I can find record of, of the now-named Black Spout, which artists had already noted in their drawings and paintings:

> Of the fissures or rents by which the great precipice is scarred, one, the largest of all, commencing not far from the eastern summit, may be descended to the base of the rocks. (*Natural History of Deeside* p. 61)

He also climbed Einich Cairn, on a trip from Deeside to Speyside in 1819, but this must already have been trodden by Keith on his way from Braeriach to Cairn Toul in 1810. I. McConnochie credits

MacGillivray with the third ascent of Braeriach in 1819, after the successes of Keith and Robson (CCJ Vol 11. p. 55-6). But MacConnochie would appear to err. It is clear from MacGillivray's own account, that he ascended to the Wells o Dee, and traversed to Speyside, by-passing Braeriach's summit, whose name, like all the other mountains in the area, he was ignorant of in 1819! He, like Keith, ascended Garbh Choire, but unlike Keith, slept out making a bed from heather and grass, putting on gloves and a night-cap and placing his knapsack over his feet. A snack from his 'scanty store', a few mouthfuls of water, and he slept. On waking he felt weak, but decided to proceed further:

> The sides of this corry were composed of sloping rocks of vast height... Here the rocks were most abrupt, but I had determined to proceed, at least to attempt the passage. Before I got to the base of the rocks I felt very weak and was obliged to stop every now and then. However, I proceeded and found myself on the very summit of this vast mass of rock...
> I had now reached the rounded summit of the ridge, and proceeding along the streamlet... I traced it to two fountains and several subordinate ones. From the two principal founts I took a glassful, which I drank to the health of four ladies of my acquaintance... Descending on the northern side of the mountain I came upon a precipitous corry down which I did not venture... On the northern side of the mountain some alpine lakes occurred... (Ralph's *Journal* No. 3 pp. 4, 5)

From Wells o Dee our traveller went to the edge of Coire an Lochan, descending north-west into Glen Einich, missing the summit of Braeriach, somewhat to the east. Only later, in 1830 on a repeat visit to the area, did MacGillivray have any idea of where he had been; he claims only to have 'crossed' the Braeriach plateau.

But there are a couple of candidates for first, rather than repeat ascents, from MacGillivray. In 1830, the scientist and a party of gentlemen went from Braemar to climb Macdhui. A little more affluent now, they were driven to the Linn o Dee to save time. The group went together to the Lairig Ghru, whence they climbed Cairn Toul. Afterwards MacGillivray and his son went direct to Macdhui, while the others bagged Braeriach; so our naturalist may never have trodden Braeriach's summit at all. After they reached the summit of Macdhui, the mist came down, which was fortuitous. For it is clear that, inadvertently, this caused them to make the first recorded ascent of Derry Cairngorm, which anyone who has trod its stony surface will recognise from the description – though MacGillivray does not name it. But follow his account, with map in hand, and you will have no doubt of his route:

> After a walk of about half-a-mile over sand and granite slabs, gravel and rough stones, we arrived at the centre of the broad top [Macdhui, I.M.], and seating ourselves on the base of the pyramidal cairn of the Trigonometers, made our evening meal. It was eight o'clock; a thick mist suddenly covered the mountains and enveloped us...
>
> Not at all dismayed, we found by our compasses the direction in which we ought to proceed... But, there is a great precipice not very far distant from us which we must avoid. [Sputan Dearg, I.M.]
>
> So we directed our course eastward, descended over a long tract of very stony ground... and passing round the head of Glen Lui Beg, crossed a stony place to a hollow between two hills, [s. from pt. 3692. I.M.] expecting to find an easy descent into the valley of the Derry. But by this time it was so dark we could not have guided ourselves with safety among the rocks and stones of the very steep declivity... [Coire Etchachan or Coire an Lochan Uaine I.M.] Turning away, therefore, we ascended a hill entirely covered with large stones [Derry Cairngorm I.M.]... and found a gradual slope leading to the valley All this long slope, however, was covered either with stones or long heath... I never once fell among the granite blocks; but this night, in the course of our most weary progress over the heather, we all slipped or tripped many times... (on) our most fatiguing descent into the Derry... We did not reach Castletown [Braemar, I.M.] till three o'clock in the morning. (*Natural History* pp. 92-4)

Virtually every other Cairngorm hill was climbed by MacGillivray, though not all were firsts. The old Monega Road goes over Glas Maol, passing but a little east of the summit. It is difficult to believe that the cattle drovers did not, on occasion, climb to the summit to see, if nothing else, what weather lay ahead, or that those intent on depredations on menial or bestial, did not use it for a lookout. Be that as it may, our Professor, on a trip from Braemar to study the flora of Caenlochan glen, stepped aside from the path he walked from Glen Cluanie to Caenlochan, and ascended a couple of hundred feet up the shoulder of Glas Maol.

> On the broad summit of Glas-mheal we had a superb view all round, including in the south and west the mountains of Perth-

shire... To the east were seen Mount Keen and Mount Battock...
On (the) summit we saw three Dotterels, and further on several
Ptarmigans. Alpine Hares were numerous... (*Natural History* p. 77)

But *Glashmeal* had already been ascended by the sturdy Colby
of the OS, in 1819. (*Account... Principal Triangulation*, 1858, p.
114.) However, in the same year of 1850, MacGillivray made an
ascent of Lochnagar by Glen Callater, the route to which passes over
the shoulder of Carn an t-Sagairt Mor. MacGillivray loved this peak,
calling it 'picturesque' and 'finely proportioned', and he also noted
that its 'elevated summit' was composed of granite. Men have been
hung on less evidence, and I think that we can assume that
Macgillivray traversed the summit of the Hill of Peter the Priest on
his way to that of Lochnagar. He was a particular man, so he would
not speculate.

Many more must have been the summits trodden by our naturalist, but as his interest was mainly in the flora and fauna, he did
not deem it of import to record or claim feats of mountaineering.
In other words, MacGillivray was still a pre-mountaineer. Though
he did not claim any mountains, the mountains claimed him. On
Lochnagar he caught a severe chill due to exposure, from which
he never fully recovered. His wife's sudden death soon afterwards
hastened his own premature demise, one of the Grim Reaper's earliest mountaineering victims in Scotland.

MacGillivray shared many of the attitudes of his times. He was
a pillar of Victorian religiosity, of the Scottish type, and on his trip
to London was shocked at the laxity of the English Sabbath. This
found expression in his attitude to the mountains, where the common, in fact, commonplace, idea of the mountains as nature's tem-
ple is expressed – an idea that is still frequent in our day. In his
British Birds he wrote:

> ...in the wilderness, the lover of Nature cannot fail to look upon
> Nature's God. I believe it in fact impossible, in such a situation, on
> the height of Ben-na-muic-dhui or Ben Nevis, for example, not to
> be sensible, not merely of the existence but also of the presence of
> a Divinity. (Quoted in *A Memorial Tribute...* 1901, p. 146)

But other attitudes he expressed were at variance with normal
Victorian social conformity. As a Highlander he sympathised with
the plight of the Clearance victims, and shared their hatred of the
sheep which replaced them. As a naturalist he also hated the sheep

economy for its destruction of the indigenous flora and fauna of the mountains, as for example when he wrote on the raven that,

> ... sheep-farmers, with guns and traps, have left but a very scanty residue of a once prosperous and respectable race. The same inconsiderable selfishness which has cleared Van Diemen's land of its aboriginal population has destroyed our magnificent Eagles and sagacious Ravens. (*Natural History...* p. 84)

Though the modern environmentalist may recoil at his killing of birds and animals for scientific purposes, such attitudes as found in MacGillivray's writings make him a pioneer conservationist.

MacGillivray was a bit of an elitist in his mountaineering. Again and again he cautions us that the best experiences are had on one's own, and he decries as profanity the groups 'from our large towns' whose aim is simply to climb Ben Lomond or another peak, feast on chicken and whisky and 'toss as many stones as they can find over the precipices' *Memorial* (p. 146). He also regretted the discovery of Deeside by the general tourist, and the changes which had occurred in the half-century since 1800. The railway to Ballater was under construction, and in the Preface to his *Natural History of Deeside*, MacGillivray bemoans that:

> The romance of old Scotland is gone forever. The quiet waters of our sequestered lakes are agitated by the paddles of the steamer; carriages roll along our mountain valleys. (p. IX)

Now, this is the common lament of middle-aged men, that things were better in their own youth. But in as far as he is pointing out that the mountains are being opened up, MacGillivray was right. And once opened up, it would not be long before the era of mountaineering, as opposed to pre-mountaineering, was at hand.

Access Problems

MacGillivray's book helped to publicise the Cairngorm Highlands, and was followed nine years later by Burton's *The Cairngorm Mountains*, written purposely as a guide to exploration. J.H. Burton was born in Aberdeen in 1809, and died in 1881. His childhood was unhappy, his father dying when he was ten. Though his doting mother lived on, a semi-insane grandfather did not help. At an early date, according to his obituarist, he was 'afflicted with an invincible aversion to society', and as a 'great pedestrian, he imbibed a taste for solitary tours'. (DNB Vol III, p. 463.) A Benthamite Liberal, he wrote for the *Edinburgh Review*, and briefly edited the *Scotsman*. A sinecure to the Prisons Board gave him security to indulge his workaholic historiographical studies. In 1853 appeared the initial volume of his *History of Scotland*, the first academic study on the theme, and the work was completed in 1870. He also wrote a biography of Hume and collected and published many historical documents. He had few friends, and might appear to those from outside the North-East as a typical dour Aberdonian. As his obituarist in the DNB put it, 'With a dry, critical intellect, he combined an intense sensitiveness... the real cause of his unfortunate irascibility and impatience of contradiction' (Loc. Cit. p. 464). Even in those days the 'loner' like Burton sought solace in the mountains, denied him in society.

Burton published his *The Cairngorm Mountains* in 1864, and it is the first, general, authoritative guide to the massif. Its main importance is to show the historian that by the mid-1860s the area was well-known, and all the major mountains regarded as straightforward tourist ascents. Indeed, there was a tourist industry on Upper Deeside by then, with hotels catering for travellers, coaches providing transport, and locals offering services as guides. The era of pre-mountaineering was ending, as soon the clubs would be founded and mountaineering emerge as a specialised sport, with its own books, equipment and ethics. Significantly, Burton refers to the growing vogue of Alpinism (whose devotees he humorously refers to as 'Alpenstockists'), by mentioning that at Loch Avon, 'An Alpine devotee – for the passes and glaciers are coming to be among our objects of secular worship – might console himself here...' (p. 53).

Burton's book is a guide, enlivened by personal experiences. It is probable that he made many first ascents of the remoter peaks, since he tells us that 'it was when in boyhood (that) I first stumbled into that grand wilderness'. As he was born in 1809, that puts his first rambles in the early 1820s, when only the major peaks had been climbed. However, from his book, we can only discover that he made many repeat ascents. In one place he tells us of a trip in summer to the Shelter Stone, where he and his party were caught in a storm. Arriving at Loch Avon, Burton's feelings have been echoed by other mountaineers since:

... the interstices in the tempest-driven clouds only showed us a

dreary, winter, Greenland-like chaos of snow and rocks and torrents. It taxed our full philosophy... to believe that we were still in
the United Kingdom... and that it was the 1st of August. (p. 55)

Here we see the emerging eye of the mountaineer, not the
tourist. Loch Avon is Greenland-like, while he comments on the
snow-covered Shelter Stone Crag (then unnamed):

The peak detached from Ben Muich Dhui shot forth from the
snow as like the Aiguilles de Mont Blanc as one needle is like
another. (p. 54)

However, my favourite Burton story concerns an earlier trip,
his first, which is the kind of magical thing that seems to happen
to small boys, out on their first mountain experience. Here I repro-
duce it, to convey all its excitement and charm – an adventure one
could have in the semi-civilized Cairngorms at that time, but now
could only be had further afield, in the Karakoram, or another of
the earth's dwindling wild places. As well as ascending Macdhui,
our wee loon also probably crossed Beinn a' Bhuird on his journey from Glen Avon to Glen Quoich:

Some note of the blunders that brought (the adventure) about may
be a seasonable warning to the unwary... I had reached the top of
Ben Muich Dhui early in the day. The little wallet of provisions
had been carelessly left on a tuft of heather where I had rested, and
I could not afterwards find the spot. Somewhat tired and faint
with hunger, I descended the rocks by the side of the cataract,
believing that Loch Avon, seemingly so small from the summit of
the mountain, was the little tarn of Etichan, which had been
passed in the ascent from Deeside. It was alarming to find the lake
extending its bulk as I approached, and to see the glens looking so
different from any of those I was acquainted with from Deeside...
a few miles below the exit of the stream from the loch, as the
extreme dimness of the valley showed that sunset was approaching, I met a drover who had gone up into the wilderness in search
of stray black cattle.
He could speak little English, but was able to give me the startling
intelligence... that I had gone down towards the strath of the Spey
instead of that of the Dee, and that I was thirty miles from the
home I expected to reach that evening. My new friend took me
under his charge and conducted me to a bothy, made of the bent
roots of pine trees, and covered with turf... so low one could not
stand upright in it... my new friend hospitably presented me with
a supper of oatmeal and water... [and] I lay down and slept.

Conscious of a confused noise and a sort of jostling, it was with some surprise that I perceived that no less than ten men had crowded themselves into that little hut and had lighted a fire. This was like a realisation of some of Cooper's romantic incidents... My new companions were not of the most agreeable cast; they were rough and surly, hiding a desire to avoid communication by the pretence of inability to speak anything but Gaelic; while, in the midst of their Celtic communications with each other, they swore profusely in the Scottish vernacular. What their pursuits were... in that wild region, was a complete mystery to me, opened up slightly by reflecting on the two great lawless pursuits, smuggling and poaching, of the fruit of neither of which, however, did I see any symptom.

It was not, however, with much regret that, after having been packed with them for some hours on the hard stumps of heather, I left them in full snore at sunrise on a clear morning, and ascended the hill dividing the waters that run into the Spey from those which feed the Dee. (*Cairngorm Mountains* pp. 57-9)

Less than a quarter of a century after Burton's *The Cairngorm Mountains*, increasing mountaineering activity led to the formation of the Cairngorm Club, and the era of the Cairngorms before the climbers was but a memory. Interestingly, the formation of a separate mountaineering club for the North-East community in the 1880s, commented on adversely in some quarters then and since, was the crystallisation of tradition. Most of the Cairngorm explorers were locals, men of the North-East: Gordon, Keith, MacGillivray, Burton – and most of them confined their main interests to their local mountains – 'Aiberdeen an a hunder mile roon', to modify the original phrase a little.

But a reaction was taking place to this opening up of the mountains which coincided with the transition from sheep to deer, and the rocketing of the rentals on Highland estates. It would be pointless to deny that landlords had long taken action against poachers in the Cairngorms. W. McCombie Smith's delightful *The Romance of Poaching in the Highlands* (1904) tells many tales of the conflict between ghillie and poacher, and the ballad, *The Poacher o Braemar*, describes the romance of the chase and pursuit:

I am a roving Highlander, a native o Braemar
I've often climbed the mountains surrounding Lochnagar...

One night I went tae Ben-a-Bhuird, my gun intae my hand
Soon there follaed aifter me six keepers in a band...

The poacher is captured and laments his impeding exile to Van Diemen's land, and the fact he will see 'the bonnie Braes o Mar' no more. Versions of the ballad (Song 253), are printed in Vol II of *The Greig-Duncan Folk-Song Collection*, ed. P. Shuldham-Shaw and E. Lyle (1983). But in fact the poacher, Grewar, or Gruer, appears to have been sent to prison in Perth and subsequently died in Forfarshire. The song was well known by the 1850s, and probably describes events in the 1820s. At any rate, our poacher, who mentions 'climbing' the mountains, knew them as well as did Keith, MacGillivray and Burton who wandered the Cairngorms at the same time. That the song is in Scots shows the decline of Gaelic on Upper Deeside. Unlike in the Western Highlands where Gaelic gave way to English, in the Braes o Mar it was replaced by north-eastern Lowland Scots; by 1900 Scots was dominant, though Gaelic was still spoken in Braemar and Inverey. Today the inhabitants of Upper Deeside mainly speak a robust Scots.

But despite actions against the depredations of poachers, access was not barred to either drovers or ordinary pedestrians, whilst the sport of deer stalking was largely for the laird's amusement. Once it became lucrative, things changed, and by the end of the century, the Cairngorm Highlands became littered with litigations pertaining to attempts to ban access. These mainly lie outside our remit, but as early as 1846, Alexander Cockburn records that he had difficulty passing Glen Tilt, 'And then at the lower end of the Glen... he of Atholl has been pleased to set his gates and keepers, and for the same reason that he may get more deer to shoot easily.' (*Circuit Journeys* 1888, p. 310-11.) This closure was challenged by a group of Edinburgh botanists, leading eventually to a court case which the Duke lost, and the restoration of access through Glen Tilt. The leader of the access agitators was Professor Balfour, whose doings are commemorated in the poem, *The Battle of Glen Tilt*. (The full poem is given in CCJ Vol 3, No 15.)

> Balfour had a mind as weel
> As ony Duke could hae, man
> Quo he 'There's ne'er a kilted chiel
> Shall drive us back this day, man
> It's justice and its public richt
> We'll pass Glen Tilt afore the nicht'.

Shortly before this, the Duke of Atholl had his own claim to a first recorded ascent, or rather his domestic retainers had. We have mentioned already that a party under General Roy's command had climbed and measured the height of Beinn a' Ghloe in 1776. An outlier of this peak had its fiery baptism as follows:

> In 1839 a great bonfire was built to celebrate the 6th Duke's wedding, when wood and tar barrels were driven up the (Cromalltan) pass to the top of Carn Liath. Another bonfire was lit there in 1861 to celebrate the coming of age of the 7th Duke, and both these celebrations had the effect of widening the track. (*Life in the Atholl Glens,* John Kerr 1993, p. 94)

But just to stay true to form, Atholl tried to close this road over the Cromalltan Pass in 1888, and again failed.

A more tragic conflict of interests took place in the 1840s, between the inhabitants of Glen Ey and the Duke of Fife, who cleared the glen of all its inhabitants for a deer forest. The ruins of their clachans lend a picturesque note to the glen, but it is worth remembering that in the era of pre-mountaineering, these ruins, like others in Glen Dee and Glen Derry, housed numerous families, from whom our travellers appear to have met nothing but good will. An excellent short account of this glen is given in 'Gley Ey, a History' by G. Ewen, in CCJ (1994) Vol 20, 103. Increasingly, such good will was not what walkers met from landowners and gamekeepers. It should possibly be re-affirmed how artificial a creation the deer-forest was. When William Collie was hired with his father in the 1840s to manage Glen Feshie, there were almost no deer on the estate. The forest was stocked by poaching fawns from Mar and Atholl estates. Later Collie stocked Strathfarrar with similar gamekeeper-turned-poacher methods, described in his 1908 *Memoir of William Collie* (1992 edn.). The deer-forest is a totally unnatural environment.

In 1878 two Aberdeen men, one of whom was Alexander Copland, later a founder member of the Cairngorm Club, went on a trip to the Cairngorm mountains, of which they published an account. They climbed Cairn Toul, slept out, then climbed Macdhui and Beinn a' Bhuird. They commented on the changing times.

> Our native Mumbo Jumbos who molest the traveller in Glen Derry, Glen Lui Beg and other wilds... [attempt] selfishly, out of excessive relish for shooting deer... to prevent the inhabitants of this country from visiting its finest scenery, and turn back in dis-

gust those who know no better. It is intolerable that this should be permitted. (*Two days and a Night in the Wilderness,* Dryas Octopetala and Thomas Tway-blade 1878, p. 7)

They describe meeting Private Road signs and threats to prosecute trespassers, commenting, 'this notification, which strikes terror into the hearts of the Cockney tourist, does not alarm us much' (p. 35). Their advice to walkers who are stopped and questioned by those 'who would shut up every hill and glen in Scotland' is to 'treat such molestation with the contempt it deserves' (p. 42). Great stuff, and so is, 'The late Duke of Athole got a lesson which some of his neighbours may have not yet quite forgot; or if they have they may get it repeated.' (*Two Days...* p. 42.)

Our bold lads also mention that they were using

... those excellent and wonderfully cheap maps furnished by the Ordnance Survey. These maps, on the one inch to the mile scale, may be had from 1s 9d to 2s each, showing every road and path the tourist need take. (Op. Cit. p. 41-2)

In addition they give the times of the trains from Aberdeen to Ballater and other handy advice. Mountaineers with OS maps and railway timetables had replaced the pioneers like Keith, who only a little over half a century before had taken three days to reach Braemar from his home, a journey that now took, by train and connecting coach, roughly as many hours.

CHAPTER 3

West Highland Wanderers

IT WAS A GLORIOUS DAY in February 1994, pure sunlight and blue sky upon the whiteness of snow. Despite all that, I had failed to climb a hill in Glen Affric, because the drift was chest high and soft as a good meringue. Exhausted, I retreated and was being commiserated with at his retirement home in Cannich by old Duncan Maclennan, gamekeeper at Affric Lodge for many, many years. A good dram, and Duncan's tales of life in Glens Affric and Cannich compensated for my setback, but so too did a story he told me about my hill of failure, Beinn Fhionnlaidh. 'That hill, now, Findlay's Hill – do you know how it got its name?' I did not, so he told me.

The First Munroist

Fionnladh was a retainer of Mackenzie of Gairloch, and a keeper in the Affric Forest. One day on his wanderings he encountered an intruder at the hunt on top of a hill. Challenged, the intruder resisted, and *Fionnladh* shot him dead with an arrow from his bow, and hence the hill was named after the keeper, Findlay's Hill. As authority for the tale, Duncan had the word of previous keepers from these glens, and I for one was disposed to let this oral tradition stand. But the date? All I could hazard then was that by the end of the seventeenth century, the Highlander had abandoned the bow, and that therefore *Fionnladh* climbed his hill sometime before 1700. Whenever it was, this made our bowman the first recorded person to have definitely ascended a Scottish hill of over 3,000 ft beyond the Great Glen. It was also further evidence that the Gael did, in fact, frequent the mountain tops. At any rate, it was Duncan's story of his fellow keeper of yore which helped germinate the seed from which this present work developed.

A couple of years later, a piece of luck allowed me to date Findlay's exploits more or less exactly. I was examining the *History of the Clan MacRae* by A. Macrae, published in Dingwall in 1899, to see if I could find any detail about the battle of Glenshiel in which the clan fought. On that there was only the information of common currency, but I noted a chapter on the oral traditions of the clan, and idly flicked through it... My eyes caught the following:

> There was once a famous archer of the Clan MacRae called *Fionnla Dubh nam Fiadh* (Black Findlay of the Deer). He was forester of Glencannich... (p. 298)

I knew I had hit pay-dirt.

A certain MacDonald of Glengarry had settled in Glen Affric, and was out hunting one day, meeting Findlay and dying the death told to me by Duncan. The corpse was dumped in *Lochan Uaine Gleannan nam Fiadh* (the green loch of the glen of the deer), which lies between and below the summits of Carn Eige and Mam Sodhail. The loch itself is at an altitude of almost 3,000 ft, and lies to the south of the hill bearing Findlay's name. Indeed the murder may have been committed on Carn Eige or Mam Sodhail, rather than on Bein Fhionnlaidh; what is clear is that our archer knew his peaks.

The upshot of the murder was a quarter-century feud between the Mackenzies and Macdonalds, which ended with the former gaining a charter to the latter's lands in Lochcarron and Lochalsh in 1607. Findlay's exploits can therefore be dated to the 1580s, meaning he beats *Cailean Gorach* of Glenlyon as the first Munroist by a decade. According to oral tradition, MacDonald of Glengarry sent a dozen men against Findlay for revenge, but the bowman's loyal wife poisoned eleven of them with fox-bait. The survivor informed Glengarry, and in a rage he sent another dozen, who Findlay killed one by one with his arrows, after luring them into his house and then calling them out. Another dozen were sent. They killed Findlay's brother, but again our archer slew the lot when they found him hunting on Mamantuirc in Glen Elchaig. Finally, Findlay's bow and arrows despatched yet *another* dozen at a battle between the clans in Glenshiel. Findlay eventually died by treachery, an itinerant MacDonald medical man thrusting a needle into his brain when he was ill at Faddoch. As the blood flowed into his mouth, Findlay said, '*Is milis an deoch a thug thu dhomh*', sweet is the drink you have given me.

However, there is further evidence from neighbouring Strathfarrar that Findlay was not alone in frequenting the heights at this period. South of the mountain Sgurr Choinnich is a gap known as the Bowman's Pass, which then climbs to Sgurr na Conbhaire approaching 3,000 ft. Iain Thomson tells us how the pass got its name:

King James VI of Scotland was entertained by Lord Colin, First Earl of Seaforth... For weapons they used bows and arrows and long spears, killing the deer as they leapt through the narrow passage, and the memory of their sport has come down to us in its name, the Bowman's pass... (*Isolation Shepherd*, 1983, p. 126)

This incident must have taken place before James's departure for England in 1603. Let us further speculate... *Sgurr na Conbhaire* is the Hill of the Dog-handler. We know that deer were hunted with wolf hounds in those days. It seems reasonable to assume that the dog-handler watched from the summit of Conbhaire, before unleashing his hounds on the deer as they forced the pass. Such stories show, I think, that the hills, including their tops, were frequented by the Gael, long before the outsiders arrived in the Highlands.

But the lands west of the Great Glen were always the least known in Scotland to outsiders. Inaccessible, inhospitable and lawless, they attracted few visitors, except from necessity. One such was General Monck, Cromwell's commander in chief in Scotland in the 1650s. Faced with a Royalist rebellion against Cromwell's Republican government, Monck made an epic tour of the West Highlands in 1654, harassing the enemy in Glen Moriston, Strathfarrar, and Kintail – where the population had fled, leaving Monck the only option of burning the houses and driving off the cattle of the Royalist Macraes. This was little-known country, and of his journey from Kintail through Strathfarrar to *Browling* (Broulin), he observed,

...the way for neere 5 miles (was) soe boggie that about 100 baggage horses were left behind... Never any Horse men (much less an armie) were observ'd to march that way. (TSGI Vol 18 p. 76)

However, in that very year of 1654, but unknown to Monck at the time, was to appear in Amsterdam, Blaeu's *Atlas*, containing work which was to make Scotland one of the best mapped countries in the world. Most of these maps were based on the pioneering travels of Timothy Pont, and his resulting sketches and notes, made over half a century before Monck's expedition. Pont's odyssey in the West Highlands, at a time of lawlessness and clan warfare, is little short of astonishing.

Peregrinations of Pont

As earlier stated, the motivation for Pont's journeys is unknown. Possibly it was simple curiosity, though it has been suggested he was a spy, sketching fortifications and castles. The frequency with which economic opportunities and resources are mentioned by Pont, e.g. iron deposits, at least suggest that he was in part prospecting. Certainly others were economically interested in the West Highlands and Islands, and shortly after Pont's visit came the attempt to 'plant' Lewis, and to develop the Loch Maree iron deposits, though these may have been coincidental occurrences.

South of the Great Glen Pont's black and white sketch maps cover most of the Highlands, but it is otherwise to the west. Indeed, from the extant maps in Stone's work we might be tempted to conjecture that he started round the Black Isle, moved up via Loch Shin to the far north-west, which is well mapped, and then hopped, possibly by boat, down the west coast, charting the areas around Loch Broom, Loch Maree and finally Kintail/Applecross, before returning to Inverness via the Great Glen and Glen Garry – which is also mapped. Apart from part of South Uist, the rest is a perfect and absolute blank. But Jeffrey Stone (personal communication, 3.12.97) cautions against such an assumption, arguing that the evidence suggests that Pont's maps of the north-west have not survived, and that he did indeed visit most of the area. And if the documents usually attributed to Pont in Macfarlan's *Geographical Collections* are his, then he certainly covered an astonishing amount of ground.

As well as noting mountains, lochs, rivers, distances and habitations on his maps, Pont was also keen to give useful information, and there are many jottings, almost certainly from personal observation, on the sheets reproduced by Stone. He tells us that there is 'a holl of 180 fathoms deep' at the head of 'Loch Erebill', which is possibly a slightly misplaced reference to Smoo cave, and cites other antiquities such as standing stones. There is information on tides and the 'good tak of herrings' at Loch Laxford. In many places he observed iron extraction, even noting at Skell in Sutherland 'here yrons made', showing local artisan skills. Several reference are given to fresh-water pearling, including 'heir perle' at the head of Loch Stack. But there are drawbacks around Loch Stack such as 'black flies seen souking mens blood', while at Edderachills, which despite his lack of Gaelic Pont gives more accurately as *Edir-da-cheules*, the map-maker observes 'many Wolfs in this cuntry'. Loch Shin impressed him because 'The mightiest and largest salmond in all Scotland are in this loch', but like many others its dreich surroundings appalled Pont, and the huge expanse of country east of the loch is simply designated as EXTREEM WILDERNES.

Pont noted many of the area's mountains, which clearly were not named by him, already carrying Gaelic or Norse names. *Bin Houpp* (Ben Hope) known since Viking times is in its correct place, and so too is *Bin moir Assynn* (Ben More Assynt). Pont made a special study of the area around Loch Maree, mapping the islands, and also making a unique and astonishing eye-sketch of the mountains to the south of the loch (Map 4a). This is, to my knowledge, the first visual representation of successive ranges of actual Scottish mountains, and because of their lay out, Pont must have climbed high on the north shore of Loch Maree to get a view of them. Otherwise, there is no way he could have seen *Bin Wreck* (Beinn Bhreac), *Bin cherkyrr* (Beinn Chearcail) and *Bin Eoin* (Ben an Eoin) with behind them respectively *Bin Rowstack* (Ruadh Stac Mor of Ben Eighe) and *Bin derg* (Beinn Dearg), with still further in the background to the south a mountain called *Liachann* (Liatach) and another I cannot identify, *Bin Yr Chory*. I would love to say that the perspective in his rough sketch could only be gained from, for example, the summit of Slioch, but it looks possibly – using the perspective of the OS map – to have been taken from a point on the eastern banks of Loch Maree opposite Talladale. Also noteworthy about this sketch is that Pont was high enough up to see Coire Mhic Fhearchair (shown as *Corymackermack*) between Rowstack and Sail Mor (which he draws but does not name) of Beinn Eighe: that is, fairly high up. Would that we knew how many other vantage points Pont climbed to get a perspective on the landscape, but we do not, though there is the possibility that the work of Project Pont may enable some useful suggestions to be made. G.E. Morris, in 'The Profile of Ben Loyal from Pont's Map', in *Scottish Geographical Magazine* Vol 102, 2, (1986), states that the profile of that mountain is 'clearly drawn (and) clearly recognisable' (p. 74), showing An Casteil and the rugged Sgor Chaonsaid, and identifying the perspective (sadly) as from the eastern shore of Loch Loyal. Use of similar methods could possibly identify perspectives on other outline hills; promising here would be *Ptalloch*, An Teallach, Pont's sketch of which (Map 4c) shows clearly the outlier Sail Liath, east of the main, jagged summit ridge – not a viewpoint possible from Loch na Sealga, and more likely to be from high ground to the south side of that loch.

The Loch Maree area clearly impressed Pont, and in a document called 'Noates and Observations on dyvers parts of the Hielands and Isles of Scotland', which has been credited to Pont, is the comment,

> Loch Mulruy (Maree) is reported never to freeze. it is compassed about with many fair and tall woods as any in all the west of Scotland... fair and beautifull fyrrs of 60,70,80 foot of good and serviceable timmer for masts... in other places ar plentie of excellent great oakes, whair may be sawin out planks of sumtymes 5 foot broad. All thir bounds is compas'd and hemd in with many hills, but thois beautifull to look on, thair skirts being all adorned with wood even to the brink of the loch... (*Macfarlane's Geographical Collections*, Vol 11 ed. Sir A. Mitchell, 1906 edn. p. 540)

While Pont clearly sees much wilderness in the West Highlands, I think citations like this show that people could be and were receptive to the natural beauty of the Highlands long before the Romantic period. Kintail, for example, is described as 'a fair and sweet countrey, watered with divers rivers covered with strait glenish woods...' by our cartographer, who is impressed by its 'divers hie mountaynes, but... ovirtopping all is SkorRoura' (Sgurr Fhuaran). Pont had a good eye here, for it is the highest in Kintail, but only just!

Pont gives little information as to the actual inhabitants, apart from mentioning clan allegiances and territories, but comments in his 'Noates' suggest they were not living in extreme poverty. Of Strath Naver, later famed in Clearance times, he writes:

> this countrey is exceedinglie well stored with fishes both from the sea and its own rivers. as also of dear, roe, and dyvers kinds of wild beasts, especially here never lack wolves... it is well stored with wood also, by transporting whereof manie are served of victual and cornis from Catness [Caithness'] 'Noates' (*Macfarlane's Collections...* Vol 11 p. 559)

And there are interesting travellers tales, for example, of Lewis, where we are told that there is a mountain where the deer have two tails, and a loch where the fish have four feet... But though sounding equally unlikely, the statement that out of half a mile of the Barvas river over 3,000 'salmond' were taken in 1585, is probably little of an exaggeration, the west coast of Lewis having some of the best salmon runs in Europe.

Despite the efforts of Pont and those who completed his work, the West Highlands was still largely a *terra incognita* to outsiders until well into the eighteenth century. One exception was the area round Loch Maree. In Blaeu's map the loch is possibly double its size, with many settlements mentioned. The area saw several iron-works set up, at the behest of Mackenzie of Kintail by Sir George Hay in the early seventeenth century, subsequent to Pont's travels. Sir George brought skilled workers, technology and capital, and the works flourished for a century, the workers eventually 'going native'. The remains of the ironworkings can be seen at the foot of Slioch where there are ruins of bloomeries and a graveyard for the work-ers. But remember, Hay was invited in by Mackenzie and under his control; what happened to the uninvited in the Highlands at this time we will deal with when we come to look at the islands, and the Lewis Adventurers, who were massacred by the natives. (For further detail on the ironworkings, see J.H. Dixon's *Gairloch*, 1886, Ch. xvii-xx.)

The Loch Maree area was the exception which proves the rule. Daniel Defoe, in his *A Tour Through The Whole Island of Great Britain* in the 1720s traversed Rannoch Moor, Glencoe and the Great Glen, but north of Inverness he hugs the coast to Wick and back, never venturing into the 'interior'. For, despite Pont's trav-els, for a long time to come virtually the only non-Highlanders who ventured west of the Great Glen were military commanders on punitive expeditions against rebels and bandits. This makes Pont's achievement all the more remarkable. And to a military expedition against rebels we now turn.

Spaniards... and a Dutchman or Two

Sgurr nan Spainteach... towering over the narrowest part of the pass at the head of Glenshiel. How did it come by its name?

They must have had severe trepidations even before they set out from San Sebastian on 8th March 1719. The three hundred Spaniards under the command of the exiled Jacobite leader, the Earl Marischal, were undoubtedly familiar with the fate of the ear-lier Spanish Armada which had sailed round Scotland to disaster. This time, as part of a Spanish-Jacobite intrigue, they were the advance guard of another proposed fleet from Spain, whose aim was to alter in favour of the Stuarts the political/religious establishment in Britain. The fate of the advance guard was sealed by that of its rearguard. The main Spanish expedition force sailed from Cadiz under the Jacobite Ormonde, and on 29th March hit a severe storm off Cape Finisterre. Horses, guns and stores were thrown overboard, many of the crewmen died, and the fleet limped back to Cadiz. The 'little rising' of 1719 would have to rely on its own resources – and the three hundred *Spaintich*.

The Earl and his Spaniards managed to reach Stornoway, but that was as far as their luck held. Joined by Lord George Murray, Tullibardine, and other exiled Jacobites from France, they waited for news of Ormonde's Spanish Armada, debated, quarrelled and finally resolved on a march on Inverness. Their little fleet set forth, was battered by a storm into Gairloch, returned to Stornoway and finally reached Lochalsh on 13th April. There a rag-tag crew of Jacobites joined them, including Rob Roy and a party of his men, though the main contingent was supplied by Seaforth, in the form of about five hundred Mackenzie and Macrae clansmen. Altogether an army of L,ooo assembled, and while most *Spaintich* marched with this force, about 50 were left to garrison Eilean Donan castle and hold the Jacobite supplies.

The lack of enthusiasm for the whole affair on the part of the 'Dons' was shown when warships of the British Navy opened fire on the castle. An anonymous report sent to Duncan Forbes of Culloden, shows that Spaniards were in a rush to abandon fort, indeed they mutinied in effect:

> ... one of the men of war went up to the house of Island Donan, and battered it with three guns for two days, and... on the Monday fifty Spaniards, who are there in Garrison, bound ane Irish Captaine, and three others, hung out a white flag and surrendered prisoners, which are all aboard... ('The Battle of Glenshiel', J.J. Galbraith, TSGI Vol XXXIV, 1927 p. 295)

The attack on the castle destroyed most of the Jacobite supplies, and left them in a pitiful situation. Their army took up a defensive position of Glen Shiel, awaiting the enemy. About 1,000 Whig or Hanoverian troops (including a Dutch contingent) had been collected from regular army units in Aberdeen and Inverness, and supplemented by Whig clans (Mackays and Munros). Under General Wightman they encamped at Cluanie, then on the morning of 10th June advanced to engage combat.

The Battle of Glenshiel is unusual in that, instead of charging, the Jacobites adopted a defensive position throughout the action, the *Spaintich* holding a fortified redoubt in the throat of the pass, and the Highlanders occupying the flanks of the surrounding hills. Tullibardine expected a frontal attack, which the Jacobite forces could ambush. Instead, Wightman sent his own Highlanders up the slopes of the hills to the sides of the pass, followed by regular troops, and outflanked the rebels, driving them back in a war of position. The Spaniards were bombarded and then, in danger of encirclement after a brief exchange of fire, they fled and the battle was over. Casualties were light, about 100 on each side. For the Jacobites it was the end to a rather inglorious military campaign. However, their army during this engagement accomplished a sequence of summit ascents which gives them a more honourable role in the early history of Scottish mountaineering.

Peter Tillemans (1684-1731) was a minor representative of the great Dutch school of painting. Like many, he had followed the House of Orange to England, where he made a good living painting hunting scenes, battles and 'landskips'. The year of the Battle of Glenshiel he painted a huge work which hangs in the National Portrait Gallery in Edinburgh. Tillemans was surely at Glenshiel. The layout and sequence of the battle, represented as a succession of scenes on the canvas, is given with great accuracy, and so too is the mountainscape, with Sgurr a'Chuillin on the left, and Sgurr na Ciste Duibhe unmistakable on the right. The latter is a modern Munro at 3,370 ft, and the artist shows the Highland host in possession of this, and other summits. This might be thought mere artistic licence, using canvas space to depict the battle sequence, but other evidence corroborates his painting. The Marquis of Tullibardine wrote to the exiled Earl of Mar after the battle that, '...several men that were to be with us (were) on the top of the mountains on each side, yet they did not descend to incorporate with the rest' (TSGI Op. Cit., p. 308). This was presumably because they saw the battle was not going the Jacobites' way. Thus we can award the first recorded ascent of Sgurr na Ciste Duibhe to a party of half-hearted Jacobites, probably Mackenzies or Macraes, who would have known the country. But the Spaniards were almost instantly to give it a repeat ascent, and to add one of their own.

As well as Tillemans' painting, there is a plan-drawing of the battle by John Bastide, a lieutenant in Montague's Foot, who took part in the conflict on the government side. He made the drawing into a broadsheet which was sold in bookshops. Bastide's plan clearly delineates the progress of the conflict, and the respective fates of the Highlanders and their Spanish allies. It shows the breastworks of the *Spaintich* being bombarded, and in the narrative of the sequence of events, lists:

11. Spaniards marching up ye Hill to retreat
12. Top of ye Hill where they fled after ye action
(*Fortress Scotland and the Jacobites*, C. Tabraham and D. Grove, 1995, p. 67.)

Bastide's 'Hills' are very roughly drawn, unlike Tillemans', but we can still work out what must have been the route of the Spaniards after defeat, aided by cartographical knowledge.

Abandoning their breastwork (whose remains can still be seen beside the A87 road where it crosses from north to south of the River Shiel, about half way between Cluanie and Shiel bridge), the Spaniards assembled and then began ascending the hills by the ground still known as *Leac nan Spainteach* (flat stone of the Spaniards). Fearful of pursuit they continued until they reached *Bealach nan Spainteach* just below the summit of Ciste Duibhe, then continued towards *Sgurr nan Spainteach* (3,129ft), and crossed the ridge to the north side which they passed in the hollow knows as *Coirean nan Spainteach*. The map evidence gives incontrovertible confirmation to the view that the Spaniards actually climbed the hill which bears their name, not simply that they engaged in combat below it. Tullibardine's letter to Mar already cited says the Spaniards 'at last all began to run, tho' half had never once had an opportunity to fire on the Enemy... But all went off over the mountains...' (Loc. Cit. p. 310). Bastide's drawing has matchstick men in retreat over the summits, following the route we have described.

Most of the Highlanders fled to the hills and safety, but the poor *Spaintich* had nowhere to go, and after a night on the bare mountain, cold and hungry, they surrendered and were shipped back home at the Spanish King's expense. Marischal and Tullibardine fled abroad again, but Seaforth was pardoned in 1726, and wisely stayed neutral in 45. Those killed in the battle are said to be buried under *Clachan Duich* below *Leac nan Spainteach*. But watch out if you are wandering the area at night, for the ghost of the *Dhuitseach*, a Dutchman reputed to be the first casualty on the conflict, is supposed to walk the battlefield at night. This tale, like many of the best ones, may be apocryphal, as the 'grave' of General Wightman used to be pointed out locally – though he was certainly not killed in the battle! But dealing only in certainties, the ascent of one of the famous Five Sisters, often first attributed to the ubiquitous Col. Colby of the OS, was actually carried out a century earlier by some half-hearted Jacobite clansmen and their *Spaintich* allies. And the feat was repeated by several of their Hanoverian pursuers, making it, in all probability, the biggest mass-ascent of a Scottish mountain before the era of club outings a couple of centuries later.

The Prince on the Peaks

I have little time for the person of Charles Edward Stuart, histrionic egoist and later drunken wife-beater, who plunged Scotland and Britain into a bloody civil war. And I have less time for the religious and political aims of the Jacobites, intending to turn the clock back to a clerical absolutism which had been decisively rejected by the mass of the British and Scottish people long before Culloden Moor. Despite this, the romance and bravery of the attempted coup of 1745-6 is still fascinating.

And credit where credit is due. Bonnie Prince Charlie was a pampered dandy who was probably unused to tying his own shoes, and a stranger to hardship. Yet after Culloden this same dandy spent more than twenty weeks in gruelling marches – many carried out at night – through country difficult now and more so two hundred and fifty years ago. He ate – when there was something to eat – most often food that was meagre and cold, the dangers of lighting a fire often being too great. He slept many times in the open, on bare hillsides or in the heather; luxury was a stone cave, such as those in Glenmoriston, or the comforts of Cluny's cage on Ben Alderside – or the (very) occasional peasant hovel, or 'sheally hut'. His footwear was unsuited to the terrain, and his clothing to the harsh climate, even though it was technically summer. Despite all this, the Pretender covered hundreds upon hundreds of miles in his wanderings until a French ship carried him off to exile, and in the course of these wanderings he has a definite claim to the first ascent of two Munros, and a very strong claim to two more. Little consolation for the loss of a crown, perhaps, but the justification for his inclusion in a work on the pre-history of mountaineering. This account will not be a detailed one of his entire travelling (of which there are many accounts, most recently *Summer Hunting the Prince*, by A. Maclean and J.S. Gibson, 1992), but concentrate on those sections and episodes where he ascended the tops.

Horn's article cited previously (SMCJ 1966) does not mention Charlie's ramblings. Steven in *The Story of Scotland's Hills* gives them just a brief, admiring nod, simply saying that the Prince 'followed more ridges and skulked past more summits than we know about now...' (p. 48-9), and the greatest height he cites for the Prince is the Window at about 3,000 ft on Creag Meagaidh, which he thinks the Pretender probably passed through. In the SMC Guide to the *Western Highlands* by J.A. Parker (1931), there is an account of 'The Wanderings of Prince Charlie' by the Rev. A.E. Robertson, the first man to complete his Munros. In a Note to this account, A.E.R. cites as his authorities the three-volume *Lyon in Mourning*, which is a collection of papers and memoirs relative to the 45 edited by Bishop R. Forbes, and a companion volume by W.B. Blaikie entitled *The Itinerary of Prince Charles Edward Stuart*, which was published in 1897. A.E.R. states:

> The above brief notes have been largely compiled from these volumes, together with a personal knowledge of the whole route traversed by the Prince on the Mainland. (Op. Cit. 4th edn. 1964, p. 130)

In fact, Robertson followed much of the Prince's West Highland itinerary, in a massive trek on the 150th anniversary of the 45 Rebellion, where, even with OS maps, he got lost a couple of times! (See the present author's 'Munros, Maps and the Minister', in *Great Outdoors*, Vol 17, 2, 1995.) However, even A.E.R. does not do full justice to B.P.C., and with Blaikie in one hand, and a clutch of OS maps in the other, we will try and redress the balance.

A.E.R. has B.P.C. leaving the Monar area on 17th July 1746 and arriving in the vicinity of Loch Quoich on the 20th, giving his route as follows:

> Sgurr a Mhuide, east end of Loch Eilt, Fraoch-Bheinn, Coire Odhar, Mam Sgurr na Choileam (O.S.Sgurr Thuilm), upper Glen Dessary, Coire nan Gall... (p. 127)

But a closer examination of Blaikie and his sources gives a fuller, and more interesting and impressive picture. The Prince's party certainly climbed Fraoch-Bheinn, an outlier of the present Corbett

Sgurr an Utha, and then advanced into Coire Odhar on the evening of 18th July. There they had an assignation to meet one of Clanranald's men, the young Glenaladale whom they had sent to Glenfinnan for intelligence. Captain Alexander Macdonald, who was with the Prince, wrote in his Journal that the meeting was to take place,

> ...about ten o'clock at night on the top of a hill, above Lochar-kaig in Lochiel's country, called Scoorwick Corrichan. (*Lyon in Mourning* Vol 1, p. 336)

Glenaladale was not there when they arrived, but in the night at about 11 o'clock (there was a near full moon) they bumped into Donald Cameron of Glenpean at Corrour (*Coire Odhar*). Cameron had been sent for to guide the Prince in Lochiel's country. It is clear that the guides each knew their own patch; Clanranald's men knew Moidart, Lochiel's knew Arkaig, Glengarry's knew Knoydart, and so forth.

John MacDonald was also with the Pretender at this point, and wrote:

> Then we came to a resolution to depart that country... and for that purpose sent an express to Donald Cameron, Glenpean, an aged gentleman, to meet us at Corrour..which accordingly we did, we proceeded under night till sunrise next morning to the top of a high mountain lying between Loch Arkeig and Loch Moror head. (*Lyon...* Vol 3, p. 377)

He thus concurs with Captain Alexander MacDonald's account that

> ...travelling all night they came at four o'clock in the morning... to a top of a hill in the Brae of Locharkaig, called Mamny-nleallum... (*Lyon..* 1 p. 337)

(When sources say 'top' of a hill, I think we should take that as the summit, especially when – as with fugitives – there was a real reason, ie, observation, to chose the highest point of any hill.)

The party spent the day on the hill, Cameron assuring them it had been searched the day before and was safe, and there they later met Glenaladale, who had failed to meet them at Corrour the previous night. At nine o'clock on the 19th the Prince set off northwards. So, what ground had they traversed?

Looking at the OS Map (No. 40), the party's route is clear. They met Cameron of Glenpean at *Coire Odhar Mor* (Corrour), below *Scoorwick Corrichan* (Sgurr nan Coireachan), on whose top they had arranged an assignation with Glenaladale. Their next steps must have undoubtedly been towards the meeting point with Glenaladale, but he had yet to arrive from Glenfinnan and they missed him. They walked for about five hours in darkness, or the light of the moon, and at daylight were at *Mamnynleallum*, between Loch Arkaig and Loch Monar. This mouthful is, according to Blaikie, Mamnyn Callum, a name initially rendered by the OS as Sgor Choileam, but which is now given as Sgurr Thuilm. And it lies, as indicated by John MacDonald, between Lochs Arkaig and Morar. Upon *Mamnynleallum* the party spent the day of the 19th July. The route from Corrour must therefore have passed over Sgurr nan Coireachan, where they had a rendezvous, and along the summit ridge of Meall an Tarmachain and Beinn Gharbh to Sgurr Thuilm. A time of five hours is a reasonable estimate of what a journey from Corrour to Sgurr Thuilm, on a moonlit night, might occupy, and is what Prince Charles' band took. There can be little doubt, therefore, that the group containing Prince Charles, John MacDonald and Alexander MacDonald did the first recorded ascents of Sgurr Thuilm and Sgurr nan Coireachan on 18th-19th July 1746. Recorded ascents... for they were accompanied by an old man, Donald Cameron of Glenpean, who obviously knew where he was going. It is therefore likely, though unverifiable, that Glenpean had been over the ground before. It is surprising, moreover, that authorities such as Robertson and Steven have failed to fully record these documented ascents. However, greater problems begin with the next stage of the journey.

On the morning of the 20th, the Prince's party arrived at Coire nan Gall at the west end of Loch Quoich; we have no details of the route, though Capt. MacDonald says it took them four hours from the summit of Sgurr Thuilm, which is incredible going. Their route must have been to Glen Dessary and then over the western shoulder of (another) Sgurr nan Coireachan; the bealach between the former mountain and neighbouring Garbh Cioch Mhor lies at about 2,500 ft, so no claims here for first ascents. On the evening the party ascended *Drimachosi* (Druim Cosaidh) to avoid detection, probably at its eastern lower end, and not its western extremity Sgurr a Choire-bheithe, which is a hair's breadth off a Munro, but would have been well out of their intended direction.

On the next day Capt. MacDonald has the party at *Corriscoridill* (Coire Sgoireadail) at the eastern end of Loch Hourn, after nearly losing the Pretender down a precipice in the dark. To get there from Druim Cosaidh, the most logical route would have been over into Coire Shubh across the ridge of Sgurr nan Eugallt – the hill of the precipices, possibly including the one which almost claimed the Pretender. Again, no claims for first ascents here, nor on the next stage of the journey. Most commentators assume the band of Jacobites got to Glen Shiel, where they arrived early in the morning of the 22nd July by passing the Bealach Coire Mhalaghain below the Forcan Ridge of the Saddle mountain. But this was the main route to Kintail, and with a township at its foot, would undoubtedly be watched; anyway, it was out of their route from the head of Loch Hourn, and A.E.R. is undoubtedly right in saying they went by the Bealach Duibh Leac, between Sgurr a' Bhac Cholais and Creag nan Damh. The bealach is around 2,500 ft, well below the 'Munro' summit of Creag nan Damh. The route from Sgurr Thuilm to Kintail was dangerous and hard, but from the documentary evidence, and likely deduction of the precise route, there is little possibility that the Prince bagged any more peaks on this section of his travels.

On the next section of his odyssey Charles certainly did scale the summits, though it is more difficult, although not impossible, to say exactly which ones. Let us here deliver the story over to Captain Alexander MacDonald (*Lyon in Mourning,* Vol 1, pp. 343-4). (Discrepancies in dates of the various accounts possibly result from the calendar change in 1752, or simply from MacDonald's faulty memory, for the dates were a little earlier than those he gives.)

Having once more got together, his royal highness and his small retinue set out, and travelling all the remainder of the night, came early in the morning of July 28th to a hillside above Strath-chluanie... They steered their course northward, and mounting up a high hill betwixt the Braes of Glenmoriston and Strathglass came very late at night to the top of it, and being very dark they were obliged to lodge there all night... being wet to the skin... and having no fuel to make a fire, the only method (the prince) had of warming himself was smoking a pipe.

About three o'clock in the morning... [various of the retinue] were sent out in quest of some trusty people... and appointed to return to the top of a neighbouring hill where his royal highness and the remainder of his retinue would meet them. Accordingly, about five o'clock in the morning his royal highness set out, and by seven came to the top of that hill, where meeting with the guide on his return [he was] given directions... to repair to a cave in the Brae of Glenmoriston in a place called Coiraghoth, where they promised to come at an appointed hour with refreshments. Accordingly his royal highness set out, and by the time appointed came to the place... where he was refreshed... and making a bed for him, his royal highness was lulled asleep with the sweet murmurs of the finest purling stream that could be, running by his bedside within the grotto, in which romantic habitation his royal highness pass'd three days... [then] they removed... into a place within two miles of them, called Coirmheadhain, where they took up their habitation in a grotto no less romantic than the former.

Both Blaikie and Robertson argue that the night on the bare mountain of 23rd-4th July was spent on Sgurr nan Conbhairean, and indeed coming from Strathcluanie and then going north it would be a logical deduction; another possibility, however, is that it could have been Carn Ghluasaid, which is also a Munro, and which could also be climbed coming from Strathcluanie and turning north. However, I feel there is a solution to the problem, despite no names for hills being given in the text. On the 24th the Prince set out for another mountain top which he reached in about two hours, and where he was met by the loyal eight men of Glenmoriston, who conducted him to the first of two caves in the Ceannacroc Forest where he lodged. According to the SMC Guidebook, *The Munros*, the walking time from the summit of Sgurr nan Conbhairean to that of Carn Ghluasaid is about one and a half hours. Allowing for a margin of error, it seems reasonable to assume that the Prince climbed both of our named peaks, but it is not *immediately* clear in what order.

However, the *first* cave Charles went to in Glenmoriston was in Coire Dho (Blaikie, p. 61). If he had spent the night on Carn Ghluasaid, there would have been no reason to then ascend Conbhairean to get to Coire Dho; on the other hand, if the Prince was on Conbhairean first, it would have been logical to proceed to Ghluasaid – which would have taken roughly the time indicated of two hours – and then to have descended eastwards to Coire Dho. I think we can therefore conclude that the Prince and his retainers did climb Conbhairean and spend a night on its summit, moving in all probability to its neighbouring Munro, Ghluasaid, early next morning, before descending to his cave.

There is another Munro on this chain, Sail Chaorainn to the

north, but I doubt it was visited by royal feet. True, there is a wonderful natural gîte, named Prince Charlie's Cave, below it, but this was his second howff in the area, resided in a few days after his summitteering. Neither can this hill be ascended directly from Strathcluanie, nor is it two hours away from any neighbouring top; the SMC Guide gives a mere half hour from Sail Chaorainn to the top of Sgurr nan Conbhaireann. No, the Heel of the Rowan was not trodden by the Heel of the Prince, but it would be churlish in the extreme to raise doubts about his ascent of its two neighbouring Munros. The available evidence indicates that B.P.C. did them, a century and a half before A.E.R. But a final point: *Conbhairean* signifies handlers of the dogs; again, I venture that this peak had been climbed in the course of the hunt, when bows and arrows and dogs, not guns, were the main means of killing deer, that is, pre-1700.

In the Central Highlands section of this work we have examined, and sadly dismissed, any claims for first ascents by Prince Charles in that area. However, he returned from east of *Gleann Mor* to the West Highlands, en route to his escape vessel. Though he did no more 3,000 ft summits, he did climb another mountain which, though lowly, I wish to mention, mainly in order to have an excuse for telling a fine story. On 23rd August the Prince spent a night on the summit of *Mullantagart* (Meall an Tagraidh), which is almost 2,500 ft, and is an outlier of the Corbett Meall na h-Eide. *Mullantagart* is the Hill of Claiming, ie, disputed hill: disputed between Glengarry and Lochiel, though finally decided in Glengarry's favour. The watershed is ill-defined, and at Fedden lived an old woman who used the dispute to her advantage. Fedden was the highest inhabited house in the area, just at the watershed where the wind whines through the hills (*feadan*, a chanter or whistle). When the factor from Glengarry came, the *cailleach* diverted the stream – and her cottage was on Lochiel's ground. When *his* factor came, the stream was re-directed and her house now stood within Glengarry lands. By this means she lived at Fedden rent free for many years, at the foot of Mullantagart. (*See Place Names of Glengarry and Glenquoich*, E. Ellice, 1898, pp. 15-17, 42-3.) The Pretender lived rent-free on the summit of the Hill of Claiming for possibly three days, before proceeding westwards to his French ship and exile, his political ambitions, and also his mountaineering exploits, at an end.

Pacification and After

The Jacobite Rebellions gave a great impetus to the search for information and knowledge about the lands beyond the Highland Line, in order to put into operation a counter-insurgency policy on behalf of the Hanoverian government. Thus 1715 was followed by the construction of the system of military roads which bear the names of Generals Wade and Caulfeild, as well as the building of fortified strongpoints like the Bernera barracks in Glenelg. William Taylor, in his *Military Roads of Scotland* (1976), makes no mention of ascents in connection with road building, but it is possible, for example on the Braemar-Perth road, that soldiers and/or engineers did ascend the hills for survey purposes, or that some of Wade's soldiers skipped up to the top of Corrieyairack Hill for a look at the view. Some mapping activities accompanied these works, but it was only after the 45 that the Military Survey, associated with General Roy, was undertaken, resulting in the mapping of all of mainland Scotland. Thus, fifty years after the 1715, the Highlands of Scotland, their topography, settlement and communications, were immeasurably better known to outsiders; and in addition – forbye the odd bandit – the *Gaidhealtachd* had been pacified. Travel was thus fraught with less difficulty or danger than hitherto.

This initial impetus provided by the Jacobite threat to exploration of the Scottish mountains, continued long after the extinguishing of that threat. A key to pacification was seen by the London/Edinburgh establishment in economic development, and the revenues from the Jacobite Forfeit estates were devoted to road building, construction of harbours and churches, and other activities such as the building of the Caledonian Canal. In this connection we encounter again James Robertson, about whom we know little except that he was appointed by the Commissioners of the Forfeit Estates to investigate the Jacobite lands, and the Highlands in general, with a view to assessing their mineralogical and botanical potential. In his first mission in 1767 Robertson visited the Northern Highlands and Islands, including Skye, and collected botanical specimens. (Our highly-regarded botanist was no ornithologist though, for on seeing a 'species of crow with a red bill and feet' he is unable to identify the humble chough.) He notes that on 20th April, 1767:

Having been instructed to make a tour thro' the north of Scotland, in order to examine the vegetable production of the various counties, I set out for Inverness. (NLS 2507 p. 1)

In the course of his wanderings he ascended for the first record-ed time, in addition to the hills of Morven and Scaraben in Caith-ness, at least three mountains over 3,000 ft. One was Ben Hope, the most northerly of the present Munros; he crossed from Loch Tongue over the mountain to *Loch Erbol* despite being ill and unable to get a guide, and in bad weather. He also ascended Ben Wyvis, whitened by a snowstorm in June.

From Strathpeffer I went to Loch Glash, passing over the top of Ben-we-vis, said to be the highest hill in Ross-shire. It is certainly an excellent scene for a botanist... On the summit I was whitened by a fall of snow, and in many lower parts of the mountain it lay underfoot to a considerable depth. (NLS p. 46)

Ben Klibreck (3,154 ft) was his other first ascent, and he records that,

having reached the summit, I saw a large flock of deer skipping along the brow of a hill below, but my view of these beautiful ani-mals was soon interrupted by a cloud of intervening fog (NLS Op. Cit. p. 54)

His diaries, in the National Library of Scotland, also mention his having navigated in a snow and hail storm, and steering by map and compass; possibly being thus the first mountaineer with rudimenta-ry mountaineering equipment. It is reasonable to assume that the maps Robertson would have used would have been those complied by Roy in his Military Survey. The relevant map with Ben Hope shows huge gaps in the terrain, and there are as yet still no contour lines, only hachures (shadings) showing gradients. Even though trav-elling in pacified times, and picking off the three Munros most acces-sible from the coastal plain, and with the benefit of Roy's carto-graphic work and a pooch full of Forfeit siller, the botanist's achieve-ments are still impressive. And Robertson's trip was not without adventures, in which the man's loneliness in an alien environment comes poignantly through. He wanders in *Strath-oikle*, passing only 'huts of turf which they call *shiel-bothies*'.

In examining this tract... I wandered for 3 days all alone till night fell, scarcely knowing wither I went. The night, which I was oblig-ed to pass in one of the miserable huts, ill compensated the fatigue of my lonely strayings thro' the day...

...he who accompanied me could not speak english, so that I was obliged, without an Interpreter, to live among people whose language I did not understand. (NLS p. 50-1)

There is little sense of sympathy for Highland culture in Robertson's *Journal*. He gives us a story about a miracle-working stone, thrown into a local loch, which was subsequently reputed to have curative powers:

This story, the offspring of ignorance and the lowest superstition, I have detailed particularly because it shows at once, better than a thousand descriptions, the state of society here. (Op. Cit. p. 68)

And he describes his relief at coming to the country after Contin which 'is peopled and cultivated' after passing the 'dreary' road from Braemore, on his way out of the Highlands:

For 18 miles of this dreary road, there is no house except one small hut midway where Travellers are refresh'd with a little *Usquebaugh*... (Op. Cit. p. 80)

Despite Robertson's travails, there is evidence that mountain ascents were becoming sought after, the kind of thing one could talk of proudly in polite society, and Ben Hope boasts the first possibly fraudulent claim to having been ascended. The mountain was visited on 28th June 1776 by the Rev. Charles Cordiner, who published his account of its 'ascent' in 1780 in *Antiquities and Scenery of the North of Scotland*. His account has been republished in the SMCJ Vol IV, No. 21, pp. 167-171. Cordiner was at Tongue, and wished to visit the antiquity of *Dun Dornaigil* (Dornadilla), possibly the best preserved broch on the mainland. He and a guide went by *Ribbydale* (Ribigill) and in all probability crossed the shoulder of Meallan Liath, moving on and ascending the eminence at 718m behind An Gorm-Loch, before descending to Strath More, wherein lies the broch. (Cf. note by C. Swan, Op. Cit. p. 171.) However, in amongst all the reverential hyperbole of 'vast chasms dug out by winter torrents', Cordiner does make the claim that:

When I first descried Ben Hope, and saw its shapeless head heaving into the horizon... I could have formed no idea that I should be under any temptation of attempting to gain the summit, yet this now became not only expedient but necessary. (Op. Cit. p. 168)

A few paragraphs of gushing prose later, he tells us that 'we soon found the difficulty of surmounting Ben Hope over', after battling though 'embryo-snows' of 'mingled sleet and rain'. Cordiner may have been under the impression, in the mist, that he had climbed to the summit of the mountain, or he may have been using 'summit' loosely, meaning a summit ridge over which passage was necessary; at any rate, he clearly did not equal Robertson's achievement in ascending the mountain.

OS Men on Hill and Glen

But we do not have to wait too long to be able to record another first ascent west of the – we are now able to say – Caledonian Canal, to vary from the constant repetition of Great Glen. This was the work of a party of military engineers led by the redoubtable Col., later Gen., Thomas Colby, Director General of the Ordnance Survey from 1820 to 1846. Born in 1784, Colby had lost his left hand in an accident which almost killed him in 1803. Despite these injuries he was a man of enormous stamina and fanatical addiction to his work of mapping. It was under Colby that the os six-inch survey was extended into Scotland, and he later worked on a similar project in Ireland. His obituary in the *Proceedings of the Institution of Civil Engineers* (1852) p. 133, commented,

> Numerous recollections are still cherished by his few surviving friends, of the extraordinary personal energy which enabled him to triumph over climate and country in the wilds of Scotland.

Unfortunately, the field journals of Colby, along with much other material, were lost when the Luftwaffe damaged os buildings in the Second World War (personal Communication from W. Debeugny os Records 14.7.97). We are fortunate, therefore, that when his biographer J.E. Portlock wrote his *Memoir of the Life of General Colby* in 1869, he asked one of these 'few surviving friends' to describe a year in the field with Colby, to be included in the *Memoir*. Major Dawson dug out his old letters home to his family, and gave an account of Colby's *Annus Mirabilis*, 1819.

> We were joined at Huntley by Captain Colby, he having travelled through from London on the mail coach. This was Captain Colby's usual mode of travelling, neither rain nor snow, nor any degree of severity in the weather, would induce him to take an inside seat or to tie a shawl round his throat... he would pursue his journey for days and nights together... with but little refreshment, and that of the plainest kind...

From Huntley, Captain Colby proceeded with us on foot, and on the second afternoon we reached the base of the mountain. Here... we made an irregular encampment for the night... A marquee was pitched for Captain Colby, in which he slept, in his clothes, on a bundle of tent linings.

On the following morning the really laborious part of the business commenced, that of conveying the camp-equipage, instruments and stores to the top of the mountain. Horses were hired for the purpose and made to carry the packages slung like panniers over their backs... but when the ground became broken and hummocky... there was no alternative but to unload the horses and carry the things on the men's shoulders... (Colby)... selected a suitable place for a turf-hovel to be built on the sloping face of the hill, with a tarpaulin roof, in which to make a fire for cooking, and for drying the men's clothes and shoes, and to serve as a place of shelter and warmth... in tempestuous and severe weather... and the theodolite itself was then brought up with special care and fixed in its position. (Qu. in *Memoir*... by Portlock, pp. 132-3)

Colby and his subordinates made two massive journeys from Corriehabbie in the summer of 1819. The first through eastern Inverness-shire, Ross-shire, Caithness and Orkney occupied twenty two days and covered 513 miles. They indulged themselves in a rest day, and then set off westwards, walking 586 miles in another twenty two days. Colby pushed himself and his men at an incredible rate, averaging twenty to thirty miles a day, and climbing a mountain roughly every other day as well. In addition they were measuring and surveying as they went. I doubt if even the fittest parties of today could equal, still less emulate Colby, and the conclusion must be that people then, more used to walking, were stronger pedestrians than we are now. Dawson comments:

Captain Colby having, according to his usual practise, ascertained the general direction by means of a pocket compass and map, the whole party set off as on a steeplechase, running down the mountainside at full speed... crossing several beautiful glens, wading the streams which flowed through them, and regardless of all difficulties which were not actually insurmountable on foot. (*Memoir*.... Op. Cit. Qu. p. 138-9)

Colby's method of travelling is almost more impressive than what he and his parties actually climbed. Steven does not mention any hills ascended apart from Coryhabbie itself. Horn (p. 161) cites that one mountain scaled was 'apparently' Creag Meagaidh. But as we have seen above (p. 76), Colby actually climbed Carn Liath after having done Carn Dearg in the Monadhliath. Horn also mentions 'one or more' of the Five Sisters above Loch Duich. But the discovery of Dawson's elusive account allows us to say definitely which one (for it was only one).

The military mappers entered the West Highlands from Fort Augustus, taking 'the line of one of the old military roads of General Roy', and then 'the parliamentary road, made by the late Mr. Telford', to Glen Moriston, travelling:

> through a desolate mountain tract, without any living beings, ... the inhabitants had been driven out to convert the district into a sheep farm, and the remains of their habitations were occasionally to be seen by the road-side (p. 142)

This was one of the peak periods of the Highland Clearances, whose most notorious expression was taking place at that very time in Sutherland, with the clearance of Strathnaver and neighbouring glens by Partick Sellar, acting on behalf of the Duchess of Sutherland. Of these events Karl Marx would later write,

> My lady Countess resolved upon a radical economical reforms, and determined upon transforming the whole tract of country into sheep-walks. From 1814 to 1820, these 15,000 inhabitants, about 3,000 families, were systematically expelled... All their villages were demolished and burned down, and their fields converted into pasturage.. An old woman refusing to leave her hut, was burned in the flames of it. Thus my lady Countess appropriated to herself 794,000 acres of land, which from time immemorial had belonged to the clan. ('*The Duchess of Sutherland and Slavery*' in *Articles on Britain*, 1978, p. 145)

This ethnic cleansing was, sadly, the backdrop to outsiders' discovery of the Highlands.

The Trigonometers arrived at Cluny [*sic*] consisting 'of only a few miserable mud hovels' one of which was their abode, where they were offered rotten salmon and slept on wooden stools. But next day, 27th July things improved:

> It may be inferred that our departure was not delayed much after daylight... on our arrival at Invershiel, at the head of Loch Duich, to breakfast, we partook with no slight satisfaction of a fine salmon, brought almost alive... We proceeded after wards to Scour

Ouran, a high mountain to the north-east, being one of the serrated main range... having built a large conical pile of stones on its summit, we returned to the inn at Invershiel to sleep. (Dawson Qu Portlock Op. Cit. p. 143)

Thus was Sgurr Fhuaran, first mentioned over two centuries before by Pont as *SkorRoura*, finally ascended.

The party moved on to Skye, where their creditable attempts will be dealt with in our next section, before going by boat to Jeanstown (Lochcarron). Dawson tells us that:

We explored that day the mountains to the north-eastward, and built piles upon some of them, passing on afterwards to the upper end of Loch Maree... (p. 146)

This is infuriating, for there is no record in the *Account of Principal Triangulation* of stations on mountains in this area; however, en route from Jeanstown to Loch Maree, there are Trig Points on Glas Bheinn (2,332 ft), and more interestingly Fuar Tholl (2,975 ft). The latter lies just west of the Coulin Pass, which is the standard route from Strathcarron to Loch Maree, which the os men would probably have taken. Fuar Tholl is also visible from the country to the south and a good choice for a survey point; I think we can argue that the circumstantial evidence points to an ascent by Colby in 1819, though the Trig Points themselves were actually erected much later.

While planning their route from Lochcarron, Dawson began whistling a light air. But it was Sunday and Captain Colby checked him, 'explaining to me the deep sense of veneration with which the people of that country regard the Sabbath. There is no doubt that I was wrong and Captain Colby right'. Indeed a local had reported Dawson to the laird, who made representation to Colby, indicating the firm grip Presbyterian sabbatarianism had gained in many areas of the West Highlands by this time. Many locals though, were glad of the work in portering for the surveyors, suspicious though they might be of the purpose of their strange instruments. And not without reason, one of the purposes of the original survey to establish a basis for land taxation!

Horn's citation of 'Slioch and other hills to the east of Loch Maree', as having fallen to the os men is beyond dispute. Hector Mackenzie, the grandfather of the more famous Osgood, told one of his sons a story, further retailed by him to Osgood, of Colby in Gairloch.

...one day there arrived Major Colby of the Engineers, who, with a sergeant and some privates, had been sent to the north-west as pioneers of the Government plans for the Ordnance Survey of Britain, a great work, hardly completed yet, though I must be writing of about the year 1816 [1819, I.M.]... Colby (was) a highly educated man of science, from astronomy all the way downwards... and I remember what high spirits he was in one day when one of his people won a prize by throwing the sun's rays from a concave mirror from the top, I think, of Slioch, to the Clova Hills in Kincardineshire through some glen or other... (*A Hundred Years in the Highlands,* Osgood Mackenzie, p. 142)

According to Mackenzie, the guest book in Kinlochewe Hotel recorded the ascertained height of Slioch, in the name of a Captain Kirkwood, R.E., and we may safely assume he was the 'one of Colby's people' who determined the height of the *Sleugach* in 1819, finding it much lower than the 4,000 ft it had been reputed.

After a couple of days loafing about with the local lairds, which Dawson clearly enjoyed, they headed back towards Corryhabbie from Kinlochewe:

exploring the country to the eastward, and building piles upon the mountains which were well placed, we descended to Loch Fannich... (p. 148)

Between Kinlochewe and Loch Fannich, and in a logical line of trajectory, lie Fionn Bhein (3,059 ft), and it is possible that it was climbed by Colby's party.

Apart from those mentioned, Colby certainly climbed Ben Lomond, Ghlas Mhaol and Ben Wyvis at various times. With seven, possibly eight Munros and a cluster of Corbetts to his credit, Colby had – with the exception of MacCulloch and possibly Grierson – climbed more Scottish hills than anyone else by 1820.

It is clear that our os men were fine chaps, able to sustain any hardship – but one. Like many before and since, they found the midges insufferable. Lightly clad in good weather, they were 'exposed in a particular manner to the baneful attacks of these venomous insects'. Even in their bedrooms they were plagued, losing much sleep from bites. Dawson states, 'We had frequently to make smoke in our bedrooms, and over our meals to drive these insects away'.

Dawson had noted, on entering the West Highlands, the clearance of natives for the sheep economy. At Loch Fannich, he noticed another innovation in land use, that of emptying the glens for hunting. This was a time of real hardship in the Highlands, and Dawson was clearly shocked when he heard that those who took the Fannich shootings 'killed at the rate of fifty brace of birds to each gun per diem, and left the birds where they fell upon the ground'.

Colby certainly worked his men hard, but there were compensations. At the end of the summer, in September 1819, Colby organised a gargantuan feast for the engineers, where 'Success to the Trig' was toasted and,

> The chief dish on such occasions was an enormous plum-pudding. The approved proportion of the ingredients being – a pound of raisins, a pound of currants, a pound of suet, etc, to each pound of flour; these quantities were all multiplied by the amount of mouths in the camp, and the result was a pudding of nearly a hundred pounds weight. (Dawson Op. Cit. p. 153-4)

The pudding took twenty four hours to cook. And was much needed, no doubt by men who had often walked forty miles in the course of a day's work. Indeed, what comes through in Dawson's marvellous account is the camaraderie of the hills, among the os men. When it snows, they stop work and have a snowball fight; at a haunted loch they engage in merry ghostly japes with a turnip lantern at each other's expense. They complain about the midges, they girn over the blisters inflicted by Colby's merciless regime... it is a bit like a cross-country bothy trip, writ large. Give the Trigonometers a thought, next time you scale a ben with the wonderful maps whose groundwork they laid. For as Wordsworth said:

> Know
> That on the summit whither thou art bound
> A geographic Labourer pitched his tent
> With books supplied and instruments of art...
> (Written... on Black Comb, 1813)

Into the Great Wilderness

Change was coming to even the remote lands to the north of Slioch, the (today) so-called Letterewe wilderness. James Hogg, the Border poet and writer, was in search of a Highland sheep farm, and in an interesting series of letters to Walter Scott describes his journeys in the far north. Hogg was no mountaineer, but he saw some wild country. The highest point he attained was the summit of the Coulin Pass from Achnashellach to Kinlochewe; thence he proceeded northwards to Dundonnell, probably roughly by Carnmore and then Shenavall. In Strath na Sheallag by Shenavall he noted the progress of market forces in the Highlands in 1804.

> I now proceeded down a glen several miles in length, which brought me into the Valley of Strathinashalloch, near the head of the lake of the same name. The valley is now only inhabited by Mr. MacIntyre's shepherds, but there were considerable crops of corn and potatoes left by the tenants who had removed last term. (*Highland Tours,* James Hogg, 1981 edn. p. 100)

Pont's sketch maps from the 1590s show widespread settlement in this now deserted area, including a clachan where Shenavall bothy now stands. The introduction of that pest, the sheep, had led to the removal of the native residents by 1804, as the old patriarchal clan system expired. This was excellent ground for crops, with ample game. Hogg mentions the 'good fishing in the river and loch', while Pont, who had earlier, from the evidence of his sketches, taken the same route Hogg later took, had scribbled on his map of the area, between Loch Sealge and a jaggedly drawn mountain, *Ptalloch*, the comment:

> excellent Hunting place wher are deir to be found all the year long as in a mechtie Parck of nature (*Pont Manuscript Maps...* p. 42)

The cartographer had also shown this whole area as extensively wooded. Pont's *Ptalloch* is the first recorded mention of An Teallach and it appears as *Ptalloch* in Blaeu's *Atlas*. By the time of John Thomson's *County Atlas of Scotland*, published in 1832, the mountain has become *Kalloch*, with its northerly summit *Kea Cloch*, in a series of cumulative erroneous transliterations, only set right when the OS men thought to ask a local. It was by the name *Kea Cloch* that the first man to ascend the mountain knew it. This man we already know as the garrulous Dr. MacCulloch, from his Central Highland exploits. The ascent of An Teallach was undoubtedly MacCulloch's finest achievement, and also the most significant ascent of a Scottish mountain to that date, especially since it was in the remote North-West, where most tourists still failed to venture.

As we have already noted, MacCulloch was a peak-bagger, out to climb as many hills as possible. West of *Gleann Mor*, however, he only claimed two mountains of later Munro status, and one of these was an innocently wrong claim.

> Ben Lair will well repay the toil of the expedition to its summit. The height of this mountain exceeds three thousand feet... But its great attractions are the views from its summit, and chiefly to the northward... through a country as apparently uninhabitable as it is uninhabited... Everything is gigantic and terrible; wild and strange and new. (*The Highlands and Western Islands of Scotland*, 1824 Vol II, p. 302)

Here we see, as in the case of other pioneers, that by the early nineteenth century the figure of 3,000 ft already had about it a magical and desirable quality, later merely formalised by Munro in his Tables. But in the case of Ben Lair as elsewhere, MacCulloch's heights were guestimates, as he does not appear to have carried a barometer with which to make calculations; the height of Ben Lair, at 2,817 ft, is well below the three thousand mark. The geologist's second error is in his description of the country to the north of his peak as uninhabitable. Certainly it was virtually unpeopled when he made his ascent, at a date we cannot be exactly sure of, but sometime in the decade and a half before 1824. But as described earlier, these glens and bens once supported a fair population.

MacCulloch also miscalculated the height of An Teallach, overestimating it by a good measure. The Doctor was travelling by boat, and moved on from the vicinity of Loch Maree to Little Loch Broom. He does not indicate the exact route he took, but from internal evidence in the account of which I append extracts for the readers' scrutiny, I suggest that he landed on the southern shore of the loch and ascended the Allt Airdeasaid burn, which has the many waterfalls he describes and is in a glen about two miles long; near its end is a 'miniature lake', Lochan Ruadh. Thence he went by Coire Mor an Teallach to the *bealach* between Bidean a' Ghlas Thuill and Sgurr Fiona, and ascended one of them. From the fact that a) he continued from the summit along a series of serrated peaks, and b) he could see clearly to the west into what is certainly Strath na Sealga 'the valley... striking for its vacuity', I think it fairly conclusive that MacCulloch made the first ascent of Sgurr Fiona on An Teallach at 3,474 ft. (This leaves the honour of the neighbouring – and marginally higher – summit, Bidean a' Ghlas Thuill to – possibly – the OS men who erected the Trig Point on it at a later date. From the *latter* hill, Sgurr Fiona would have prevented MacCulloch seeing much of

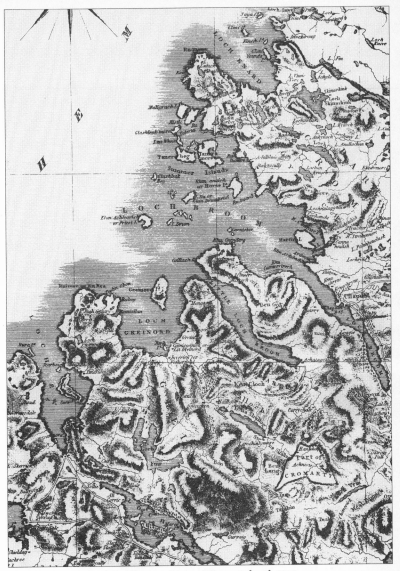

John Thomson *Ross and Cromarty* [part], 1816
Thomson's *Atlas* here shows that the 'Great Wilderness' to the north of the Loch Maree
was still little known. (Fionn Loch, as *Loch Fuir* wildly out of shape, and Loch Fada missing,
as are the mountains such as A'Mhaighdean to its north.) Shenavall, *Shenwell*, is still there,
showing 250 years of continuous habitation since Pont's visit.
(Ian Mitchell)

what he describes.) Let the reader follow the geologist's somewhat overblown prose, through which his merited awe at the mountain is nevertheless clear, and make up his or her own mind.

From this mountain there descends a torrent of great size, with a length of almost continuous cascades... I will only call it two miles... The forms of rocks which accompany its course are bold, broad, and various; while the wild trees... add variety to its ornament... hanging over the deep ravine...

So deep is its course in some places, in the ravine which it has cut for itself, that the water is invisible... At one point... the river, thundering down in a thousand falls, becomes a gentle stream... till at length, forming a miniature lake, its waters subside to repose.

Of the height of these falls, it is not easy to form an estimate; but of two or three which I could more particularly examine, the altitude cannot be less than one hundred and fifty, and two hundred feet... One series, forming a continuous fall to the eye, could not have been short of eight hundred.

In ascending, we were at length caught in a trap, where there was no resource but to return, or to cross the torrent... John talked of leaping the fall. It was very well for him; but what chance had I against a Highlander, with legs like a deer and muscles like fiddle strings... In the turning of a handspike, he was on the other side... I sighed and looked and looked again, but honour won the day, and I never struck the ground with half so much satisfaction...

... taking a new course through a lateral valley, we found ourselves in the region of snow, on a brilliant frozen plain... The summit of the mountain, extending to five or six hundred perpendicular feet above this point, is a narrow and rocky ridge, serrated into peaks, and of a very marked and picturesque character... The effect of the valley on the west side, which separates (Kea Cloch) from Loch Greinord, is more striking from its vacuity than if it had displayed the utmost intricacy of form... I proceeded for some distance along the giddy ridge, in hopes of seeing its termination; but all continued vacant, desolate, silent, dazzling and boundless. Of the height of Kea Cloch I cannot speak with precision, having forgotten to bring up the barometer. But though it seems to have been completely overlooked by mapmakers and travellers, it must be among the highest mountains of the west coast, if not of Scotland...excepting perhaps Ben Nevis. (*Description* Vol 11, pp. 312, 317)

We leave MacCulloch at the peak of his achievement; but we will meet him once more, before our journey's end.

The Turn of the Natives

We have been dealing with outsiders, *Goill*, surveyors, geologists and map-makers on the mountains. Soon we will be dealing with actual proto-mountaineers themselves. Is there still a place in these pages for the return of the native, or are *Fionnladh Dubh* and his like a mere memory by this time?

Meall a' Choire Ghlais is an outlier of the Munro Sron a' Choire Ghairbh (3,066 ft), to the south. According to Edward Ellice:

> The monument on the top of the hill is a favourite place for luncheon with stalkers, and it was probably here that Alastair Dubh [Black Sandy], a famous Glengarry stalker and a certain noble lord, were one day sitting and admiring the scenery. Sandy, who had not much English, was anxious to impress his visitor with the extent of Glengarry's property, and suddenly addressed him as follows: 'All that you see' – then struggling for suitable words and waving his hands in the air he panted out – 'and all that you do not see, that's Glengarry's! (*Place Names in Glengarry and Glenquoich*, 1898 p. 14)

Let us first relate that a similar phrase about 'all you can see and cannot see' was often applied to the land of Glengarry's neighbour, Lochiel. But if everything from the top of the mountain was Glengarry's, then Black Sandy climbed the hill before 1838, when half the Glengarry lands were sold to Ellice's father; this would also square with Sandy having 'little English', as many travellers commented on the general monoglot nature of Highland society before the mid-nineteenth century. We can assume that from Meall a' Choire Ghlais Sandy would have made the easy trip to the summit of Sron a' Choire Ghairbh, the summit proper; this supposition is strengthened by Ellice giving the height of the hill with the monument as 3,066 ft, which is the height of the main top, Sron a' Choire Ghairbh. It is possible Ellice confused his peaks, and Sandy sat contentedly many a time on the actual 'Munro' summit.

The Glenquoich hills are fascinating, but infuriating. Ellice Snr. built a shooting lodge at Glenquoich, now submerged under the raised loch, and there he entertained Richard Cobden and Edwin Landseer amongst others, indeed a roll call of Victorian polite society. A 1930s reprint of Ellice's *Place Names* contains some extracts from the Visitors' Book, which was compulsory for guests to fill in, but none are of mountaineering interest. My efforts to locate the Visitors' Book involved writing to the Ellice descendants, who still own some land in Glengarry. Jean Ellice replied (20.6.95. personal communication) but commented, 'I do not have any of the materials you ask for'. I also visited the remaining Ellice lodge at Invergarry, now a hotel, but knowledge of the book was vague, though there was talk of a fire destroying some estate records... It is inconceivable to me that in the 1840s and 50s none of Ellice's visitors climbed any of the neighbouring hills, but we will possibly never know if they did, or which they did.

One of Ellice's tenants was a bandit, Ewan MacPhee. MacPhee had been an army deserter and lived as a robber and rustler on an island on Loch Quoich. He was reputed to have killed a couple of people, and the locals feared *and* admired him – for he rustled sheep, which caused depopulation. MacPhee knew the hills well, crossing the mountains to Knoydart to steal a wife, who became his loyal servant, shooting at and dispersing on one occasion some agents of Cameron the sheep-grazer, who came to poind MacPhee's goats. The bandit was 'away on the mountain', and his wife's exploits were covered in the *Inverness Courier* (10.3.1842):

> They were not, however, allowed to carry away their booty without resistance from MacPhee's wife. Seeing her flocks all carried away by the ruthless shepherds... she, alone, with a loaded rifle, hovered about the enemy and fired several times at them. They fled precipitately before the modern *Helen MacGregor*... [I am indebted to Angus Mackenzie for this reference, I.M.]

MacPhee's local mountain was Gairich: is it conceivable that he did not climb this hill, en route to his depredations on Loch Arkaigside, or Knoydart? Ellice was tickled pink when he inherited MacPhee, and often had a dram with the ageing bandit, who eventually died in prison (for a fuller account of MacPhee, see I. Mitchell, '*Ewan MacPhee of Loch Quoich: the Last Highland Bandit*' in WHFP 12.5.95).

Or what, further north, of Jaimie Macrae, whose parents had come in the hungry 1840s to squat on an island in Loch Monar? The family crofted, but their main business was illicit distilling.

> [The Macraes] got squatters' rights by building a house on an island in the loch. Their son Hamish Dhu [Jaimie] carried on the business after the death of Alistair [his father] until 1900, when

he turned in his own equipment to the gaugers (excisemen I.M.) for the reward! He was certainly the last illicit distiller on a large scale. The local lairds turned a blind eye to his doings, and the folk of Strathfarrar would delay the gaugers heading for Monar, while sending warnings to the MacRaes. (*Mountain Footfalls; A Calendar of the Scottish Hills*, by I. Mitchell, 1996 p. 57)

The Macraes' bothies were latterly on Meall Mor, the huge whaleback slope of Lurg Mhor. Jaimie watched for the gaugers while his father distilled, often cooped up for days when it snowed, for fear of leaving tracks. They were poachers too, and again, I find it incredible to think that local summits were not ascended in the chase, or as look-out points. But what is certain is that, like MacPhee, *they knew the hills in all their aspects, including in all probability, their summits*. Speculation perhaps? Perhaps... perhaps not.

Before we head a bit further north, let us leave this region by visiting Mealfuarvonie, a fine little hill overhanging Loch Ness. For here we have a handed-down tradition that the mountain (let us give it that title) was ascended before it became the Invernesians' Sunday stroll:

> It was also believed that there was a connection between [Loch Ness] and a well at the top of Mealfourvonie [*sic*], and an ancient legend says that a herd-boy threw his 'glocan' (a piece of stick with a stone fastened to one end) at a cow near this well, and that the stick, disappearing in the well, was found long afterwards at Bona, near Inverness. ('*Story and Song From Loch Ness-Side*, Alexander MacDonald, 1914, 1982 p. 13)

Possibly some caver could test this for us?

Traditions of Gaels on the summits exist further north too. Dixon, in his *Gairloch* already cited, tells us why an outlier of the rugged Corbett Beinn Airidh Charr bears the name Martha's Peak, or Spidean Moirich:

> It is said that a woman of that name having climbed the peak sat down and began winding thread on her spindle. The spindle fell from her hand down the steep rocks to the north-east. Martha tried to recover the spindle, but fell over the rock and was killed. Hence the name. (Op. Cit. p. 315)

A tall tale you might think; what would a woman go to a mountain top to spin for? But *Beinn Airidh Charr* is the Hill of the Rough

Shieling. The woman was obviously at the summer pasture, and, watching the animals, got on with her spinning after choosing a good viewpoint.

In the same area as Martha had her accident, there are other tales of at least the lesser summits being visited by local people, before the mountaineers. Osgood Mackenzie tells us of a cave, *Uaimh Bhraodaig*, half way up Beinn an Eoin, which was familiar to both poachers and gamekeepers in his uncle's time (i.e. early nineteenth century) and also of another gamekeeper hunting eagles 'on the top of Bathais Bheinn' (our present Baosbheinn) (*A Hundred Years...* p. 124). Osgood Mackenzie's own accounts of his mountaineering are scanty, though he does tell us that – in pursuit of the hunt – he ascended the summit of Beinn a' Chaisgan Mhor, a fine hard hill, but short of Munro status, above Carnmore. Mackenzie describes the 'flat, smooth top 2,800 ft up' where he downed a master stag in the 1850s. As well as climbing this hill, Mackenzie visited Carnmore, and the reader who has bothied there might like this description of its state a century and a half ago:

> We arrived in the gloaming at Carn Mor, to find things in a terrible mess in the bothy. It seemed that a few days before... a passing herd of cattle belonging to the laird, being bothered with the heat and flies, had pushed open the door of the bothy and taken refuge in it, which was not difficult as the door was hanging by one hinge... The smell made the house almost unbearable, and had it not been a wet night we should rather have laid ourselves à la belle étoile... The fire, which consisted of heather and bog-fir, was at one end of the bothy against the gable, and I lay on the earthen floor on a bed of heather... (*A Hundred Years...* p. 121)

However, despite his roughing it, and his interest in Gaelic and gardening, we should make it clear that Osgood Mackenzie does not deserve the title of the Good Laird often ascribed to him, for he was a one-man ecological disaster, responsible for wiping out several native species on his lands, and virtually eradicating others by deliberate policy, in his pursuit of game. In 1868 he alone killed a total of 1,900 birds and animals by proud boast:

> To plough through the frenzied orgy of blood letting described in this book (*A Hundred Years...*) is a stomach churning experience. And we are not just talking of game... We are also talking about what he classed as 'vermin', and systematically eradicated with his keepers; foxes, badgers, pine marten, sea eagles and ospreys –

whose eggs he took, wild cat and polecat all reduced or wiped out with trap and dog and strychnine.. (Ian Mitchell *Mountain Footfalls,* Op. Cit. p. 70)

Thus fared the land, in the hands of its 'natural' custodians...

Tourists Discover the Wild West

Enough, I hope, has been hinted at in this interlude in defence of the honour of the Gael in his mountains, for us to return to the explorations of those who came to the hills from outside, and give them in turn their due. It remained the case that the West Highlands were less known than the other mountain areas well into the mid-nineteenth century. Peter and George Anderson's tourist *Guide to the Highlands and Islands of Scotland*, cited earlier, gives us little on this area, barring a description of Suilven, and an extended account of *Scurrvullin* in Strathconon, which they evidently climbed and were ecstatic about, possibly making the hill's first ascent. The *New Statistical Accounts*, so useful in the Central Highlands, are disappointing here; for example, the Rev James Russel of Gairloch, ignorant of the work of the os men under Colby, is uncertain whether Slioch is over 3,000 ft, though he thinks 'it cannot be less' than that, while the Rev. Simon Fraser of Kilmorack thinks *Scour-na-lapich* 'almost equals' the height of Ben Nevis! It is interesting to look at the aforementioned 'Table of Mountains in Scotland' (p. 47), printed as an appendix to *The Scottish Tourist*, (ed.) W. Rhind in 1825, in relation to mountains west of the Great Glen. The Table lists about 200 mountains, many of which are Lowland or Border hills now listed as Corbetts, Donalds, etc. But there are about 30 recognisable as present-day Munros. All but *one* of these, which include the honey-pots of Nevis, Lomond, Cairngorm and others, lie *east* of the Great Glen, and *Benweavis* (Wyvis) is the only one in the wild west. (Rhind includes Mealfourvonie at 3,060 ft, but this merely confirms his ignorance of the West Highlands, as it is in reality well below even Corbett level.) In 1834, in his notes to *The Lakes of Scotland,* John Leighton confirms this perspective of the unfrequented west, commenting that, 'Few tourists ever think for a moment of crossing the Murray Firth' (p. 153) – though he himself did.

His book contains an engraving of Fionn Bheinn, which Leighton evidently climbed, possibly for the first time, though the os men *might* have been there; he writes, 'the mountain is green to the very top, full of springs of water and affords the finest feeding for sheep' (p. 154). Leighton moved on to Kinlochewe, where the 1832 Reform Bill was still unheard of, there not being a single newspaper subscriber in the area, and admired the local mountains. Pont, in the 1590s, had noticed the Ruadh Stac summit of Beinn Eighe, and drawn a rough sketch of it; apparently, almost 250 years later, it was still unclimbed. Or if it was, it was not so by Leighton, who left it well alone:

> The file mountain is exceedingly remarkable. It seems, but we did not ascend it, to be composed of quartz rock and entirely destitute of verdure (p. 158)

Indeed of all areas, Torridon is most barren of early recorded ascents; as barren as the slopes of Beinn Eighe, whose resplendence in the moonlight quite overwhelmed Leighton. Others were impressed by Beinn Eighe, but also left it alone. Henry Cockburn commented in his *Circuit Journeys* (1888 edn.) that 'I have been on a good many Scotch hills', including Ben Lomond, Nevis, Ben More, Ben Ledi and Goatfell (p. 172). And of the view from Kinlochewe to Beinn Eighe he writes admiringly, 'I know of few such mountain prospects' – though he made no attempt on it. But even Torridon has a rumour of a mountain ascent before the mountaineers, which claim I am prepared to concede – a rival claim to that of the *gruagach* who is reputed to plot her evil in Beinn Alligin's summit snows...

Just below the summit of Beinn Alligin is a deep gash noted and avoided by all walkers. This is called *Eag Dhubh na h-Eigheachd*, the deep gash of the crying or wailing. The local legend has it that shepherds used to hear a wailing or cry of despair from this gash, which only ended when one of their number, descending to investigate, fell to his death. The spirit of the mountain appears to have been appeased by this unintended sacrifice, and the wailing ceased. (*Torridon Highlands,* Brenda G. Macrow, 1953 p. 42.) This incident happened, evidently, after the coming of the sheep (since the men were shepherds) but before the os men came to collect place-names, as the term appears on original os maps. So, between *c.* 1800 and *c.* 1850, Torridon shepherds used to pass regularly by the top of this gash, overlooked by a point called *Sgurr na Tuaigh*, 100 feet below the summit of Beinn Alligin. It is simply beyond belief that none of them breasted the summit.

MacCulloch is the first real 'bagger' or 'ticker' to rush to print – the first who ascended Scottish mountains because they were there, and also because they were seen as the plum ones to climb (usually the biggest and or the most spectacular in any area). This attitude spread, and by the middle of the nineteenth century it was common to establish one's credentials at the beginning of any mountain travel book, by listing one's tally of hills. Thus, in his *Autumnal Rambles Among the Scottish Mountains* (1850), by the Rev. Thomas Grierson, we are given a list of the hills he has climbed in Scotland and northern England, which is as impressive as that of MacCulloch. The bulk of Grierson's walking was done in Galloway, Arran, the Lake District, and more especially the Central Highlands and Cairngorms, which we have more conveniently dealt with elsewhere in this work. Here we will briefly review his experiences in the Western Highlands.

There were a series of articles in early editions of the SMCJ, entitled '*The Rise and Progress of Mountaineering in Scotland*' by various hands. The fourth in the series, in SMCJ III (1895), is by W.A. Smith, and has some notes on Grierson. He claims that,

> Mr. Grierson got as far north as Sutherland and ascends Ben More in Assynt; but we shall not follow him there... (p. 254)

Just as well, for it would be difficult. Grierson makes no claim to Ben More Assynt, either in his Preface, or in his little narrative itself. What he does claim is Ben More in Perthshire, which may have confused Smith; pity, as the Assynt Ben More would have been a first ascent. The only eminence of significance Grierson climbed west of the Canal was Ben Wyvis. Now this had become a standard tourist climb by this time and had a large cairn ('The Monument') on the summit. However, it is worth going over Grierson's account, for it shows how haphazard the attitude of hill-baggers was at this time; we are far from seeing mountaineers in action. Apart from a watch, they carried no equipment – no map, no food, no compass, no barometer, and they completely underestimated the ground. Had there not been a moon, the descent of Grierson's party would probably have ended in fatality – as he himself mused, when, after thirty-three miles walking in fourteen and a half foodless hours, he was supping at the hotel in Dingwall. Here is an extract from his account of the ascent.

We crossed the river by a wooden bridge, and passing some cottages, directed our steps to the summit of Ben Wyvis... and, to our mortification, found it covered with newly-fallen snow. Showers of snow fell all day on the mountain... Upon asking a shepherd the best mode of ascent, he told us we could not reach the "Monument" as he termed the Cairn, that day, and that we were sure to be benighted. That put us on our mettle, and we never stopped for three or four hours... till we came to the bottom of the last ascent, which was fearfully rugged, and the upper part covered with snow.

... It was now half past four, and before we got to the top, it must have been at least six; but we were actually afraid to look at our watches, as there was now a certainty of our being benighted. The snow fell fast, and lay several inches deep... we had to struggle with our hands as well as feet. The difficulty was now to find the 'Monument', for we could not see above fifty or sixty yards in any direction. We agreed to separate, that we might have three chances instead of one... After a considerable time, our young friend shouted, 'I have found it!'....

(*Autumnal Rambles*... 2nd edn. 1851 pp. 74-5.)

Grierson's slapdash methods exclude him from being termed a mountaineer; he himself describes his status as 'mountain-lover', but in the following extract we see that all that is wanted is a bit of professionalism, a few clubs to be founded and equipment to be patented, and we will be in the era of the mountaineer proper. For in relation to what he says below, we mountaineering legatees of Grierson have been there, seen it, got the tee-shirt.

Many, no doubt, will be disposed to marvel at the folly of men, reputed sane, voluntarily exposing themselves to such hardships as to hunger and fatigue. To this *I reply, that unless they are mountain lovers* [my emph. I.M.], fired with the noble ambition of standing at the very top of society, it is utterly hopeless of me to attempt our justification (p. 78)

Three Men on the Mountains

Historical actors do not usually carry out their activities with a view to posterity. This is true in the macrocosm of history and in the microcosm of mountaineering history. Most mountain lovers, then as now, were not also aspiring authors, and have left no account of their struggles. But as more people visited the mountains, more people wrote about them – for secondary gratification, for fame, or even at this stage, for filthy lucre. How many accounts, written up in private diaries, or submitted for publication but rejected, must there be of men (or women) and mountains meeting in the early nineteenth century? Many of these would have been subsequently lost, but occasionally we get a glimpse of what has vanished.

Ministers everywhere... The Rev. A.E. Robertson, First Munroist, was merely the latest in a long line of men of the cloth who tramped the hills in the nineteenth century, their leisurely lifestyle, wealth and social status giving them great advantages. (See *The First Munroist*, P. Drummond and I. Mitchell (1992) for the social background of Victorian mountaineering.) Three sons of a Borders minister who introduced them to hill walking, turned into unsung pioneers of Scottish mountaineering – though, to be fair, only one of the sons himself became a minister, the other two becoming publishers and lay preachers. William, Charles and Robert Inglis served their apprenticeship in the Scottish hills in the 1840s, going on to climb Galdhoppigen in Norway in 1859, after having made the first Scottish ascent of Monte Rosa in 1857 – only the sixth ascent. These men are as near to crossing that line from mountain lover to mountaineer as we can get.

Going through scattered notes, the son of Robert, J.G. Inglis (in SMCJ XVI, p. 288), is able to present an impressive list of their expeditions and ascents in Scotland, covering the period 1846 to 1863. As well as repeating standards like Macdhui, Nevis, Schiehallion, Ben Hope, Ben Lomond and others, the brothers would have a good claim to the first ascents of the following mountains: Ben More Assynt (1863) and Beinn Dearg near Ullapool, either 1863 or 1872. *Ben Screel* (Sgriatheal) and *Cralic* (A' Chralaig) were also climbed on one or other of these trips, though there are few details, and the former had been climbed by Stuart and Lightfoot. However, most interestingly Inglis comments:

> In their Scottish ascents they very early embraced the cult of the 3,000 ft peak... in jottings of my father's tours, going back to 1846, only peaks over 3,000 ft are ever mentioned by name... (p. 288)

These splendid fellows kept padding about till the 1880s, and all died within three months of each other in 1887-8. Charles was clearly the *primus inter pares* of the brothers, 'the keenest and most experienced mountaineer of them all', and could apparently tramp 70 miles non-stop. Claims were easily made, for no-one, in those days, would have dreamt of questioning the word of a *gentleman*. They apparently scrambled as well as bagged, and their editor comments:

> A 'Glencoe Ridge' (Aonach Eagach? editor's insert, I.M.) and a narrow 'Ben Nevis Ridge' are mentioned in the seventies; the tale of the latter, if I mistake not, was responsible for sending Dr. Inglis Clark on one of his early adventures (p. 289)

Charles, apparently for the purposes of reading it aloud in a Victorian soiree (what fun! – see what mountaineering videos have killed off?), preserved an account of one of the brothers' trips, which his nephew J.G. Inglis published in SMCJ in the 1920s, seventy years after the events took place. Written in 1856, '*A Pedestrian Excursion in the Highlands*' is an absolutely splendid, three-men-on-a-mountain style account of a steamer trip to Fort William, followed by a walk to Skye, and I recommend all readers to study the entire opus, for which the résumé here can only be a poor substitute.

The first incident of interest is when they arrive at 'Glen Affaric'; then the Lodge was (probably) the present gamekeeper's cottage, as the imposing Affric Lodge was built by Lord Tweed-mouth *c.* 1870. A servant emerged and invited the gentlemen in for lunch, saying it was the tenant, Colonel Ing's instructions that any passing stranger should be offered refreshment, given the lack of places of hospitality in the district. After discussion, they accepted, and then proceeded about a mile up the glen, where,

> ...there was a track leading up the mountain side, which we followed. The climb, though long, was not difficult, and in due time we found ourselves on the perfectly naked top of Mam Soul... the dense mist effectually prevented us seeing any further than a few yards around (SMCJ XVI, p. 15)

If they had climbed Mam Sodhail, the Inglis' would not have been the first ascent. Even leaving aside the possible ascent by Black Findlay of the Deer about 1580, discussed above, there were indisputable prior claims. There are extensive remains on the summit of Mam Sodhail. The men of the Ordnance Survey occupied the summit from 29th July to 31st August 1848. Colonel Winzer of the OS was then on the mountain, making trigonometric observations, and established the height of the mountain at 3,862 ft. Winzer describes the structure they built. 'The station is on the highest point of the mountain, and is marked by a stone pile 23 feet high and 60 feet in circumference', and additionally mentions the discovery of 'a pile on Carnet (Carn Eighe) three-quarters of a mile north' (*Account of the Principal Triangulation,* 1858, p. 27). Duncan MacLennan, the former Affric keeper, had already suggested to me that this was a pre-OS structure, probably a watchers' bothy, and Winzer's evidence confirms that Carn Eige at least was ascended by bothy builders and watchers before 1848.

It is inconceivable that – even in mist, the brothers Inglis could have 'missed' these large structures. The small cairn the brothers saw was in all certainty on the summit of Ciste Dubh (3,606 ft), about half a mile south west of the top of the hill they had wanted to climb. Their route was up Coire Leachavie to the col, and then passing the cliffs of Ciste Dubh on their left, to its summit.

They were now, and not for the last time, hopelessly lost. They headed north, probably down Ghleann a' Choilich, in the direction of Loch Lungard (now fused into Mullardoch) and the Lungard cottage, where they hoped for shelter. Eventually, more by luck then skill, they found it, and Charles describes the scene. A voice cried in the mist, 'That's the wrang gate [direction, I.M.]; gang roon the ither side'. The cottage was occupied by the family of Sword, a Borders shepherd, who showed them Highland hospitality:

> The gudewife and the whole family were roused, sheep dogs included... the fire was kindled afresh; the kettle hung on the crook and the gudewife got out a large dish of curds and cream to 'keep us going until the tea would be ready'. After tea we retired to rest, and they gave us the best end of the house, indeed their own sleeping room, a homely clean apartment. (SMCJ XVII, p. 23)

In the morning, refreshed, they accepted Sword's advice after accepting of his hospitality, as to the route to follow towards Craig, their next stop. This day was a beautiful one, but again they got helplessly lost. In part the reason was they were using maps and guides which bore little relation to the terrain, these 'differed from each other, and from the country before us', (XVII p. 257) as Charles put it, while his nephew years later commented that 'this stage of the journey was utterly unintelligible and untraceable for a long time' (XVII p. 254). The Inglis' problem might have been explained if they were using Black's *County Map of Ross and Inverness*, which places An Socach four miles out of position. I will only accompany the trio on the first stage of their journey; readers fond of mazes and puzzles can read the whole account *in situ* in the SMCJ, until the men's arrival at Craig, where there was 'only (!) herrings, milk and potatoes, on which we dined heartily' (SMCJ XVIII p. 12).

Having accidentally missed Mam Sodhail, the brothers on the following day climbed another peak, whose name they were unfamiliar with, but it is clear that they ascended An Socach, at just over 3,500 ft, as is clear from the account.

> [Sword] also mentioned that when we reached the col at the head of Coire Lungard, a fine view would be obtained by climbing the hill just east of it...
> ...as the mountain on the other side of the glen shut out all view of what lay to the north-west, we decided to climb 'Sword's hill'.
> After a long time we reached the top of the range and saw into the new hill country on the other side. We admired much the grand view from this point (SMCJ XVII, p. 256)

We might speculate that the 'long time' taken to get to 'the top of the range' took the brothers past An Socach, possibly to An Riabhachan, almost 200 ft higher – and visibly so – than An Socach. But that would be mere speculation; what is certain is that the brothers Inglis made the second recorded ascent of An Socach, the border shepherd Sword having beaten them to it, on a previous, unspecified occasion, or possibly several such.

Sgurr na Lapaich, or *Scournalapich* in then-current use, the highest point in this whole range of mountains east of An Socach and north of Mullardoch, had been climbed by another OS party, led by a Sgt. Donelan, on 15th July 1846, and they had stayed on the summit till October. Again, today's walker can find their constructions, or the remains of them, still on the mountain.

> The site of the station of 1845 is 100 feet west south west of the highest peak of the mountain, and is covered by a pile of stones 22 feet high and about 11 feet in diameter (*Account*... Op. Cit. p. 35)

Further north, the brothers showed the internationalising of the climbing language by describing the hills around Loch Maree as the 'Ross-shire Alps'. But ignorance was still bliss, for when the climbed *Sleoch* they thought it was 4,400 ft high; again they carried no barometer, nor as far as I can make out, no compass either. Despite their obsession with mountains over 3,000 feet, they seemed to not know of Colby's previous measurement in 1819 of Slioch. But they did establish an organic link with the trigonometers. On a very hot day they acquired a local guide. But the heat and the rapidity of the brothers' movements caused the guide to faint, and he had to be revived with water splashed on his face. The guide was clearly an old man, for Charles comments:

> Our guide remarked that he had accompanied the sappers and miners when they were surveying the district, and acted as their guide and assistant, only he could never understand what they were doing with their little telescopes mounted on three legs,... He also said the country people were very suspicious of their intentions. (SMCJ XVIII p. 15)

We may find the good-humour poked at the inhabitants of the Highlands here a little offensive nowadays, but unlike certain others, the Inglis' can be excused from looking down on the Highlanders. We will take leave of our worthy trio, though meeting them on the Cuillin later, with Charles' account – full of admiration – for the locals' beliefs and integrity, on the day after the brothers had climbed Slioch.

> Next day being Sabbath we attended the Gaelic Church: though not understanding one word, we were very pleased with the attention and primitive appearance of the congregation. In the course of the day some gentlemen expressed their disgust at not being able to get a boat to go out on the loch for love or money. It spoke very much for the character of the poor people about, that none of them could be found willing to sell his conscience for money. (Loc. Cit. p. 16)

We are on the verge of the mountaineering world, the Highlands have changed beyond recognition from the days when Black Findlay roamed, cutting down without qualm his chief's enemies, answerable only to the chief and himself. Strangers have arrived, taking the shootings in the glens and bringing their servants, or leasing the grazings and putting in shepherds from the *saoghal mor*, the lands of the non-Gael. More of the locals can speak English, and act as guides for walkers, ghillies for fishermen, or provide the mountain and general tourist with accommodation. The mountains before the mountaineers were occupied, high and low, by the Highlander; the displacement of the natives – except in the occasional role of a servant – from the mountains was one of the consequences of a whole complex of social changes, inside the Highlands and outside, which cleared the way for the emergence and institutionalisation of mountaineering as a sport. From the Mountains before the Mountaineers, to the Munros after the Munroists, might sum up the Highlands' trajectory.

But, as in the Central Highlands and the Cairngorms, the emergence of mountaineering was fraught with access problems west of the Great Glen. One of the most notorious controversies featured the American multi-millionaire, and Railway Robber Baron, Walter Winans, who leased the deer forests of Glen Affric, Strathfarrar and Kintail, a total of 200,000 acres. His shootings took place on a vast scale, and were little more than mechanised slaughters of the deer. To ensure stag numbers he built an enormous fence of hundreds of tons of metal from Kintail to Loch Monar, a distance of about twenty miles. To transport the materials he had a 30-ton boat, *The Flyer*, built and transported overland to Loch Monar to ferry materials for the fence. In 1887 the *Inverness Courier* reported that some of his staff had given unwelcome intruders into his domain a physical drubbing, and employees on the estates he rented were forbidden to give accommodation to walkers. These were often molested physically if they strayed off designated rights of way, in case the deer were disturbed.

But Winans met his match, though not at the hands of any walker. Winans had forbidden the tenants at Kintail to use the peat cuttings, forage for timber in the woods, or own any animals which could compete for grazing with the deer, in an attempt to make the locals' lives intolerable, admitting, 'What I desire is to rid the cottages of their inhabitants'. But this was the time of the Crofters' War, and one of the activists in the local Land League, Murdoch MacRae, decided to give Winans a run for his money. He allowed a pet lamb onto Winans' land, which led to a series of court cases that *Murchadh Ruadh* eventually won. This, with the passing of the Crofters' Acts which gave the peasants security of tenure and access to grazing and fuel rights, led Winans, in disgust, to give up his leases in the West Highlands. Winans went, and all that remains today of his schemes are rusting sections of abandoned deer fence, Winans' Dyke. *Murchadh Ruadh* is buried in the Kintail Kirkyard beside his forebears, below the mountains he fought for access to, and where his descendants still live. Remember him as you walk. Visit his grave.

CHAPTER 4

Island Itinerants

PARADOXICALLY, GIVEN THEIR SITUATION of geographical remoteness, the islands of the Hebrides were easier to visit than many parts of the mainland, before the mountaineers. Even once mountaineering had become an institutionalised sport in the later nineteenth century, Skye for example would be visited oftener and earlier than Glencoe or Ben Nevis. For this, the Islands had to thank the element which divided them from the mainland, the waters of the Minch.

It was not until the railways opened up the Highlands, beginning with the Inverness line in the 1850s, that mainland transport became relatively easy. True there were roads, but no vehicles using machine power till virtually this century; coach travel was slow and unreliable. But from the 1820s, the islands of the inner and outer Hebrides could be reached by steam-powered vessels, and even before that the relative ease of travel by ship meant it was easier to go from Glasgow to the islands than to many points on the mainland.

Sir Donald Munro, Dean of the Isles, appears to have visited virtually every inhabited island off the Scottish coast, according to his *A Description of the Western Isles of Scotland, Called Hebrides* (1549), which gives ecclesiastical, genealogical and topographical information on the Hebrides, written in a robust Scots tongue. To travel as far and see as much on the contemporary mainland would have been a much greater feat, showing that it was relatively easier to visit the islands.

Easier, but not initially necessarily safer. James VI had despaired of civilising the Hebrides, and in the later sixteenth century sold Lewis to the Fife Adventurers, a company which attempted to settle the island with Lowlanders and to turn it to economic usefulness. After a few years, the natives rose and massacred/expelled the settlers. James was so despairing of the clansmen, that he actually thought of selling Lewis to the Dutch, whose fishing fleet was already ploughing the waters of the Minch.

Early Voyagers

But just as the Vikings had found it easier to conquer the islands than the mainland, so too did the pacification of the islands actually precede that of the mainland Highland area. Though there was widespread Jacobitism in the 1715, hardly anyone from the islands joined the rebellion of 1745 – which was a mainland, indeed largely Central Highland, affair. Banditry too declined in the islands before the mainland, possibly simply because opportunities for raiding the richer Lowlands were less available, and clan warfare faded earlier too. One does not want to exaggerate this picture, but it is significant that, at a time when no such rival existed regarding the mainland Highlands, there appeared in 1703 a *Description of the Western Islands of Scotland* by Martin Martin. This was a publishing success, and the events of 1715 caused a Second Edition to be rushed out in 1716.

Martin was a Skyeman of the tacksman or factor class, lowland educated, who made his journeys in the 1680s and 90s, possibly using Blaeu's *Atlas* based on Pont's voyages a century before. He was mainly interested in chronicling the 'Antient Customs' of clan society, which Martin saw were already in decline, and his book is a prolix account of superstitions, customs and practises, not without occasional doubts as to its accuracy. His other aim was to rescue the Highlander from being portrayed as a savage, and he comments:

> They are generally a very sagacious people, quick of Apprehension, and even the Vulgar exceed all those of their Rank and education, I ever yet saw in any other Country. They have a great Genius for Musick and mechanicks... They have very retentive memories... The unhappiness of their Education, and their want of converse with foreign nations... deprives them of the opportunity to cultivate and beautify their Genius... And on the other hand... they are to this day happily ignorant of many of the Vices that are practis'd in the learned and polite world...
> (*Description*... Martin Martin 1716, 1934 edn. p. 240-1)

For present purposes, Martin is of limited usefulness. He visited every island from Arran to Lewis in both the inner and outer Hebrides, but it is clear that – apart from a journey across Lewis – he generally hugged the coast of the islands he visited. Scenery does not figure among his items of interest, and still less do the mountains of the Hebrides, though some lesser ones on Skye (see below) are named. However, Martin prepared the way, and later in the century travellers were forever comparing their observations with his, and commenting on Martin, which was a semi-official guidebook. And after the 45, these travellers no longer had to rely on Blaeu's *Atlas*, as a more reliable guide to the islands and seas of the west coast of Scotland had appeared.

It is well known that after the last Jacobite Rebellion, the Hanoverian government, not knowing it was the last, ordered not only a massive campaign of military fortifications to be undertaken, and additions to the military roads network, but also the mapping of the Highlands in the Military Survey of 1747-55. What is much less well known is that, having failed to intercept the arrival of the Prince in, or his escape from, the Hebrides, the same regime ordered the charting of the seas for the Navy. The work was entrusted to Murdo Mackenzie, an Orcadian (despite his Highland name). In the 1770s he published a series of Nautical Charts, covering the west coasts of the entire British Isles. Mackenzie definitely ventured further inland than Martin, for the triangulation method obliged him to set up land-based markers. Elizabeth Bray describes how it was done:

> Small parties of natives would have been despatched up prominent peaks... cairns were built on each peak. Mackenzie himself must have toiled up the key bens, for these were the triangulation points... On each wind swept peak he would take a reading of the other triangulation points, reading off the angle on his sextant. (*The Discovery of the Hebrides*, 1986 Ch. 4, p. 65)

The increased safety resulting from these charts, added to the romance of the recent wanderings of the Prince and motives geological or other, soon brought the island itinerants from the decks of their boats, to the exploration of the glens, and the ascent of the bens. Keeping the best (Skye, need I add?) till last, let us look at the conquest of the lesser island peaks first.

Though possibly sailed around early, the islands of the western seaboard had their summits assailed late. Even though – with the exception of Ben More in Mull – none of the peaks of the islands outside Skye rise over 3,000 ft, many, such as those of Arran and Rum, are the equal in difficulty of all bar a handful of mainland summits. Cruising doon the watter from Glasgow we come to Arran, an island early pacified, colonised and visited by Lowlanders, to whom it is visible from much of central Scotland. So it is hardly surprising that Goat Fell has one of the earliest claims of any Scottish mountain to having been climbed. Lugless Willie Lithgow (1582-1650) was an adventurer and traveller, who lost his ears when he fell foul of the Inquisition and was tortured horribly in Spain – though other accounts say it was the action of outraged brothers, concerned for family honour. For Willie had been forced to leave Scotland after seducing a girl of good family, and he subsequently walked 36,000 miles in Europe, North Africa and the Middle East. He wrote an amusing and successful account of his travels, which appeared in 1632, entitled *Totall Discourse of the Rare Adventures and Painefull Peregrinations of Long Nineteen Years*. In his book, he appears to have climbed Goat Fell, which, as a walk, would have been well within the powers of a man of his pedestrian prowess. He describes 'This Ile of Arraine' as:

> ...sur-clouded with Goatfieldhill which with wide eyes over-lookethe our Westerne Continent, and the Northerne Countrey of Ireland; bringing also into sight in a cleare summer's day, the Ile of Manne and the higher Coast of Cumberland. A larger prospect no Mountaine in the world can show, poynting out three Kingdoms at one sight... (*Totall Discourse*... 1906 edn. p. 428)

And someone, if not Lugless Willie, had climbed the hill to know this. He spent 'certain days' at 'Braidwicke' Castle with the 'Marquesse of Hammilton' in 1628, and thus had the opportunity for an ascent. And he certainly had the ability. Lugless or no, Oor Willie had 'cros'd the Alpes at six severall parts' (p. 10) in the course of his travels, including 'the steepe and Snowy Mountayne of Mont Cola di Tenda, the Highest Hill of the Alpes' (p. 295), when traversing the Ligurian Alps in 1612.

Arran became an early resort for the wealthy of central Scotland, especially Glasgow, and Goat Fell in particular would have been ascended frequently. The ubiquitous Dr. MacCulloch visited the island, and sometime between 1811 and 1824 climbed the highest peak, commenting,

'The ascent to the top of Goatfell is gentle and easy and will well repay the visiter' (so-spelled), though he did point out the summit's deficiency, '...not quite attaining 3,000 ft' (*Highlands and Western Islands*... Vol 11 pp. 26, 30). The doctor was impressed by Arran, which he thought presented 'a rugged, mountainous character, unequalled in Scotland, except by the Cuchillin hills in Skye' (Op Cit p. 26) – a plaudit more mountaineers today might be willing to attach to Rum. After climbing Goatfell, MacCulloch proceeded to *Ben Hiush* and *Ben Breach*. He also admired – but did not climb – the 'acute and rocky pyramid of Kid Voe...' (p. 34), which might puzzle the reader till he deconstructs the geologist's atrocious Gaelic as Cir Mhor! Doing Goatfell became quite the thing for the Glasgow bourgeoisie on holiday. John Nichol, later Professor of English at Glasgow University, recalls his first ascent in 1836 at the age of three – on the back of a Mr Douglass, the family's host at Corrie, though Nichol records that he later climbed the mountain himself on foot. (*Memoir of John Nichol* W.A. Knight, 1896 p. 23.)

The Squire from Flint

In bad weather today, the sailor has the option of the route by the Crinan Canal from Arran towards the inner Hebrides. Not so in the days of Thomas Pennant, who in 1772 visited Arran, without however, climbing anything, and then, fearful of heavy seas round the Mull of Kintyre, crossed Kintyre on horseback and joined his ship again at Gigha. For Pennant was no sailor, but a landlubbing Flintshire squire of independent means and scientific ambitions, publishing his *British Zoology* in 1761 and becoming a member of the Royal Society. He had already visited Scotland in 1769, and two years later published *A Tour in Scotland*, where he made the famous comment, 'North Britain was as little known to its Southern brethren as Kamschatka'. The success of this account prompted the second journey to the islands in 1772, which appeared as the *Voyage to the Hebrides*, and enjoyed even greater success.

The main significance of Pennant's voyage is that, shortly after leaving Gigha, he made the ascent of the highest of the Paps of Jura, Beinn an Oir, the only peak on the island to breach the 2,500 ft contour. Dean Munro had known the names of Jura's peaks over two centuries before, commenting, 'The greatest hills in this iyle are chieflie Bencheelis, Bensenta and Benannoyre...' (Description, 1934 edn. p. 489). Pennant's account of his ascent of *Beinn-an-oir* is minutely observed:

> Cross, on foot, a large plain of ground, seemingly improveable, but covered in deep heath... See the arctic gull, a bird unknown in

South Britain... After a walk of four miles, reach the Paps... for there are three; Beinn-a-chaolois, or the mountain of the sound; Beinn-sheunta, or the hallowed mountain; and Beinn-an-oir, the mountain of gold. We began to scale the last; a task of much labour and difficulty; being composed of vast stones... and all unconnected with each other. The whole seems a cairn, the work of the sons of Saturn...

Gain the top, and find our fatigues fully recompensed by the grandeur of the prospect from this sublime spot; Jura itself afforded a stupendous scene of rock, varied with little lakes innumerable... On the summit are several lofty cairns, not the work of devotion, but of idle herds, or curious travellers. Even this vast heap of stones was not uninhabited; a hind passed along the sides full speed, and a brace of ptarmigans often favoured us with their appearance.

(*Voyage to the Hebrides,* 1790 edn. Vol 1, pp. 247-9)

Pennant mentions Bank's computation of the South Pap at 2,359 ft, adding 'Beinn-an-oir far over-topped it', without hazarding further.

Several points stand out in Pennant's narrative. Firstly, although we are in the high Augustan and pre-Romantic period, when order in nature was seen as being as important as order in society, and when the English landed gentry's idea of the beautiful was ornamental parkland, it is clear that Pennant saw grandeur and sublimity in the scene from the mountain's summit; not all shared the opinion of Johnson and those of kindred spirit, that the Highlands were sterile and ugly. Too often the Doctor's negative views on Highland scenery have been taken to represent all his countrymen, and all his contemporaries.

Secondly, climbing a mountain for pure enjoyment is not yet a self-justified activity. Pennant feels obliged to lecture us on whin dykes and volcanic activity while he is admiring the view. Before the mountaineers, it was still necessary to have an ulterior motive, or an alibi, for climbing the hills.

And finally, an early ascent, but *not* the first. The cairns on the summit, which Pennant speculates are the work of 'herds' or previous travellers, prove the peak had frequent correspondents before Pennant's pioneering trip. Moreover, the name of one of these is known. The Rev. Dr. John Walker (1731-1804) was on Jura in 1764, and wrote:

In Order to ascertain the Height of the paps of Jura, I filled a Barometer on the 27th June, on the Shore of the Sound of Ila... We set off at 10 o'Clock; and it cost us Seven Hours of excessive fatigue, to get to the summit of the highest mountain... the Perpendicular Height of the Mountain turns out to be 2,340 English feet above the level of the Sea. (*Report on the Hebrides of 1764 and 1771* ed. M. Mackay, 1980 p . 114)

Though Walker underestimates the height of Beinn an Oir, we must take him at his word that he climbed the highest Pap, and not one of its satellite peaks, especially as he states that 'some Highland gentlemen' acted as his guides, and presumably they would know their peaks.

It was probably on 30th June 1772 that Pennant climbed his hill; readers may be puzzled as to the reference to Banks and another Pap in his account. But Pennant was writing after his own tour was completed, and after he had received intelligence that the famous geologist Banks – en route to Iceland where his party *inter alia* climbed Hecla and estimated its height at just under 5,000 ft – had climbed, on 6th August 1772 the 'south-Pap' of Jura (Beinn a' Chaolais) and estimated its height by barometric methods. Thus two of the trio of Paps had ascents within a little over a month, from two scientists who were also friends. (If the reader is worried about the Rev. Walker, he is not lost, we shall meet him again soon.)

As both a scientist and an improver, Pennant was genuinely appalled at and sympathetic to the poverty of the islanders, and more than whin dykes came to his notice, and was brought to that of his readers. It was midsummer and the harvest still a while off, and Pennant was horrified to see women and children collecting shellfish as their basic fare (in Gaelic those living such are called *sgalagan*, a term of opprobrium). He describes the regular habitations of the Jura folk as,

> ... scenes of misery, made of loose stones; without chimnies, without doors... a pothook hangs in the middle of the roof, with a pot pendant over a grateless fire, filled with fare that may rather be called permission to exist, than a support of vigorous life...
> (*Voyage...* Vol 1 p. 262)

Our squire also noticed the still vibrant system of transhumance, and visited a group of summer shielings, where the women and children mostly from the populated east coast of the island spent the summer pasturing the beasts on the west coast. The map today shows *Airigh Mhic-'ille Mhoire* just south of Loch a Chnuic Bhric beside the Sound of Jura. It was from these shielings, which he describes and which his servant sketched, that Pennant set off to climb Beinn an Oir. The ruins of these shielings lie around the loch today, and in Jura in 1994 I met an old man, Donald Darroch, who had been at the *airigh* there as a boy.

Pennant moved on through Jura Sound, and sailed round Mull, and to Canna and round Skye, where he did another climb, ascending *Beinn-na-Caillach*, which he describes as follows:

> After ascending a small part, find its sides covered with vast loose stones, like the Paps of Jura, the shelter of ptarmigans... the top flat and naked, with an artificial cairn of a most enormous size, reported to have been the place and sepulchre of a gigantic woman in the days of Fingal. The prospect to the west was of desolation itself, – a savage series of rude mountains, discoloured, black and red, as if by the rage of fire... The serrated tops of Blaven affect with astonishment; and beyond them the clustered height of Quillin, or the mountains of Cuchullin, like its antient hero, "stood like a hill that catches the clouds of heaven... (*Voyage* Vol 1, p. 330)

Whether the Mountain of the Old Woman was named after a female Fingalian long in the tooth or, as another legend has it, a Norse princess who wanted to look over the sea towards her homeland when dead, remains forever a mystery. However, what is certain that the mountain, which exceeds 2,400 ft, did not receive its initial ascent from Pennant. Someone, indeed probably many hands, had built the cairn, which locals regarded as always having been there.

Pennant was a humane man, genuinely interested in Highland life and customs, and impressed by the good qualities he saw in its inhabitants. He ends his book with a plea to the Highland chiefs to become improvers on the southern model, training their people in useful arts and developing industries which could gainfully employ them. But the Lowland model of improvement was not to be applied here. Pennant would have been horrified had he lived to see Jura, which still had a population of several thousand at the time of his visit, reduced by clearance and emigration today to around 200. But even Jura was favoured compared to Rum.

Ethnic Cleansing

Pennant did not visit Rum, though he sailed past it. However, the Rev. Dr. John Walker did, and claimed a surprisingly early ascent of one of Rum's main peaks. In his *Report on the Hebrides of 1764 and 1771*, Walker records that in pursuit of botanical specimens, he landed on the island, and climbed Askival, though underestimating its height by 500 feet.

> From (Loch Scresort) I made a Journey to the highest of these Mountains, named Ascheval. From the Shore we ascended through deep Mosses, whose Surface would scarcely carry us, and then passed through several deep, pathless Glens, so narrow, as the Bowels of the Earth so mangled with Torrents, as to appear hideous. The rest of the Ascent was clambering amidst broken Rocks and falls of water; but among these Rocks and among the straggling Junipers, I found such a Variety of rare Alpine Plants, as amply requited the Fatigue of the Journey. Some of them, the Inhabitants of the highest Alps in Switzerland, and others of Lapland and Spitsberg. This Mountain by the nearest Computation, is about 2,100 Feet high, above the level of the Sea. It is divided at the Top into a great Number of detached Rocks, which shoot up perpendicularly like Spires... Near the Summit it is connected with the neighbouring Mountain, by a Rocky Ridge, in some places so sharp, that a Man may lean his Breast over it, and look down an inaccessible Precipice, between eight and nine hundred Feet high (*Report...* p. 196)

John Walker was a Kirk of Scotland minister of the Moderate party, who became Professor of Natural History at Edinburgh University in 1779. This opened him to a charge of pluralism, and his parishioners at Moffat tried to get rid of him, saying 'he spent the week hunting butterflies, and made the care of souls a bye-job on a Sunday'. He was disciplined, but re-instated in his post, going on to become Moderator of the Kirk in 1790, though being struck blind in 1796 (*Fasti*, 2 p. 217) – doubtless the Evangelicals in the Kirk saw this as a judgement! He was chosen by the Commissioners of the Annexed Estates to tour the Hebrides, as another in the legion of surveying improvers, and was also sponsored by the SPCK on his journeys, to inquire into the religious condition of the islands, especially with regard to residual Episcopalianism and Catholicism. There is no doubt that Walker preferred such work to the dreary job of saving souls in Moffat. Aside from Beinn an Oir and Askival, he climbed no more hills, though he did notice the Clisham, under-estimating it at 2,000 ft, and mentioned the *Quillin* in Skye.

Later our old friend Dr. MacCulloch visited Rum several times, though without much pedestrian success. He commented in 1824 that:

> ...on seven or eight occasions that I have passed it, there has been a storm, and on seven or eight more in which I have landed it was never without the expectation of being converted into a cold fish... (*Highlands and Western Islands*... Vol IV, p. 61)

MacCulloch may have been piqued that he was unable to attempt an ascent of any of the Rum hills, but he has nothing but praise for the native inhabitants, commenting that he would rather be shipwrecked there than anywhere else. Let us give him the floor.

> Again attempting Rum we landed at Scuir More... it blew a hurricane, and all hopes of re-embarking vanished. With the assistance of the villagers of Guirdil, the boat was hauled up dry, and we made up our minds to remain a week... But we should not have starved, while there was a Highlander who had a potatoe. We were at least in as much danger of being devoured by kindness. One hoped, that if I visited his neighbour, I should also come to him... in ten minutes the potatoe kettle was put on the fire... I was taken into the parlour and regaled with tea...

Of another occasion he writes,

> I met a young man in the usual shepherd's dress, and accompanied him to his house, to remain as long as it should please the elements of Rum. When shall I go into such a house in England, and see such smoky shelves covered not only with the books of the ancients, but of the moderns; books too not lying uncut, but well thumbed and talked of? But I had met with such things too often to be surprised... (Op. Cit. Vol IV, pp. 53, 62)

Two years after MacCulloch's book appeared, almost the entire population of the island of Rum was forcibly cleared. Three hundred people were packed into two vessels, the *Highland Lad* and the *Dove of Harmony*, (names ironic indeed) on 11th July 1826, and transported to Nova Scotia. A witness recalled,

> He... would never be able to forget it till his dying day. The wild cries of the men and the heart-breaking wails of the women and children filled all the air between the mountainous shores. (Qu. in *A Boyhood on Rhum,* Archie Cameron, 1988, p. 4)

Doubtless amongst the evicted were those, including the shepherd-scholar, who had shown MacCulloch such kindness; the result is that today on Rum there are no descendants of the original population, to compare with Donald Darroch and a handful of others on Jura. (Archie Cameron's family were introduced as shepherds for the animals which replaced the people.) After such an atrocity, it is difficult to return to a history of mountaineering ascents.

Things worsened on Rum, before they got better. After a series of failures as a sheep farm, the island was bought by the notorious Bullough family, to be used as a sporting estate, during which period it became known as the Forbidden Island. The Bulloughs were self-made Lancashire textile people of limitless wealth, who built a fantasy castle on the island and entertained lavishly, but forbade their dependants to give shelter or sell supplies to any who landed uninvited. Until 1914 the plutocracy and aristocracy were entertained at Kinloch Castle, enjoying its exotic hothouse plants and fauna, including turtles, and being entertained by opera and ballet performers brought in the Bullough yacht, until their world crashed with so much else in 1914. Even in the inter-war period, when the family was in straitened circumstances, walkers and climbers were not welcome.

But those with connections could enter this elite world. As Sir Hugh Munro, Scottish laird and oft-failed Tory M.P., commented in the SMCJ in 1891, he was able to visit the island and obtain accommodation. 'This February, through the introduction of a friend, and the kindness of the proprietor, the late Mr Bulloch...' (Loc. Cit. Vol I No. 6 p 259) – small wonder the early SMC felt little need to agitate on access issues, when 'introductions' could open doors closed to others. Munro was able to climb the hills of Ainshval, Askival and Sgurr nan Gillean, all of which exceed 2,500 ft, and describe them in his article. I would dearly love to believe that some of those evicted in 1826 had known them as well. Certainly, when the Ordnance Survey arrived on the island in 1877, they found Kenneth Maclean, the last survivor of one of the only families which escaped the clearances, to be the sole source of place-names on the island, including those high on the mountains, which he had possibly visited. (*Rum: Nature's Island*, Magnus Magnusson, 1997, p. 24.) Had the OS arrived much later, we would not know the names of the hills, glens and bays on the island.

The exploits of MacGillivray the naturalist in the Cairngorm

Mountains have been covered earlier in this work. When a youth MacGillivray regularly walked home to his uncle's in Harris, where he had been placed as an infant, before returning to Aberdeen, the city of his birth, to study. Harris did not suffer clearance to the extent of Jura, Rum or even Skye, and sustained a viable community at this time. In Harris he wooed his wife, and sought specimens for his collection of birds and other fauna, but he also engaged in pedestrianism, as was the current phrase. In his *British Birds,* (1837), Vol 1, pp. 306-7, written much later in life he recalls his ascent, and the earliest on record, of the highest mountain in the Outer Hebrides, the Clisham in his native Harris. The account is appended, and note that even at this early date, the magic figure of three thousand crops up, and is given as one of the mountain's important features (though MacGillivray erred in estimating the hill as almost 400 ft higher than it really was).

> Having in October 1817... left Borve in Harris, (we crossed) Loch Tarbert to a place called Urga. We remained there for a night, then continued our journey, proceeding up a long, craggy and bleak valley, in which is a very dark-coloured lake [Loch Bhoshmid, I.M.], famous for a goblin beast which is seen on it in summer in the form of a black mass having three humps. The wind was exceedingly keen, the hail came on in great showers, and the summits of the mountains were covered in snow.... having resolved to ascend the highest hill, in order to witness a Hebridean snow-storm in all its glory, I proceeded towards Clisheim, the height of which is estimated at somewhat more than three thousand feet. In spite of hail and snow, and the furious whirlwinds or eddying blasts that swept the mountain, I made my way, though not without labour, to the summit; and well was I recompensed, for there I enjoyed a very sublime spectacle.

MacGillivray can see the whole of the Long Island, as well as the mountains of Ross-Shire and the 'pointed hills of Skye', but the price for such delight is pain:

> Having gazed on this splendid scene till nearly frozen, I descended with considerable difficulty into a deep valley, where I encountered a fall of snow so dense as to render me apprehensive of being smothered by it. I felt too... the benumbing effects of the cold, my feet and fingers having become almost senseless... However, by walking and running I soon recovered heat enough, and after passing the deep glen of Langadale... discovered tokens of cultivation at the distance of three or four miles.

Though the Clisham is the only hill greater than 2,500 ft. in the Outer Hebrides, there are several over 2,000, amongst which the pride of place must go to Beinn Mhor on South Uist, a hard day if combined with its neighbour Hecla. The first recorded ascent of the hill was by Corp. Jenkins of the Ordnance Survey in 1851. Jenkins calculated its height at 2,034.5 ft, and commented on the 'immense precipice along the north side' of the mountain where he established an OS station. But it is clear that there had been a previous ascent by trigonometers, since Jenkins says, 'The stations of 1840-1 and 1851 are identical' (*Account of the Principal Triangulation* (1858), p. 6).

Mull of the Cool High Bens

Mull has often been visited for the wrong reasons, either as somewhere to be got over to get to Iona, whose attractions outshine for many those of the larger island, or later, as something to be sailed round to get to the famous Fingal's cave, discovered by Banks en route to Iceland in 1772. Few of the pious Christians or free thinking geologists on passage gave much attention to Mull itself, but there was one of the scientific persuasion, who, in 1784 was instrumental in getting Ben More its first recorded ascent, the first of any peak over 3,000 ft outside the mainland.

Barthelemy Faujas de Saint-Fond was born in 1742 into a French landowning family, and studied law and natural history, becoming the Royal Commissioner for Mines. He survived the Revolution, even benefited from it, gaining a Professorship of Geology in 1793 at Paris from the Republican government. In his early thirties he read Bank's and Pennant's accounts of Scotland, and these fired his curiosity, especially regarding Staffa. His *Travels in England, Scotland and the Hebrides* was published in France in 1797 and translated into English two years later. His accounts of his meetings with famous British scientists of the period are fascinating, and travelling through Scotland he comments on the state of agriculture, visits the lead mines and foundry at Tyndrum, whose state of repair he commented unfavourably on, and like many others is impressed, even moved, by Highland generosity and hospitality. But...

Faujas de Saint-Fond failed in his attempt to climb Ben More (which may account for some of the pique with which he dismisses the mountain as hardly worth the bother), finding like many others that the heather and bogs of Scotland's hills are more exhausting than the greater height of their continental counterparts. Amongst his enthusiasms, Faujas counted experiments in ballooning, and possibly he would have wished such flight was at a more advanced stage when he attempted Ben More. His American companion, William Thornton, was however made of sterner stuff and carried on to the summit and its first recorded gracing. But again, as it is possibly becoming tedious to point out, it is clear that the young man who guided them was intimately familiar with the ground, and one can have little doubt that Mr. Campbell had – possibly on several occasions – already ascended the mountain. It is appalling that in numerous cases where a local guide is named in the original accounts of a climb, the subsequent writers ethnically cleanse him out of it. For example, though Saint-Fond clearly gives his guide's name as Campbell, neither Horn nor Steven in their accounts of the ascent of Ben More do – he is simply the nameless local, the ghillie or the guide, of no significance. Robbing the Highlander of his name robs him of his dignity and equality.

Another point essential to mention to avoid confusion is that, although sharing the same surname, our *William* Thornton is another than *Thomas* Thornton, who two years later would by a remarkable coincidence ascend Sgoran Gaoith and Creag Meagaidh. But as to the route taken by our transatlantic cousin on Ben More, Saint-Fond's account is too general to allow us to speculate with any degree of usefulness:

> ...I had determined to set out at sunrise to visit the high mountain of Ben More, and William Thornton, whose taste for Natural History was growing, wished to accompany me. The house of Mrs. Campbell, of Knock, is agreeably situated at the foot of a high mountain... Mr Campbell was then at Oban, but we were received with affability by the mistress of the house, who offered us tea and rum. We begged that she would procure a guide to direct our way to the top of Ben More, but her son, a youth of seventeen or eighteen years old, was willing to accompany us himself. This young man, who had a very good figure and was dressed in the Highland costume, immediately presented us with fowling pieces, saying... we should certainly find some black-cocks; for he could not imagine that we wished to climb so rugged a mountain,

for any other purpose than the pleasures of the chase, which he passionately loved himself. He was therefore much surprised when I took out my hammers, and told him that l had come to examine the rocks of the place....

As we intended to return to Aros in the evening, we lost no time in beginning to scale the steep sides of Ben More. In my journeys among the High Alps I never found so much difficulty as here. Almost impenetrable heather, above a soil saturated with water on the lower ground, the middle and the summit of the mountain which rises like a sugar loaf. It is impossible to make progress except by following the small gullies which the rivers have worn... I had reached a great height, when, wearied with seeing only the same lavas, and meeting with no other plants than the toilsome heather... I resolved to go no further. But William Thornton, braving every thing and desirous of gaining the highest summit, climbed to it. Upon the whole, the mountain of Ben More... does not repay the trouble of ascending it. (*Travels...* pp. 89-92)

Did the Frenchman have a little sour grapes, perhaps, with his evening meal?

'Queen of them all'; Surveys and Setbacks

In much of our recent literary voyaging Skye, and especially the Cuillin, has been visible, and it is now time to go there and examine the history of mountain exploration in what the Alpine and Himalayan mountaineer Frank Smythe called the only real mountain range in Britain. Others have given the Cuillin even greater praise, and Ben Humble claimed that 'they have no equal in all the world', a verdict that normally only *Sgitheanaich* would have the courage to utter. However, Humble's experience of and admiration for the Cuillin meant that he spent a great deal of time investigating the history of its exploration and ascent. His classic *The Cuillin of Skye* (1952) devotes much of its contents to the pre-mountaineering history of the gabbro pinnacles of Skye, and thus it is the only area of Scotland aside from Nevis, where a reasonably systematic account exists of exploration and first mountain ascents. Humble was able to carry this out because of the lateness of mountain exploration in Skye. With one possible exception, no Skye peak was ascended till Victorian times, and the majority of those who carried out their climbs left accounts of their ascents. We are greatly indebted to Humble today for his pioneering survey, and it intends no disservice to him that we aim to complete the traverse of the ridge again, giving more detail from the explorers' accounts.

Skye had many visitors, welcome or otherwise, but the first to mention its mountains was Dean Munro in 1549, who wrote, 'In this ile... maney grate hills principally Euilvelimi and Glannock' (*A Description...* p. 503). Cuillin and Glamaig are meant. Pont visited Skye in his peregrinations, and the entry in Macfarlan's *Geographical Collections* on 'Skie or Skianach' is most likely from his hand. In Vol II, it says of Skye 'ther ar mountaynes in it '(p. 531), but none is mentioned by name. Another anonymous account of the island from *c.* 1630 tells of 'a mountaine of great hight (sic), covered with snow all summer' in the 'west wing' of the island. But our credulousness in this might be undermined by the writer's statement that the snow on the hill congeals into 'crystalls', which ladies then wore! (*Collections*, Vol 11, p. 222.) The Cuillin was put on the map when Blaeu's Atlas appeared in 1654, based on Pont's surveys. The sheet on Skye shows the Culluchin or Gulluin hills, but in the wrong place, lying roughly between present day Braes and Portree. The hills mentioned by name are *Bin na Kailly* (Cailleach) and *Klammaig* (Glamaig) wildly misplaced. No individual peak on the main Cuillin range, the so-called Black Cuillin, is named.

By the time we come to Martin Martin a century after Pont, the main range has become Quillin, and he also identifies *Bein-na-Kaillaich* and *Bein-vore-scowe* (Marsco) among outlying peaks, but does not name any separate summits on the main ridge, unless *Scornifrey* be one, and Bruach na Frithe be meant (*Description...* p. 196). A copy of Martin Martin accompanied Boswell and Johnson on their later trip to Skye. Of course, the flight of the Pretender, gradually assuming a roseate romantic glow, and the heroic antics of Flora Macdonald gave further impetus to the lure of Skye, as did the increasing flow of travellers' tales, such as that of Pennant already discussed. The latter's mention of Blaven on his 1772 tour, incidentally, is the first separate mention of a Cuillin main peak I have located.

Many visitors tended to agree with the comment of James Robertson, who also visited the island at this time, that despite the prevailing poverty, 'Perhaps there is no part of the inhabitable globe where so few bodily imperfections are to be seen' as Skye ('James Robertson', A Mitchell, *Proceedings of the Society of Antiquaries,*

Vol 32 (1898) p. 11). That comment might receive short shift in Lewis, however. Robertson visited Skye in 1768, in his own words 'In compliance with the directions I had received' – in all probability again from the Forfeit Estate Commissioners who sent him on similar journeys to the Central and Western Highlands. His *'Remarks Made in Tour through Several of the Western Isles and West Coast of Scotland'* is lodged obscurely in manuscript in the *Communications to the Society of Antiquaries*, 11 (1785-1799), having been read to the society in several parts during 1788. Attention was first brought to Robertson's *Journals*, and to many other accounts of Scotland by early travellers, by Arthur Mitchell in his 'A List of Travels, Tours etc., Relating to Scotland', in *Proc. Soc. Antiqu.* Vol. xxxv (1900-1).

Unlike Robertson's other *Journals*, this one, though of great social interest, is of little mountaineering value. My hopes of discovering previously unknown Cuillin first ascents, by the man with half a dozen mainland first ascents to his credit, were dashed! Robertson first visited Arran, where he climbed *Goatfield* and proceeded some way along the ridges of the other hills, describing them as 'very dangerous to walk along' (p. 6). On Mull he merely comments that 'The isle is very mountainous..' (p. 19), without attempting any peaks. On Skye he finds the *Bod Store* 'a most beautiful natural obelisk', commenting that its name means 'the prick of Store' (p. 25). Presumably it was sanitised to *Bodach*, Old Man, by the prudish Victorians? Robertson has a great time on the island, saying the Skye folk are musical, hospitable and 'drink a great deal of spirits' (p. 27), and he accepts without question their own estimation of Skye Gaelic as the purest spoken in Scotland. But sadly, the only comment he makes on the mountains of the Misty Isle is the following:

> This Isle is mountainous, especially towards the north-west, from Corrychatichan to near L. Bracadale, between these places nothing can be seen but very high mountains (p. 24)

The publication all three extant *Journals* of Robertson would be a great service to Scottish cultural history; of all such I consulted during work on this book, they were the most valuable and interesting.

In 1773 Boswell and Johnson arrived in Skye, and their accounts of their travels will never lose their interest. Pennant had compared Lowland Britain's ignorance of the Highlands, with

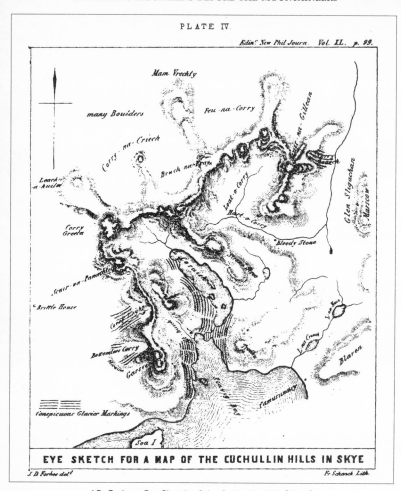

PLATE IV.

Edin.ᵉ New Phil Journ. Vol. XL. p. 99.

EYE SKETCH FOR A MAP OF THE CUCHULLIN HILLS IN SKYE

J.D. Forbes: *Eye Sketch of the Cuchullin Hills* (1846)
The best map till the O.S. men arrived. Shows many prominent features, such as the
Bloody Stone and Brittle House, but only three of the main peaks on the ridge, and
some of the major corries. Bruch-na-Fray and Scuir-na-Gillean were first climbed by
Forbes and Macintyre.
(Ian Mitchell)

their ignorance of Kamtchatka; for Johnson the parallels used
were Borneo and Sumatra – though both books did much to combat this ignorance. But for mountaineers the journey of the Doctor
and his acolyte was of limited value. Johnson did not like mountains, or mountain scenery, a 'wide extent of hopeless sterility' in

his memorable phrase. Johnson does not even mention the Cuillin, but – because of the legend associated with the hill – does deign to notice Beinn na Caillich in a back-handed way, 'The hill behind the house we did not climb... to climb steeps is very laborious and to descend them dangerous'. Boswell on the other hand ascended Dun Caan on neighbouring Raasay, and does not seem to be incredulous at the locals' claim that it was higher than the Cuillin, whereas at 1,351 ft it is less than half the height. Estimation of heights appears a serious weakness amongst many early travellers, as the reader cannot fail to have observed. Boswell does, however, notice and comment on the Cuillin, bringing to bear his experience of mountain scenery elsewhere, and like so many Scots since, comparing mountains abroad to the hills of home:

> From an old tower near this place [Ullinish], is an extensive view of Loch Braccadale... and on the land side, the Cuillin, a prodigious range of mountains, capped with rocky pinnacles in a strange variety of shapes. They resemble the mountains of Corte, in Corsica... (*Tour to the Hebrides* (1773) Vol 1, p. 241)

The Cuillin proper underwent few attempts at ascent in those days, indeed Beinn na Caillich rather became Skye's trade route after its ascent by Pennant. It was climbed in 1800 by the geologist Robert Jameson, who recorded his feat in his *Mineralogy of Scotland*, noting at the same time the 'dark, lurid and terrible summits' of the Cuillin. Dr. MacCulloch also repeated the ascent of the Hill of the Old Woman, and made several attempts from Coruisk at the summits of the Cuillin, failing each time. He excused himself, as have many later mountaineers when faced with failure, by claiming mission impossible, though he did climb part of the way up Sgurr na Stri. MacCulloch mentions no individual peak on the main Cuillin either, though Thomson's map of 1824 shows *Bruachnafrea*.

The doctor also engaged in fine hyperbole over Coruisk itself 'a place which, excepting the shepherd of Strathaird, mortal foot had never trod... here the sun never shone since creation...' and so forth. Such a view of Coruisk was repeated by Walter Scott when he visited the area in 1814. Scott's visit, and his account of it in his *Northern Lights* (p. 95), as well as his poem *The Lord of the Isles*, did much to popularise Coruisk. Scott was rowed from Camasunary, and walked from Scavaig a way up Loch Coruisk. The artists came, Robson and Daniell, and drew the scene. But like today's day-trippers from Elgol, none ventured past the landing stage and its environs, not even Turner in 1831. By then, Coruisk must have been about the most painted scene in the Highlands, this again, in the days before photography, spreading its fame. Daniell's painting is my favourite. Daniell (1769-1837), was elected R.A. in 1822. The painting is one he did to illustrate Richard Aytoun's *A Picturesque Tour Round Great Britain* (1814).

While we might feel these tourists were over-cautious in their approach to the Cuillin summits, let us remember that the os party led by Colonel Colby, fine hardy men all, considered themselves defeated in 1819 when attempting Sgurr nan Gillean, and they argued that ladders and ropes would be necessary for an ascent.

> ...we... were completely foiled in the attempt, and that was proba-
> bly the only instance in which Captain Colby was ever so foiled.
> Nothing I have seen can, for savage grandeur, compare with these
> mountains... We gained... a ridge which reaches out from the per-
> pendicular cliff with a superb column at the extremity of it, and so
> narrow is this ridge that... we were obliged to sit astride upon it...
> (Dawson, in Portlock *Colby...* Op. Cit. p. 144-5)

Let us speculate a little where Colby, Dawson and company got to. Dawson mentions they were headed for 'the summit of the Coolin Hills', which they attempted from Sconser. Sgurr nan Gillean, reputed at this time the highest peak, could have been their only target. At one point, Dawson mentions that they were 2,000 ft. above the corrie 'on the south side' of the ridge they gained; this can only mean they were somewhere between Sgurr nan Gillean and Bruach na Frithe, either the Bealach nan Lice or the Bealach a' Bhasteir; no other location fits. However, Dawson also mentions they were blocked by perpendicular rocks; from these cliffs the 'ridge which reaches out... with a superb column at the end of it' emanated. I feel this argues that they attained the Bealach a' Bhasteir between Sgurr nan Gillean and Am Bhasteir, and, blocked by the West Ridge of Gillean, proceeded some way towards the aforementioned 'superb column' – since they talk about being 'obliged to sit astride' the ridge, unnecessary at the *bealach*. (The Bealach nan Lice location does not work; try it.) As the Trigonometers were aiming for Gillean, and as Am Bhasteir is clearly lower to the eye, they would still have regarded this as a 'failure.' Dawson, Colby and company definately attained the crest of the Cuillin Ridge, and proceeded a little along it; it is not too far fetched to argue from the evidence of Dawson's account that they possibly ascended the then-unnamed Am Bhasteir, having 'failed' on Gillean.

The trigonometers consoled themselves by ascending *Scour-na-Marich* by Sconser. This is Sgurr Mhairi, the summit of Glamaig, (the greedy woman, presumably Mhairi herself), and it was the first recorded ascent of the 2,537 ft. mountain. Thus, despite the emergence of Coruisk as a veritable tourist honey-pot, with guides from Sligachan walking devotees there and back, and boatmen ferrying them in from Elgol and all the airts, the summit ridge of the Cuillin was still, when Victoria ascended the throne – if we can borrow and more accurately apply MacCulloch's exaggerated phrase regarding Coruisk itself – 'a place which mortal foot had never trod' – with the exception of a party of trigonometers. This was to change when a young Scottish geologist made his first of three trips to Skye in 1836.

The Fabulous Forbes

In 1845 Professor J.D. Forbes delivered a paper to the Royal Society of Edinburgh 'on the topography and geology of the least known portion of a yet little known island of our own country, the isle of Sky' ('On the Topography and Geology of the Cuchullin Hills' in *Edinburgh Philosophical Journal* (1846) p. 77). In this paper he not only produced the first scientific geological account of the Cuillin, where he demonstrated conclusively the existence of ancient glaciers in the range, but he also appended the first map of the mountain chain of any reasonable accuracy, from his own hand, and gave the first reliable estimates as to the heights of the hills, which had been regarded by previous visitors as anything from 1,000 to 10,000 ft! Prior to Forbes' visits the mapping of Skye was unreliable. General Roy's Military Survey had dealt with the mainland only, and for a long time the *Yle of Skie* in Blaeu's *Atlas*, (with no Sleat and the Cuillin in the wrong place), was the best that was available. As late as 1800 maps appeared which omitted to show Loch Coruisk at all, and the topography of the hills was mainly guesswork. Forbes' paper, and its map, revolutionised the mental map of the Cuillin.

J.D. Forbes came from an old Aberdeenshire family which was Episcopalian and had been staunchly Jacobite in the eighteenth century. He frequently visited the family estate at Pitsligo in the North East, but he was born in Edinburgh in 1809, where he was raised and, despite a rather erratic education, became Professor of Natural Philosophy at the University at the astonishing age of 23, part of that flowering of Scottish culture and scientific enquiry now dubbed the Scottish Enlightenment. Active in many fields of science, and designer of the first ever earthquake seismometer, his scientific status lies in his studies of glaciation. In 1843 he produced his *Glaciers of the Alps*, followed in 1850 by the first accurate map of the *Mer de Glace* on Mont Blanc, for which he was elected an honorary member of the Alpine Club in 1858. He also visited Norway and produced *Norway and its Glaciers* in 1851, where he noted that the northern mountains were 'commonly called the Kjolen range', which might possibly suggest a Norse origin for the Cuillin, as a ridge of mountains like the keel of a boat.

Neither the *Dictionary of National Biography* nor the *Encyclopaedia of Scotland* record Forbes' mountaineering feats. In Walt Unsworth's *Encyclopaedia of Mountaineering* he merits a mention (but not a separate entry) as an enemy of fellow geologist and mountaineer, Tyndall. But as well as his work on mapping the Mer de Glace, Forbes crossed the Col du Geant, at over 11,000 ft the highest pass in the Alps, and no mean feat then. He had already walked from Lake Geneva to Lake Como and back in 1832 and visited the Dauphiné Alps in 1839 and 1841, the former trip being '...one of the earliest journeys made in that wild tangle of peaks by a British traveller' (*James David Forbes; Pioneer Scottish Glaciologist*, F. Cunningham, 1990, p. 31). He was the first Briton to climb a virgin Alpine peak, the Stockhorn (later Wandfluhhorn) at 11,796 ft in the Valais, and in 1841 with his mentor Louis Agassiz climbed the Jungfrau, which took seventeen and a half hours, the guides carrying a 22 foot ladder for the *bergschrunds*, and copious supplies of wine; steps were cut the last 900 feet, which took two hours. A magnificent achievement for the times, and enough, one would have thought, to merit Forbes a more prominent place in mountaineering histories, even without his performances on the Cuillin.

Forbes visited the Cuillin as a scientist who made an important contribution to the geology of Scotland and earned himself a firm place in mountaineering history. He was clearly impressed by the Cuillin, and spoke of their 'wild and romantic forms... their sides and peaks presenting more appearance of inaccessibility than... any other mountains in Britain'. Before Forbes' first visit in 1836, the Cuillin were deemed by many, including Dr. MacCulloch and the OS men, as unclimbable, at least by non-artificial means. Even the local ghillie, Duncan MacIntyre, had been defeated on his own and with others in his attempts to climb Sgurr nan Gillean. MacIntyre must have had a good eye for routes, for in 1836 he hit on what is now known as the Tourist Route to the summit of Sgurr nan Gillean, and Forbes himself had a good eye for heights, for he estimated (without a barometer) the distance of the summit above sea level as 3,000 ft. He enjoyed the climb, remarking that 'I have never seen a rock so adapted for clambering'. In his account, Forbes gives the date of the ascent as 1837 in one place, 1836 in another; the former is possibly a printer's error, and the date was without doubt, 1836.

> The chief peaks of the Cuchullins are of not very unequal eleva-
> tion; and having been unprovided with any telescopic level, I am
> not prepared to affirm that Scuir-na-Gillean (or, rock of the young
> men...) which forms the bold and magnificent termination of the
> group towards Loch Sligachan is, beyond doubt, the highest of the
> chain. One very acute summit of the western range, named on the
> map, Scuir-na-panachtich (smallpox peak) appears to be as high...
> The ascent of Scuir-na-gillean was deemed impossible at the time
> of my first visit in 1836. Talking of it with an active forester in the
> service of Lord MacDonald, named Duncan MacIntyre, whom I
> engaged to guide me... he told me that he had attempted it repeat-
> edly without success, both by himself and also with different
> strangers... but he indicated a way different from those which he
> had tried, which he thought might be more successful. I engaged
> him to accompany me, and next day (July 7.) we succeeded in
> gaining the top; the extreme roughness of the rocks... rendering the
> ascent safe, where with any other formation, it might have been
> considerably perilous (EPJ Op. Cit. p. 80-1)

It should be noted here that it was *MacIntyre* who found the route, and that also he had tried Gillean not only with clients, but also on his own several times; further proof, if it is by now need-ed by the reader, that many Gaels did have an interest in ascend-ing the hills they lived amongst. Forbes' sharp eye is, however, evi-dent is his reservations about Gillean being the highest Cuillin. *Scuir-na-panachtich* which he judges to be as high is almost exact-ly the same height as Gillean.

Forbes came back to Skye in 1843, but was unable to visit the Cuillin, and eventually returned in May 1845 for an extended study of the geology of the hills into which he made several journeys of exploration and investigation, including the first circumnavigation of the entire range. He was able to give a detailed description of the geology of the hills and to argue convincingly on the role of glaciation in their formation, finding, in a wonderful Victorian phrase, 'amidst the splendid hypersthene formation, indisputable traces of glaciers'. To his account in the *Edinburgh Philosophical Journal*, Forbes appended his sketch-map of the range. This was astonishingly accurate in its general outline, and also named the hills which his guide, MacIntyre, knew. MacIntyre told Forbes that Gillean was from 'young men', from an early attempt by local youths to climb the peak – a now challenged interpretation, many favouring the rival Norse, Peak of the Gills (ravines). *Garsven* at the southern end of the range in named, but the only two other main peaks known to MacIntrye were *Bruch na Fray* (Bruach na Frithe) the peak of the deer forest, and *Scuir na Panachtich* (Banachdich) Milkmaid, or Smallpox Peak. Interestingly, many of the peaks were clearly not only unclimbed, but unnamed, indicating that the summits of the Cuillin were unknown to the islanders, though the passes and corries might be. Forbes also included points of reference such as Brittle House, Camasunary and the Bloody Stone as well as using hachures to indicate steepness. A remarkable achievement, especially since a pioneering one, and one of which Forbes was justly proud, saying 'I am aware of no (other) attempt to trace the topography of these hills'. He dismissed his rival MacCulloch's efforts with the rather uncharitable comment, 'his favourite method of studying geology was from a boat'!

On the 1845 visit, Forbes persuaded MacIntyre to try a new route. They ascended Bruach na Frith, descended into Lota Corrie, and ascended Sgurr nan Gillean from the west. Having this time brought a barometer, Forbes made the first accurate assessment of the heights of the Cuillin peaks. Considering the barometric fall since he set out, his results are surprisingly accurate:

> In 1843 I was in Skye with a barometer, but had not an opportunity of revisiting the Cuchullins; but in May, 1845, I ascended the lower summit, nearly adjoining, marked Bruch-na-Fray in the map, and wishing to ascertain the difference in height of Scuir-na-Gillean, I proposed to Macintyre to try to ascend it from the west side. It was no sooner proposed than attempted. It was impossible to do otherwise than descend into the rugged ravine of Loat-o-

Corry... which cost us a severe scramble, and then face an ascent, which from a distance appeared perpendicular; but aided by the quality of the rocks already mentioned, we gained the Scuir-na-Gillean from the west side, although on reaching the top and looking back, it appeared like a dizzy precipice. My barometrical observations were rendered somewhat unsatisfactory (by) the great fall (in the barometer) during the ten hours that I had been absent... (But) by direct comparison of my observations on the summit of Scuir-na-gillean, with Mr Necker's almost simultaneous observations at Portree... it is probably that the true height of Scuir-na-Gillean is between 3,200 and 3,220 feet. Bruch-na-Fray is probably about 40 feet lower (EPJ Op. Cit. p. 82)

Forbes' estimate is just over 30 feet too much, Gillean is 3,167, but that is an error of roughly 1%, excellent considering the conditions.

Forbes' achievement is astonishing – as a geologist making the first general survey of the Cuillin, and as a cartographer producing a map which would not be bettered till the first OS map of Skye was published, forty years later. And as mountaineers there must be a certain regret that his interest in mountains was first and foremost a scientific one, for he had the capacity for mountaineering greatness, as his experience on the Cuillin and skill on uncharted glaciers in the Alps and Norway testifies. Increasing ill health caused him to gradually reduce his mountain explorations, and Forbes died in 1868, when, (aside from Blaven off the main ridge), the Cuillin ridge was still unclimbed barring the two northerly summits he had climbed with MacIntyre.

Forbes had been a rambler since his youth beside the Pentland Hills, and he ascended many other Scottish mountains. Thus he climbed Ben Macdhui and Lochnagar in the Cairngorms, though he did not like 'the round lumpish Grampians [which] offer no interest except the exercise of climbing them...' (J.C. Shairp, *The Life and Letters of J.D. Forbes,* 1873 p. 175). He also ascended Schiehallion – and Ben Nevis, which he climbed and also circumnavigated, pioneering on the mountain the technique of step cutting in snow, a skill he had learned in the Alps:

...as we approached the head of the glen, we got only glimpses of snow fields and broken rocks above us; and at length we were immersed in the fog, which fortunately was not very deep. We kept on the rock as long as we could, and at length found that there only intervened between us and the ridge a short steep ascent of drifted snow, most truly Alpine. It was too late to think of receding, and it was too far; so assuming my new mahogany tripod as an Alpine stock, I proceeded foremost to make steps in the most approved Swiss fashion, to the no small edification of my companion, who had never seen such an operation before. The upper few yards were so steep that I actually could not get one foot stuck into the snow before the other, and had to get along sideways... (Forbes qu. in Shairp p. 186. The ascent was in May 1848.)

Forbes accompanied his letters to his wife with a map of his wanderings round Ben Nevis. 'I shall make you a little drawing...' he says, but this appears now lost. However he does say that in the course of a walk from Kinloch-Leven, where 'there is typhus fever...', by Lochs Eilt and Treig to Fort William, he 'got a view... from Scuir Eilt...' (Shairpe p. 186, 187). This is Sgurr Eilde Mor in the Mamores, and another first recorded ascent, though small beer to Forbes' other achievements.

Forbes was a hairsbreadth from being a mountaineer. Only the fact that his scientific work still took pre-eminence over his pedestrianism prevents us calling him Scotland's first true mountaineer. As his biographer puts it in relation to one of his continental expeditions, 'Indeed Forbes was in no doubt that, although he enjoyed the exercise, such (careful taking of scientific observations) were the principal purpose of his journeys' (*Forbes...* Cunningham, Op. Cit. p. 24) – and this was as true of the Cuillin as of the Jungfrau. *Travels Through the Alps of Savoy* (1843), like all his other works, is fundamentally a scientific, not a travel, opus. Tyndall, on the other hand, moved from geology to mountaineering for its own sake, and attempted a couple of times to gain the Matterhorn summit before Whymper in 1865 (see Unsworth pp. 352-3).

However, in places Forbes began to develop, not merely the skills of a mountaineer, but the philosophy of one as well, to whom the activity was justified in itself:

[The mountains'] solitude is the parent of reflection, and draws forth to daylight the capacities of that dimly seen inward being, which now begins to assert its claim to individuality, but which, amidst the buzy turmoil of life, might remain a secret and a puzzle even to itself... The young mind in particular seems to discover a link between its powers of conception and the greatness of the objects to be conceived. The seeds of a poetic temperament usually germinate amidst mountain scenery; and we envy not the man, young or old, to whom the dead silence of sequestered nature does not bring an irresistible sense of awe... (Qu. in Shairp p. 314-5)

It is with a sense of awe at his achievements, that we move on from Forbes to those who followed, his map in their hand, in his wake.

Repeats, Drunkards and the Cuillin Crofter

In the later nineteenth century, Colin Philip (SMCJ XIV) noted that, while in Torridon he had collected hundreds of names from locals as to the higher features of the hills, in Skye such nomenclature was limited to the main corries and passes between the peaks. A poverty of nomenclature expressing the poverty of the soil. One suggested derivation of Cuillin is actually 'worthless', ie, of no economic value for transhumance, given the poor soil cover. The few names known to Forbes' guide MacIntyre seem to add weight to this view. But in 1855 appeared Johnstone's *County Atlas of Scotland*. Topographically this was no advance on Forbes, and it was less detailed, but it did contain additional names. It is inconceivable that Johnstone could have invented the named *Scurvadie* (Sgurr a' Mhadaidh), *Scurnanack* (Sgurr nan Eag), or the delightful *Scurduniedaawin* (Sgurr Dubh na Da Bheinn), which are clearly native names. Later John Mackenzie was to record that the Pinnacle of Sgurr Dearg was known to the locals as An Stac, and Macrae, who guided Nicolson (see infra) knew the names of Sgurr Dearg and Sgurr Dhu. Philip thus exaggerates when he claims, in relation to Cuillin names, that 'many of the peaks, including the highest, had none'. Nevertheless, half the Cuillin summits were actually unnamed before the mountaineers, a situation unique in Scotland. Eventually, after 1880, the mountaineers proper would be naming the peaks they first ascended, as they went: Sgurr Thearlaich, Sgurr Mhic Coinnich... But let us return to the early days of exploration.

Forbes mentions an attempted repeat ascent of Sgurr nan Gillean which got to 200 ft of the summit in 1844, and also claims that Colby's OS men did actually ascend the peak and plant a marker on it, though Humble rather pours scorn on this idea in his *Cullin of Skye*. The first definite repeat, unguided this time, would appear to have been by the Inglis bothers in 1856 (Humble, Op. Cit. p. 20 gives 1857), the formidable trio whose wanderings on the mainland we have already dealt with. Their route was a circuitous one; by Glen Sligachan and Harta Corrie, and joining the ridge between Sgurr Beag and the summit of Sgurr nan Gillean where the present tourist route reaches it from the opposite side, though they descended by Forbes' route. The brothers rejected the offer of a guide, since the man who offered his services had never been to the summit, and had no idea how to get there, by his own admission!

The next year of 1857 saw more than a repeat of past glories, however. It also witnessed the first recorded ascent of Blaven, that outlier of the main Cuillin ridge by Loch Slapin. Its ascenders were an unlikely duo. The first was the poet Algernon Swinburne, decadent, iconoclast and homosexual sybarite. The other was John Nichol, Professor of English at Glasgow University. They had met at Balliol, and Swinburne joined the 'Old Mortality' society dominated by Nichol, dedicated to ultra-radical ideas. Both were atheists and republicans, and – though it is not clear if Nichol was himself gay – both were inveterate drunkards.

Swinburne visited Nichol in Glasgow in the summer of 1857 and much of the time was spent in a drunken stupor. However, Nichol was a bit of a pedestrian, and as well as youthful walks in Arran, he had rambled in Ireland and the Lakes, whose attraction was for Nichol in their association with the poetry of Wordsworth. Nicol also, in a letter to his wife, further records having seen the sun rise over the Pyrenees, though exactly from how far is not stated! His only real claim to mountaineering fame is the ascent of Blaven – possibly an appropriate hill, for at that time Camasunary at the foot of the mountain housed a drying out station, or what we would today call an Alcohol Rehabilitation Centre. But this was not the aim of their visit. Probably attracted by the apparent easiness of ascent (though we do not know their route), they were certainly attracted by the false impression that Blaven was the highest mountain on the island, as Nichol states in his account of their visit. This view of Blaven's height seems to be one the drunken duo have shared with no-one else, a figment of their imaginations. Also note that, according to Nichol, while the hospitality of the Highlander is still legendary, market forces are beginning to creep into relations between visitors and visited, in a way that travellers before 1857 have not really commented on. Slowly, the tourist to be charged is replacing the stranger to be given hospitality. (We do not know who 'Jack' is.)

Observatory, 3rd September 1857.

My Dear Jack —,
...Swinburne has been with me for a fortnight or so, and we have just returned from a trip to Skye... In Skye itself certainly the most wonderful spectacles are the bay of Scavaig and the head of Coruisk... The splintered shafts of the Coolin hills seem to rise right from the entrance of the bay.
We climbed Blaven, the highest peak in Skye, with no great danger. But if you are ever in the north of Skye, don't try to get up the Quiraing without a guide... Our furthest point was Uig, a city of farms... After much labour we alighted on the inn. It looked like a stable, or rather a byre... We had cream and butter, and ham and eggs, yea lamb chops and tea... generosity is not uncommon here. On the other hand, guides and boatmen have their wits well sharpened by tourist corruption, and 'the cry of the children' is something to be heard along the road, though not to the same extent as in Ireland. (*Memoir of John Nichol*, ed. W. Knight, 1896, pp. 155-6)

Forbes had been made an honorary member of the Alpine Club, largely because of his work on Alpine glaciers, on the Club's formation in 1857. One of the Club's early members, A.C. Weld, visited Skye in 1859, but as Humble comments, 'he did not put up much of a show' (p. 20). Weld underwent the 'ennui of four days' residence at Sligachan' in terrible weather, and his only achievement was the first recorded ascent of Sgurr na Stri, an eminence of over 1,600 ft, which had earlier defeated MacCulloch. Here Weld admired the view of the 'wondrous Cuillin', but it was many years before mountaineers proper followed him to Skye. However, before their coming, there were a couple of very improper mountaineers, whose exploits should be recorded, and whose explorations made the climbers' tasks easier, when one of them became a guide.

Most of the career of the famous Cuillin guide, John Mackenzie, belongs to the period subsequent to the pre-history of Scottish mountaineering. With the Pilkingtons, with Collie and others he became a partner in much of the exploration and ascent of the Cuillin after 1880. His tale is a fine one, and has been told in several places, by Humble for example in *The Cuillin of Skye*, and in the biography *Norman Collie*, by Christine Mill (1987); or at least told in part, for much of it will never be known. Mackenzie kept no log book, as did Alpine Guides, and the Guest Books in the Sligachan Hotel, which Humble did look at, have subsequently been lost.

I will resist the temptation to tell John's tale again – it lies mostly outside my present remit. But not all of it. Even before the gentlemen mountaineers came to the island, John was exploring:

> However, there was a mountaineering crofter in Skye, and I wonder how many of its people have ever heard of the man buried in Struan Churchyard, after whom one of the most dramatic peaks, Sgurr Mhic Choinnich, is named? A man who spent 50 summers on the Cuillin, and took part in much exploration and in many first ascents. A man famed beyond the boundaries of Skye in his lifetime.
>
> John Mackenzie was born on a croft at Sconser in 1856. He must have been an unusual child, for at 10 he climbed Sgurr nan Gillean on his own – at a time when Skye was virtually unvisited by climbers – and then at 14 took part in the first ascent of Sgurr a' Ghreadaidh. His fame spread and... he supplemented his living by guiding tourists and climbers on the Cuillin. ['John Mackenzie; Skye's famous Man of the Hills', Ian Mitchell WHEP. (25.12.92) – this contains a brief account of John's later achievements.]

The ascent of Sgurr nan Gillean at 10, alone, is amazing, that of Ghreadaidh, which has claimed several lives, at 14 is astounding. However, on the latter ascent he was accompanied by an experienced mountaineer, W.N. Tribe, who later made the first British ascent of the Romsdalhorn in Norway, as well as of several routes in the Lake district. But we should mention that this later President of the Bristol Stock Exchange himself was only 15 when he set out with Mackenzie to do the Peak of the Thrashing – which both of them soundly deserved for their scrape! (Walt Unsworth, *Encyclopaedia of Mountaineering*, 1975, p. 349.) Sadly, details of these ascents by Mackenzie – unsurprisingly – do not survive.

The Sheriff

Mackenzie straddled two worlds, that of the pioneer and that of the mountaineer. But just before the period of pre-mountaineering closed in Skye as it did on the mainland, the last of the pre-mountaineers was to carry out a campaign of ascent and exploration on the island which puts even Forbes' achievements there into the shade. And like Mackenzie, Alexander Nicolson whose name is forever linked with the Cuillin, was a native of the Misty Isle. Nicolson is well known for the quatrain, similar to many panegyrics composed by Hebridean exiles,

> Jerusalem, Athens and Rome,
> I would see them before I die;
> But I'd rather not see any one of these three
> Than be exiled forever from Skye.

Unlike Mackenzie, who was a crofter, Nicolson was a landlord, and also unlike the man from Sconser, Nicolson has left us detailed accounts of his summitry. But let us start with an account of his varied life, itself a mirror of social developments in the Highlands in the middle and later nineteenth century.

Alexander Nicolson was born in 1827, son of the proprietor at Husabost, and his early education was from private tutors. He went to Edinburgh University, intending to enter the Free Kirk ministry, and graduated B.A. in 1850; but he abandoned the study of theology and spent the next decade in various posts. For a while he lectured in logic and philosophy at the University, and was one of the sub-editors of *Encyclopaedia Britannica*. He was editor of the *Edinburgh Guardian* and later of the *Daily Express* which, despite its name, was radical and Liberal, a viewpoint Nicolson retained all his life, though becoming a Liberal Unionist in the 1880s due to his opposition to Irish Home Rule.

Neither his journalistic nor his academic career took off and in 1860 he was called to the bar, again without much impact. He had little business and made ends meet by legal journalism, and publishing articles and poems in the *Scotsman* and the *Gael*. Finally he was appointed Sheriff-substitute at Kirkudbright in 1872, transferring to a similar post at Greenock in 1885, retiring on ill health grounds four years later. Hardly a meteoric success story!

What is intriguing about Nicolson is that – just at the time he was appointed to Kirkudbright – he turned down the offer of Chair of Celtic at Edinburgh, which Blackie had been largely instrumental in establishing. Nicolson was a fine Gaelic scholar, later working on a new Gaelic Bible for the SPCK, and a great admirer of the poetry of the Glenorchy Bard. He would later cite Duncan MacIntyre's Gaelic poetry against those who argued that the Gael had no love for his hills, or interest in ascending them; so there must have been such denigrators even then! Nicolson's obituary in the *Scotsman* said that 'he was of a lethargic constitution which impaired his energy', which possibly explains his lack of interest in an academic career. The epitome of the convivial bachelor, Nicolson certainly put more effort into the playing of shinty, and membership of various Edinburgh Highland societies, than he ever did to any vocational pursuit. When he died, he left a modest middle-class estate of £762 to his sister, who lived with him.

The Sheriff also acted in various civic capacities. Many will know that he was one of the six experts appointed to serve in the Napier Commission, looking into the causes of the crofters' agitation of the western seaboard. Nicolson spent several months in 1883-4, during which the Commissioners' boat, the *Lively*, sank in Stornoway harbour, working on the report which laid the basis for the Crofters' Act of 1886. But he had already served in a similar capacity in 1865, when appointed to the Scottish Education Commission, with a remit to visit virtually all the inhabited islands off the west coast, and to report on the state of their schools. His report helped to lay the basis for the Education Act of 1872.

It was these journeys which gave Nicolson the opportunity to compare his native isle with the other Hebrides. This he did with generosity, but ultimately producing a verdict that few Hebrideans bar his fellow *Sgitheanaich* would agree with, though probably most mountaineers would:

Mull – has beauty and grandeur
Jura – Queenly in state, but lacks variety
Tiree – too flat, but many charms
Barra – rough and boggy
Lewis – boggy
Harris – almost like Skye in mountain grandeur
Staffa and Iona – a universal sense of wonder
Skye – Queen of them all.

It was in the year of his travels as an Education Commissioner, 1865, that Nicolson's mountaineering career began – at the relatively late age of 38. At this time, the Cuillin was still largely virgin, only four of the eleven main peaks on the range having been ascended; Nicolson was to double this number by 1874. In an article written many years later, Nicolson recalled 'Skye and Sgurr nan Gillean in 1865' (SMCJ Vol 11 No 3, pp. 99-108). This text, interestingly, records one of Scotland's first mountain casualties, an Englishman who ascended Gillean without a guide, and was killed by a fall on the descent. The text contains a detailed guide to the ascent by the normal route on the mountain. Compared to the precision and clarity of Forbes' early Victorian prose, the High Victorian prolixity of Nicolson is sometimes irritating. I will summarise. Nicolson climbed Gillean three times. The first time in 1865 was only the fourth recorded ascent, and he was 'guided by the gamekeeper at Sligachan, son of the man, Duncan MacIntyre, with whom Principal Forbes made the first known ascent... (p. 106). Nicolson (alone) repeated the ascent in 1872 and than again 'several years later'. The first ascent was the significant one, for he descended from the summit to Coire a' Bhasteir by the 'horrid cleft' later to be known as Nicolson's Chimney, now more used as a means of ascent (and which Nicolson used on his third visit to the mountain):

> ... I proposed that we should try the north-west ridge, and go down into Coir-a-Bhasdair... We proceeded carefully down that pinnacled ridge till we came to a cleft which seemed to be the only possible way of getting to the bottom, and down which the only mode of progression was crawling on our backs... (p. 106)

But despite this, possibly Skye's first rock-climb-in-reverse, Nicolson's achievements were not in climbing Gillean, nor in Bruach na Frithe or Blaven, which he also ascended, but in those peaks he ascended for the first time.

Venturing one day into Coire Lagan, Nicolson saw a fine peak, which he resolved to climb. This peak was, several years later, discovered by Norman Collie to be the highest point on the Cuillin and was named Sgurr Alasdair in honour of Nicolson's ascent – though he himself had modestly named it *Scur a Laghain*, and I think his wishes should have been acceded to. Here is Nicolson's own account, from the magazine *Good Words* (1875), which was an evangelical magazine edited by Norman Macleod, Queen Victoria's chaplain in Scotland. *Good Words* is full of cloying Victorian religiosity, uplifting texts and pious drawings. But Nicolson's text appeared in it by no mistake. He was a devoutly religious man, and saw the mountains as the cathedrals of creation. In his article cited on Sgurr nan Gillean, he states:

> It is all very well to know that the 'hypersthene' on which you plant your foot is of such and such a chemical structure, and affords the most splendid footing... But I also know, or at least believe, that it was not a blind and fatal Force, but an intelligent

Person that did in the beginning create the heavens and the earth, that did in due time order the upheaval of Scoor-nan-Gillean... the only power to keep my foot from sliding originates not in a soul-less Force, but a Paternal Mind. If Professors Tyndall or Huxley (prominent freethinkers, I.M.) should call me an ass for this, I don't care... *'Sgurr nan Gillean...* (p. 105-6)

Turning to the account of Sgurr Alasdair given in *Good Words* let us honour the shepherd Macrae, as Nicolson does – rather than omitting to mention him at all, as is the case with Humble in his account, *Cuillin of Skye* (p. 28-9). The first ascent of the peak which bears Nicolson's name was a joint venture. Note, too, the first close sighting of the so-called Inaccessible Pinnacle by Macrae and Nicolson, though it had been noted and named on Admiralty charts beforehand:

There is only one peak of all these that is really inaccessible, and that is the summit of Scur Dearg. It consists of a pillar of rock, about fifty feet above the rest of the ridge, and nearly perpendicu-lar. It might be possible, with ropes and grappling irons, to over-come it; but the achievement seems hardly worth the trouble...

I had been told at Glen Breatal that another peak, a very beautiful one... had never been ascended, and had foiled the Ordnance men. This naturally stirred my desire to attempt it, which I did accom-panied by a shepherd, A. Macrae... He too had never been up it, and had never heard of any body having done it. We first went up Scur-na-Banachdich, a charming climb... We found no difficulty in any part of the ascent.

From this peak we went on, down and up to Scur Dearg, and made the acquaintance of that formidable horn aforementioned... at this point our progress along the ridge was barred... [they descend from the ridge into a corrie, I.M.]

This corrie is called *Corrie Laghain*, and the tarn, *Loch a Laghain* and the peak, for which my companion had no name, I proposed to call *Scur a Laghain*... The climb up on the other side of the cor-rie was stiff and warm... We did it however, without much diffi-culty; one or two places requiring good grip of hands and feet, but on the whole I have been in worse places... There was no sign on the top of any one having been on it before, and of course we thought it our duty to make up for that by erecting a cairn... (*G.W.* Op. Cit. p. 458)

Nicolson's greatest achievement, however, was to come in 1874 with the ascent and descent of Sgurr Dubh which Humble claims 'was the finest thing done in climbing in Britain up to that time, and might well be reckoned as notable as Whymper's first ascent of the Matterhorn' (*Cuillin of Skye* p. 33). A little special pleading, perhaps, but nevertheless the reader can judge that here we are dealing with an epic of endurance, route finding and navigation.

Scur Dubh is one of the most formidable of the Coolin peaks, and was reputed "inaccessible". The ascent of it, or rather the descent was, on the whole, the hardest adventure I have had among these hills. I came over with a friend from Sligachan to Coiruisg... and we commenced the ascent about four in the afternoon from the rocks above Loch Scavaig. Considering the sun was to set that evening about seven o'clock... it would have been extreme to have attempted such an excursion so late in the day, had not the barometer been set fair, and the night been that of the full moon, of which we wished to take advantage for a moonlight view of Coiruisg. The ascent is a very rough one, up the corrie between Scur Dubh and Garsveinn, and partly along the banks of the 'Mad Burn.' The corrie is well named the Rough Corrie ('Garbh Choire')... About half way up we were overtaken by a shower of rain... When it cleared a little, we saw that the ridge above was covered in mist but, trusting in the barometer, we held on, expecting that by the time we got to the top the mist would have passed away, which it did. The last quarter of the ascent was very hard work, and not quite free from danger. It was about seven when we found ourselves on the summit, a very narrow, rocky ridge...

We had not much time to admire the view, as the sun had just set behind the black battlements... The descent was tremendously blocked with huge stones, and the tarn at the bottom of the corrie is surrounded by them. About halfway down we came to a place where the invaluable plaid came into use. My companion, being the lighter man, stood above with his heels well set in the rock, holding the plaid by which I let myself down the chasm. Having got footing, I rested my back against the rock, down which my lighter friend let himself slide till he rested on my shoulders...

From eight to half past ten we descended in almost total darkness, for though the moon rose about nine... we were all the way down in the deep shadow of the peak behind us. Most of the way was among shelving ledges of rock, and in one place it seemed to me that there was no going further ... and we tried in all directions before we ventured on the experiment of wriggling down the wet rock, in a perfectly vermicular [worm-like] manner... I certainly never in the same space of time went through so much severe bodily exercise as in that descent from Scur-Dubh to Coiruisg. My very finger-tops were skinned from contact with the coarse-grained rock. But the difficulties of the descent were compensated for when we got, with thankful hearts, into the full flood of the moonlight on... the valley above Coiruisg. (*G.W.* pp. 459-60)

The ordeal of the duo was not over, as they still had to face the walk in the dark back to Sligachan, which they reached at three o'clock in the morning exhausted, but without further serious mishap. Nicolson is sometimes credited with the traverse of the Dubhs, but as he only mentions one peak, I think Sgur Dubh Mor was his sole summit that day. He possibly reached the ridge between that latter eminence and Sgur Dubh na da Bhein – the 'last quarter... not quite free from danger' being the ascent to that point from Garbh Corrie. The descent was probably by Coir an Lochain, since Nicolson mentions a 'tarn' on the way back down to Coruisk.

Nicolson did no more first ascents, though he continued to visit Skye every other year, and did much to publicise the island by articles such as those in *Good Words*. He commented of Skye that 'Here a day is worth two in most places' and the thousands of mountaineers who have followed in his footsteps since would doubtless agree.

By the 1880s we are in a different world from Nicolson's of the early 1870s, with the Cuillin receiving as many ascents in an average week as it had in the previous half century. The Pilkington brothers, family fortune made in glass-making, arrived in Skye. Alpine Club members, they pioneered guideless climbing in the Alps, and made many first unguided ascents, including the Meije and the Guggi route on the Jungfrau. They, especially Charles, were mountaineers, and on Skye made the first ascents between 1880 and 1887 of the so-called Inaccessible Pinnacle and Pinnacle Ridge, as well as Clach Glas and Sgurr Mhic Coinnich, which they named after John Mackenzie who climbed with them. But the Skyeman, honoured though he was, was a survivor from a previous epoch. And I often wonder if, when accompanying the gentlemen from Sligachan Hotel to the various summits of the now explored, mapped and named Cuillin, Mackenzie thought back to the days when, a boy, he had been on Sgurr nan Gillean and Sgurr a' Ghreadaidh. Which had been the finest days of his life? That life ended in 1934, the Cuillin before the mountaineers now no longer alive even as memories in the mind of an old man in Sconser.

CHAPTER 5

The Highlands Today

OUR MAGICAL MYSTERY TOUR IS over. What, apart from an absorbing interest in and astonishment at the feats of the pre-mountaineers, can we take from it? Study of the past with an eye to the present is what distinguishes the historian from the antiquarian, and I would hope the researches in these pages have thrown some light on our contemporary concerns.

Around 1580, when our survey began, the Highlands of Scotland were seen by outsiders as an area of almost impenetrable physical terrain, of trackless mountains and bogs. Further, the inhabitants were regarded as living in the barbarous, pre-civilised state of society compared to that obtaining in the Lowlands and England. The Highland barbarians were also seen as likely to be robbers, reivers and rebels into the bargain. Their uncivilised dress, and even more uncivilised language, marked them off, ghettoised them into a national apartheid, where many Lowlanders regarded them as not Scottish, but Irish – an alien, intrusive element in national history and culture.

By the time our story ends, around 1880, a revolution in ways of seeing the Highlands, had taken place. Accessibility led to increasing numbers of visitors who regarded the Highland landscape as the epitome of grandeur, the quintessence of the sublime in nature, a heaven rather than a hell, finding expression in the works of writers like Scott, painters like Landseer, and critics such as Ruskin. By his participation in the colonial wars of British imperialism, the Highlander – from being a rebel – had become a hero, and those who remained behind in the glens were seen as quaint and picturesque, the embodiment of treasured values supposedly destroyed by increasing urbanisation and industrialisation.

Most astonishingly, the bric-a-brac of Gaelic society, the bagpipes, the tartan, as well as the picture postcard/shortbread tin images of the Highlands became, not (as they had been) the brand of the criminal, the mark of the outlawing of the Highlander from mainstream Scottish tradition, *but the generally accepted embodi-*

ment of that tradition. This is not simply because the majority of pedestrians, in previous centuries as in this, have been English rather than Scots, and might lack a proper appreciation of the matter. This skewered view has been accepted *both* by outsiders, and by the 'Tartan Army' of Scots themselves. This travesty of the national tradition produces terrible consequences in popular culture in Lowland Scotland, whose own socio-economic and ecclesiastic traditions are now largely unknown, and most people imagine all Scots wore kilts, spoke Gaelic, and were Jacobites. (See 'Museumry and the Heritage Industry', George Rosie, in *The Manufacture of Scottish History,* 1992 ed. I. Donnachie and Christopher Whatley.)

But this fabrication of Scottish history is a disaster not only for the Lowlands, which becomes an historical bastard, without patrimony, but for the Highlands themselves. For the romanticised, trashy version of their own history that the Gael is served up is offered as a sop, a compensation, for the fact that the remaining Gaels live in an area where the land ownership system is an anachronism which symbolises their own expulsion from, and lack of access to, the land of their forebears. Instead of land rights, the Gael has tourist trinket shops. Enthusiasm for some kind of radical land reform in the Highlands is increasing, and our study shows, if anything, that it is not only in the interests of those who live there, but also in the interest of the mountaineers who today visit, that this land reform take place.

All through this study, I have tried, while narrating the basic tale of exploration and ascent, to emphasise two related threads of argument.

The first is the degradation of the environment from 1580-1880, in the Highland region. From the former date to the later, there was a loss of native species of animal and bird life, a reduction in tree cover, and a depletion of soil fertility, either due to over-grazing or the abandonment of cultivation. The Highlands were never the Garden of Eden the Gael liked to think them, blinded by love like *Donnachadh Ban* regarding his wife's beauty. But today, with its main crop being bracken, the Highlands are more like the Biblical desert, an ecological disaster-zone. And comparison with other areas, with similar climates but different land-holding systems such as Norway, shows that this need not necessarily be the case. The responsibility for this must lie with those who have had custodianship of the land, the clan chiefs, turning themselves gradually into landed proprietors, (together with those who have bought into this world from outside) – and with the system of land ownership the legatees of the clan chiefs created. One of the most encouraging things to develop in the Highlands over the last twenty years or so is the spread of various kinds of social ownership of land, the spread of Crofters' Trusts, and the purchase of land by conservation and charitable bodies, such as the John Muir Trust, with a remit to repair damage and restore biodiversity.

Land ownership in the Highlands cannot be made to pay commercially, and we can hopefully look forward to the spread of social ownership and the euthanasia of large-scale private landownership over time; and in that time come to accept the view of Marx, that private ownership of landed property is as absurd of the private ownership of human beings.

And this brings me to my second point. Poaching of game led to violent and armed conflicts, from the days of Black Findlay in Glen Cannich in 1580, until the early nineteenth century when shoot-outs between poachers and gamekeepers were not uncommon. But that aside, *until quite late on in the nineteenth century, I can find no recorded instance of an 'access problem'*. The access issue arose with the emergence of two roughly parallel developments in the middle of the nineteenth century. These were: the increasing numbers of people who were on the mountains for pedestrian exercise, and the conversion of large areas of the Highlands into deer forest, whose rental value was many times that of sheep-walks. It was this last, despairing attempt of landlordism to make the Highland estate pay a commercial dividend, which not only led to the serious further ecological degradation of the terrain through over-grazing, but also to the attempts to prevent access; Cockburn in Glen Tilt, Blackie on the Buachaille, Copland in Glen Lui, all found themselves molested in the name of the sacred rights of deer-shooting. Luckily, the response of the Scottish mountaineering community over the years has been simply to ignore these attempts to prevent access. There have been exceptions, such as the Scottish Mountaineering Club (SMC), which, from its inception, printed in its publications *caveats* such as the following:

> It is essential at all times to respect proprietary and sporting rights, especially during the shooting season, and to avoid disturbing game

in deer forests and grouse moors. (SMC Guide *Western Highlands* (J.A. Parker, 1964 edn. p. 148 – or any SMC publication.)

The legal situation as regards access in Scotland is a little clouded, according to the various accounts one reads. While it would appear that there is no legal right to roam, it would also appear there is no legal right to bar access either – providing no damage is done by the person claiming access. I am unaware of any major successful prosecution of mountaineers or hillwalkers for trespass, damage, breach of the peace or other in Scotland; if there have been such, they are few and have had limited impact. Every major judgement, from the Glen Tilt case in the 1840s, to the Glen Tanar affair in the inter-war period, has upheld the right of access.

There are possible blind alleys to avoid in the access debate. For example, well intentioned though it may be, the activities of the Rights of Way Society have the danger of being seen as channelling the access issue into corridor routes, glen paths, drove roads, etc, making them a special case: a position which landlords have no difficulties with. I have on occasion been challenged for being 'off the right of way', and though I was unimpressed, others, less well informed, might not be.

Apparently more fruitful are the efforts to gain access agreements, or concordats, with landowners, such as that which received so much acclaim between various outdoor bodies and the Letterewe Estate in Wester Ross. But I doubt if more than a tiny minority of landlords, playing the environmental lord bountiful, would conclude such wide-ranging agreements as that of Letterewe; the majority, with commercial interest at heart, would resist. There has recently been established an Access Forum in Scotland, comprising, under the umbrella of Scottish Natural Heritage, various outdoor groups, as well as the Scottish Landowners Federation and the Association of Deer Management Groups. This has produced an Access Concordat which is extremely vague, and does little to advance access. It talks of the 'acceptance by visitors of the needs of land management', and 'reasonable constraints' for this to be carried out. In other words, (*and for land management, read deer-stalking*), this Concordat asks us to accept restrictions on our activities, so that a land usage which has been a social disaster and an ecological nightmare can take place. This Access Forum has produced a pamphlet, *Caring for the Hills*, which shown its leanings. Walkers are told to minimise path erosion; nothing about estates bulldozing tracks. Walkers are told not to disturb wildlife; nothing about estates' illegal trapping and poisoning of the same. Walkers are told to 'make a contribution to the local economy', when we already do so, a *contribution that is greater than that made by deer-stalking or sheep farming*.

And even if pigs could fly and the bulk of Scottish landowners would agree to some kind of agreement like the Letterewe one, where conservation appears to assume major importance, we are still subject to the whims and hostage to the priorities of the landowners. They could change their minds, with changing economic circumstances, or individual estates could change hands and policies change. But more fundamentally, the objection to making any voluntary agreements with private landowners is that this accepts and legitimises their ownership and usage of the land. This ownership and usage are what we should be challenging. Concordats are fine with Crown Lands, Crofters' Trusts and (despite past mistakes) the National Trust, bodies which in one way or another represent social ownership. They are not what is needed with private landowners, native or foreign. What is required with them, and what they are trying to avoid with their current charm offensive (as they admit) is compulsion, with legal backing.

With the arrival of a new government committed – in theory- to action of the land issue and access in particular, we have to expect and demand nothing else than a legally enshrined right to roam, on the Scandinavian model. That is the *de jure* codification of what the *de facto* situation was before the Aggravated Trespass legislation – and the abolition of that pernicious piece of legislation. Further, we should demand the abolition of deer-stalking (along with other blood sports), to be replaced by a scientific cull, and economic penalties on landowners for failure to comply.

I have my doubts that this government, or any other, will adopt more than a piecemeal approach to the land issue, preferring to avoid a root and branch attitude. But I cannot see that ultimately, in Scotland, this would make much difference. The area of the Highlands is so vast, and the numbers using it so great, that it is difficult to see how access could be prevented, either physically or legally. If we allow our historical right to roam to be diluted in any way, it will be because we have been intimidated or duped, and found not worthy of enjoying that essential part of our heritage which those mentioned in this book established by the sweat of their brows and the tramp of their feet.

Appendix

CHRONOLOGY OF ASCENTS OF SCOTTISH MOUNTAINS.
(*c.* = approx. date; ? = uncertain; ?? = more uncertain.)

o. A.D. *c.*	Bennachie and Tap o Noth ascended
84	**Battle of Mons Graupius**
?	Cruachan ascended by Fingalian warrior?
?	Ben Ledi ascended by Druidical worshippers?
?	Schiehallion scene of Pictish ritual?
843	**Union of Picts and Scots**
1070 *c.*	Creag Choinnich (Braemar) ascended
1250 *c.*	William Mhic Fhearchair wanders corries of Beinn Eighe, Mullach Coire Mhic Fhearchair?
1375 *c.*	Cruachan mentioned in Barbour's *Bruce*
1559	**Protestant Reformation**
1560s	*Domnhall Mac Fhionnlaigh* ascends Sgor Ghaibhre, Carn Dearg, Stob Coire Sgriodain?
1580s	*Fionnladh Dubh* climbs Beinn Fhionnlaid in Affric
1580s	Peregrinations of cartographer Pont. Sketches Torridon mountains
1590s	*Cailean Gorach* climbs Stuchd an Lochain, Glen Lyon
1603	**Union of Crowns. Exit Jamie the Saxt**
1618	Taylor ('Water Poet') climbs Mount Keen, Deeside
1628	'Lugless' Willie Lithgow ascends Goatfell?
1644	Creag Leacach ascended by Campbell marauders?
16??	An Sgarsoch summit scene of cattle markets
1690s	Ian Mackerachar – *Lonavey* – Climbs Carn an Righ
1707	**Union of Parliaments**
1715	**Jacobite Rebellion**
1719	Sgurr na Ciste Duibhe Sgurr nan Spainteach ascended by units of Jacobite Army and Hanoverian pursuers.
1720 *c.*	Alexander Graham ascends Ben Lomond?
1745-6	**Jacobite Rebellion**

1746	Sgurr Thuilm
	Sgurr nan Coireachan
	Sgurr nan Conbhairean
	Carn Ghluasaid climbed by Charles Edward Stuart and companions
1749	Sergeant Davies murdered on outlier of Carn Bhac
1764	Beinn an Oir
	Askival, climbed by Rev. Walker
1767	Ben Hope
	Ben Klibreck
	Ben Wyvis climbed by James Robertson
1758	William Burell's companions ascend Ben Lomond
1750s *c.*	Duncan MacIntyre climbs Beinn Dorain and ? Creag Mor
1750s *c.*	James MacIntyre climbs Cairngorm with Jacobite flag
1769	Ben More (Perthshire) ascended by 'party of astronomers'
1771	James Robertson ascends Ben Nevis
	Mayar
	Ben Avon
	Lochnagar?
1770s	Meall Ghaordaidh
	Beinn Heasgarnich
	Meall nan Tarmachan?
	Ben Cruachan?
	Beinn Sgulaird
	Beinn Sgritheal
	Bidean nan Bian, all climbed by John Stuart, some with Lightfoot
1774	Nevil Maskeleyne? and William Roy climb Schiehallion
1776	Ben Lawers falls to a party of Gen. Roy
1776	Beinn a' Ghloe; party of Gen. Roy
1784	William Thornton and Mr. Campbell ascend Ben More, Mull
1786	Sgor Gaoith climbed by party of Thomas Thornton
1786	Carn Liath, Stob Poite Coire Ardair, and Creag Meagaidh climbed by Thomas Thornton and unnamed local guide.

1780s *c.*	Stuic a' Chroin ascended by hunters
1789	**French Revolution confines English tourists to Scotland**
1800s *c.*	Aonach Eagach ridge part-traversed by fox-hunters
1800s *c.*	Beinn Alligin ascended by shepherds; fatality ensues.
1810s *c.*	Ben Chonzie
	Ben Vorlich (Lomond)
	Ben Cruachan
	The Cobbler
	Beinn Lair
	An Teallach (Sgurr Fiona)
	Beinn a' Bheithir all climbed by John MacCulloch.
1810s *c.*	Ben Alder
	Beinn Achaladair
	Beinn Udlamain
	Beinn a'Chreachain?
	Ben Vorlich (Loch Earn), all ascended by Thomas Grierson
1810	Beinn a' Bhuird
	Braeriach
	Cairn Toul
	Ben Macdhui climbed by Rev. George Keith
1813	Carn a' Mhaim ascended by George Fennel Robson?
1817	Clisham ascended by William MacGillivray
1819	Capt. Colby, Col. Dawson and os party
	Carn Dearg in Monadh Liath
	Glas Maol
	Sgurr Fhuaran (Kintail)
	Am Bhasteir?
	Slioch climbed by Dawson, Kirkwood and ? Colby
1820s *c*	Sron a' Choire Gharbh climbed by Black Sandy?
1820s *c.*	Gairich climbed by bandit Euan Macphee?
1830	Derry Cairn Gorm ascended by William MacGillivray and party
1834 *c.*	Fionn Bheinn ascended by John Leighton
1830s?	Ben Ime and Ben Narnain climbed by Robert Christison
1836	J.D. Forbes and Duncan MacIntyre climb Sgurr nan Gillean
1839	Carn Liath climbed by servants of Duke of Atholl

1844	Carn a' Chlamain climbed by Queen Victoria and party
1845	**Formation of Scottish Rights of Way Society**
1845	Forbes and MacIntyre climb Bruach na Frithe
1846	Sgurr na Lapaich. OS party under Sgt. Donelan
1848	Sgurr Eilde Mor climbed by J.D. Forbes
1848	Mam Sodhail ascended by Col. Winzer (OS)
	Carn Eighe previously ascended by deer-watchers.
1850	Carn an-t Sagairt Mor crossed by MacGillivray ?
1850s *c.*	Mr. Sword, shepherd, climbs An Socach (Ross-shire)
1857	Blaven ascended by Nichol and Swinburn
1857	**Formation of Alpine Club**
1863 or 72	Ben More Assynt
	A' Chlaraig (Affric)
	Beinn Dearg (Ullapool) all climbed by Inglis brothers
1867	John Stuart Blackie climbs the Buachaille Etive Mor
1870	Sgurr a' Ghreadaidh ascended by John Mackenzie and W. Tribe
1873	Sgurr na Banachdich; A. Nicolson
1873	Sgurr Alasdair, by A. Nicolson and A. Macrae
1874	Sgurr Dubh Mor, by A. Nicolson and 'a friend'
1887	**Formation of Cairngorm Club**
1888	**Formation of Scottish Mountaineering Club.**

Bibliography

Abrahams, A.P.	*Rock Climbing in Skye* (1908)
Access Forum, The	*Caring for the Hills* (1997)
Alexander, William	*The Cairngorms* (1950 edn.)
Anderson, P. and G.	*Guide to the Highlands and Islands of Scotland* (1827)
Anon.	*The Scottish Tourist's Companion* (1823)
Anon.	*The Scottish Tourist's Pocket Guide* (1838)
Anon.	*Mar Lodge Estate; An Archeological Survey* (1995)
Aytoun, Richard	*A Picturesque Tour Round Great Britain* (1814)
Black, Ronald I.M. (ed.)	*Poems from Watson's Bardachd Ghaidhlig* (1997)
Blackie, John Stuart	*Notes of a Life* (1869)
Blaikie, W.B.	*The Itinerary of Charles Edward Stuart* (1897)
Boswell, James	*Tour to the Hebrides 2 vols* (1773)
Bray, Elizabeth	*The Discovery of the Hebrides* (1986)
Brooker, W. (ed.)	*A Century of Scottish Mountaineering* (1988)
Brown, Hamish	*Hamish's Mountain Walk* (1980)
Brown, T.G. and Lloyd, R.W.	*Mountaineering; Catalogue of the National Library of Scotland* (1994)
Bryce, James	*Memories of Travel* (1921)
Burt, Edward	*Letters from a Gentleman in the North of Scotland* (1974)
Burton, J.H.	*The Cairngorm Mountains* (1864)
Calder, George (ed.)	*The Songs of Duncan MacIntyre* (1912)
Cameron, Archie	*Bare Feet & Tackety Boots* (1988)
Campbell, Duncan	*The Lairds of Glenlyon* (1886)
Cash, C.G.	'The First Topographical Survey of Scotland' S.G.M. Vol XVII (1901)
Christison, Robert	*Life* (1885) – includes *Autobiography* (c.1880)
Clarke, Alexander Ross (ed.)	*Account of... Calculations of the Principal Triangulation* (1858)
Close, C.	*The Early Years of the Ordnance Survey* (1969)
Clyde, Robert	*From Rebel to Hero* (1995)
Cockburn, Alexander	*Circuit Journeys* (1888)
Collie, William	*Memoir of William Collie* (1992)
Copland, A.	*Two Days and a Night in the Wilderness* (1878)
Crocket, Ken	*Ben Nevis* (1986)

Cunningham, F. — *James David Forbes; Pioneer Scottish Glaciologist* (1990)

Defoe, Daniel — *A Tour Through The Whole Island of Great Britain* (1724-6)

Dixon, J.H. — *Gairloch* (1886)

Donnachie, I. & Whatley, C.(eds.) — *The Manufacture of Scottish History* (1992)

Drummond, P. and Mitchell, I. — *The First Munroist; A.E. Robertson* (1992)

Drummond, Peter — *Scottish Hill and Mountain Names* (1991)

Dunbar, J.G. (ed.) — *Sir William Burrel's Northern Tour, 1758* (1997)

Ellice, E. — *Place Names of Glengarry and Glenquoich* (1898)

Ewen, G. — 'Gley Ey, a History' *C.C.J.* Vol XX (1994)

Ferguson, Adam — *Essay in the History of Civil Society* (1767)

Fforde, K. — 'Bonnie Dundee's Six Weeks in Lochaber' *T.S.G.I.* Vol LVIII (1994)

Fontane, Theodor — *Beyond the Tweed* (1965 edn.)

Forbes, J.D. — 'On the Topography... of the Cuchullin Hills' *Edin. Phil. Jour.* (1846)

Forbes, J.D. — *Norway and its Glaciers* (1851)

Forbes, R. — *The Lyon in Mourning*, 3 Vols (1895)

Forsyth, W. — *In the Shadow of Cairngorm* (1900)

Galbraith, J.J. — 'The Battle of Glenshiel' *T.S.G.I.* Vol XXXIV (1927)

Geikie, Archibald — *The Scenery of Scotland* (1887)

Gordon, Seton — *Highways and Byways in the West Highlands* (1935)

Gordon, Seton — *Highways and Byways in the Central Highlands* (1948)

Grant, John — *Legends of the Braes o Mar* (1876)

Grierson, Thomas — *Autumnal Rambles Among the Scottish Mountains* (1850)

Hawker, Peter — *Diary of Colonel Hawker 1802-53* (1971)

Hogg James — *Highland Tours* (1981 edn.)

Holloway, J and Errington, L — *The Discovery of Scotland* (1975)

Hope, John — 'Letter to W. Watson' *Phil.Trans.Royal Society* (1769)

Horn, D. B. — 'The Origins of Mountaineering in Scotland' *S.M.C.J.* Vol XXVII (1966)

Howse, D. — *Nevil Maskeleyne, the Seaman's Astronomer* (1989)

Humble, Ben — *The Cuillin of Skye* (1952)

Inglis, Charles — 'A Pedestrian Excursion in the Highlands' *S.M.C.J.* Vol XVI,II,III (1920s)

Johnston, W and A.K. — *County Atlas of Scotland* (1855)

Keay, J. and J. — *Encyclopaedia of Scotland* (1994)

Keith, George Skene — *General View of the Agriculture of Aberdeenshire* (1811)

Kerr, John — *Life in the Atholl Glens* (1993)

Kinsley, J. (ed.) — *Poems of William Dunbar* (1964)

Knight, W.A. — *Memoir of John Nichol* (1896)

Lees, Iain C.	*On Foot Through Clydesdale* (1932)
Leighton, John	*The Lakes of Scotland* (1834)
Lemprière, C.	*Description of the Highlands of Scotland* (1731)
Lenman, Bruce	*The Jacobite Cause* (1986)
Lightfoot, John	*Flora Scotica* 2 Vols (1777)
Lithgow, Willie 'Lugless'	*Totall Discourse of..Painefull peregrinations...*(1906 edn.)
MacCulloch, John	*Highlands and Western Islands of Scotland* (1824) 4 vols
MacDonald, Alexander	*Story and Song from Loch Ness-side* (1914)
Macfarlane, Walter	*Geographical Collections* (1908) 3 Vols, (ed.) A. Mitchell
MacGillivray, William	*Natural History of Deeside* (1855)
MacGillivray, William	*History of British Birds* (1837)
MacGillivray, William	*Journals* (unpublished)
MacGillivray, William (ed.)	*Memorial Tribute to William MacGillvray* (1901)
Mackenzie, Osgood	*A Hundred Years in the Highlands* (1921)
MacLean, A. and Gibson, J.S.	*Summer Hunting the Prince* (1992)
Macrae, A.	*History of the Clan Macrae* (1899)
Macrow, Brenda G.	*Torridon Highlands* (1953)
Magnusson, Magnus	*Rum: Nature's Island* (1997)
Marren, P.	*Grampian Battlefields* (1990)
Martin, Martin	*Description of the Western Islands of Scotland* (1934 edn.)
Marx, Karl	'The Duchess of Sutherland and Slavery' in *Articles on Britain* (1978 edn.)
McCombie Smith, W.	*The Romance of Poaching in the Highlands* (1904)
McConnochie, A.I.	'The Eastern Cairngorms' *C.C.J.* Vol 1
McEwan, P.J.M.	*Dictionary of Scottish Art and Architecture* (1988)
Michie, J.G.	'The Benchinnans' *C.C.J.* Vol II
Michie, J.G.	*Deeside Tales* (1872)
Mill, Christine	*Norman Collie* (1987)
Millar, A.H.(ed.)	*Forfeit Estate Papers* (1906)
Mitchell, A.	'James Robertson' *Proc.Soc.Antiqu.* Vol 32 (1898)
Mitchell, A.	'A List of Travels, tours etc., Relating to Scotland.' *Proc. Soc. Antiqu.* Vol xxxv (1901)
Mitchell, Ian	'The Murder of Sergeant Davies' *W.H.F.P.* (14.2.97)
Mitchell, Ian	'Ewan MacPhee of Loch Quoich' *W.H.F.P.* (12.5.95)
Mitchell, Ian	*Mountain Footfalls; A Calendar of the Scottish Hills* (1995)
Mitchell, Ian	'The millionaire, the crofter and the pet lamb.' *W.H.F.P.* (10.2.95)

Mitchell, Ian	'John Mackenzie; Skye's Man of the Hills' *W.H.F.P.* (25.12.92)
Moll, H.	*The Shire of Lenox* (1724)
Morris, G.E.	'The Profile of Ben Loyal from Pont's map.' *S.G.M.* 102 (1986)
Munro, Donald	*A Description of the Western Isles of Scotland* 1549 (1934)
Munro, Jean	'The Clan Period' in The Ross and Cromarty Book (1966)
Murray, Sarah	*A Companion and... Guide to the Beauties of Scotland* (1799)
Nicolson, Alexander	'The Isle of Skye' *Good Words* (1875)
Nicolson, Alexander	'Sgurr nan Gillean in 1865' *S.M.C.J.* Vol II
Nicolson, Marjorie	*Mountain Gloom and Mountain Glory* (1959)
O'Donoghue, Y.	*William Roy* (1977)
Owen,T. and Philbean, E.	*The Ordnance Survey* (1992)
Parker, J.A.	*The Western Highlands* (1931)
Pennant, Thomas	*Voyage to the Hebrides* (1790 edn.)
Philip, Colin	'On the Nomenclature of the Cuillin Hills' *S.M.C.J.* Vol XIV.
Portlock, J.E.	*A Memoir of the Life of Major-General Colby* (1869)
Ralph, Robert	*William MacGillivray* (1993)
Ralston, I. and Shepherd, I.	*Early Grampian; a guide to the archeology* (1979)
Rhind, W.	*The Scottish Tourist* (1825)
Robertson, A.E.	'The Wanderings of Prince Charlie' in Parker, J.A. Op.cit.
Robertson, James	*Journal* of 1768 Communications to Soc. Antiquaries (1785-9)
Robertson, James	*Journal* of 1767 N.L.S. 2507
Robertson, James	*Journal* of 1771 N.L.S. 2508
Robson, George F.	*Scenery of the Grampian Mountains* (1814)
Ross, Charles	*Travellers Guide to Loch Lomond* (1792)
Roy, W.	'Experiments and Observations...with the barometer.' *P.T.R.S.* Vol LXVII (1777)
Ruskin, J.	*Works* (1903) Vol III
Ruskin, J	*Modern Painters* (1904), Vol IV 'of Mountain Beauty'.
Saint-Fond, B. Faujas de	*Travels in England, Scotland and the Hebrides* (1799)
Sandby, William	*Thomas and Paul Sandby* (1829)
Schama, Simon	*Landscape and Memory* (1995)
Scott, Walter	*Waverley* (1815)
Scott, Walter	*Rob Roy* (1819)
Scott, Walter	*Northern Lights* (1814)

Seymour, W.A. (ed.)	*A History of the Ordnance Survey* (1980)
Shairp, J.C.	*The Life and Letters of J.D. Forbes* (1873)
Skelton, R.A.	'The Military Survey of Scotland' *S.G.M.* Vol 83 (1967)
Smith, Robert	*Grampian Ways* (1980)
Smith, Robert	*Land of the Lost* (1997)
Smout, T.C.	*A History of the Scottish People* (1969)
Smout, T.C.	*A Century of the Scottish People* (1986)
Steven, Campbell	*The Story of Scotland's Hills* (1975)
Stevenson, D.	*The Covenanters* (1988)
Stoddart, John	*Remarks on Local Scenery and Manners in Scotland* (1801)
Stone, Jeffrey C.	*The Pont Manuscript Maps of Scotland* (1988)
Stone, Jeffrey C.	*Illustrated Maps of Scotland* (1991)
Tabraham, C. and Grove, D.	Fortress Scotland and the Jacobites (1995)
Taylor, John	'Pennyles Pilgrimage' in Hume-Brown, P. (ed.) *Early Travellers in Scotland* (1891)
Taylor, William	*Military Roads of Scotland* (1976)
Thomson, John	*County Atlas of Scotland* (1832)
Thomson, Derek	*An Introduction to Gaelic Poetry* (1974).
Thomson, Iain	*Isolation Shepherd* (1983)
Thorton, Thomas	*Sporting Tour* (1804)
Turner, Jane	*The Dictionary of Art* (1996)
Unsworth, Walt	*Encyclopedia of Mountaineering* (1975)
Various Authors	*The Munros; S.M.C.Guide* (1985)
Various Authors	'The Rise and Progress of Mountaineering in Scotland' *S.M.C.J.* Vol III (1894)
Victoria, R.M.	*Journal of our Life in the Highlands* (1868)
Walker, John	*Report on the Hebrides of 1764, 1771* (ed.M.Mackay 1980)
Walker. A.S. (ed.)	*Letters of John Stuart Blackie to his Wife* (1909)
Watson, A. and Clement, R.D.	'Aberdeenshire Gaelic' *T.S.G.I.* LII (1983)
Wilkinson, Thomas	*Tours to the British Mountains* (1824)
Wyness, Fenton	Royal Valley (1968)

Acknowledgements and Dedication

I WOULD LIKE TO THANK the following for their invaluable help; all improved the book, none are responsible in any way for a single error or omission. Iseabail Macleod subjected the entire manuscript to a thorough critique, as did Peter Drummond. Bruce Lenman read the draft and gave me his weighty *imprimatur* by agreeing to provide a Foreword. Rennie MacOwan read the section on the Cairngorms and made useful suggestions. Jeffrey Stone made valuable comments on Pont, while Wayne Debeugny aided my researches into Roy and Colby. Robert Ralph facilitated my inquiries into MacGillivray, by making available his unpublished typescripts of some of the naturalist's *Journals* held in the library of Aberdeen University. At a time when the manuscript division was closed, the staff at the National Library of Scotland allowed me exceptional access to the unpublished *Journals* of James Robertson. Ronald Black brought my attention to the poem *Oran na Comhachaig*. And as always, *Seonag Mairi* helped a Saxon with Celtic *Gestalt*.

I would, however, like to dedicate the work to the staff of the Mitchell Library, in Glasgow. At a time of re-organisation and financial stringency, they helped me with every request and inquiry, with an unfailing courtesy and professionalism, the epitome of excellence in public service. Without the Mitchell, people like myself who are not based in academic institutions, could not do our research and write our books. Would that this Public Reference Library, unique in Europe in the range of its collection, were adequately resourced financially, instead of suffering cutbacks in provision.

Some of the material in the book was originally published in the *West Highland Free Press*.

Index

Some other books published by **LUATH** PRESS

WALK WITH LUATH
Mountain Days & Bothy Nights
Dave Brown and Ian Mitchell
ISBN 0 946487 15 4 PBK £7.50

Acknowledged as a classic of mountain writing still in demand ten years after its first publication, this book takes you into the bothies, howffs and dosses on the Scottish hills. Fishgut Mac, Desperate Dan, Stumpy and the Big Yin stalk hill and public house, evading gamekeepers and Royalty with a camaraderie which was the trademark of Scots hillwalking in the early days.

'The fun element comes through... how innocent the social polemic seems in our nastier world of today... the book for the rucksack this year.'
Hamish Brown, SCOTTISH MOUNTAINEERING CLUB JOURNAL

'The doings, sayings, incongruities and idiosyncrasies of the denizens of the bothy underworld... described in an easy philosophical style... an authentic word picture of this part of the climbing scene in latter-day Scotland, which, like any good picture, will increase in charm over the years.'
Iain Smart, SCOTTISH MOUNTAINEERING CLUB JOURNAL

'The ideal book for nostalgic hillwalkers of the 60s, even just the armchair and public house variety... humorous, entertaining, informative, written by two

men with obvious expertise, knowledge and love of their subject.' SCOTS INDEPENDENT
'Fifty years have made no difference. Your crowd is the one I used to know... [This] must be the only complete dossers' guide ever put together.'
Alistair Borthwick, author of the immortal *Always a Little Further.*

The Joy of Hillwalking
Ralph Storer
ISBN 0 946487 28 6 PBK £7.50

Apart, perhaps, from the joy of sex, the joy of hillwalking brings more pleasure to more people than any other form of human activity.

'Alps, America, Scandinavia, you name it – Storer's been there, so why the hell shouldn't he bring all these various and varied places into his observations... [He] even admits to losing his virginity after a day on the Aggy Ridge... Well worth its place alongside Storer's earlier works.'
TAC

LUATH WALKING GUIDES

The highly respected and continually updated guides to the Cairngorms.
'Particularly good on local wildlife and how to see it' THE COUNTRYMAN

Walks in the Cairngorms
Ernest Cross
ISBN 0 946487 09 X PBK £4.95
This selection of walks celebrates the rare birds, animals, plants and geological wonders of a region often believed difficult to penetrate on foot. Nothing is difficult with this guide in your pocket, as Cross gives a choice for every walker, and includes valuable tips on mountain safety and weather advice.
Ideal for walkers of all ages and skiers waiting for snowier skies.

Short Walks in the Cairngorms

Ernest Cross

ISBN 0 946487 23 5 PBK £4.95

Cross wrote this volume after overhearing a walker remark that there were no short walks for lazy ramblers in the Cairngorm region. Here is the answer: rambles through scenic woods with a welcoming pub at the end, birdwatching hints, glacier holes, or for the fit and ambitious, scrambles up hills to admire vistas of glorious scenery. Wildlife in the Cairngorms is unequalled elsewhere in Britain, and here it is brought to the binoculars of any walker who treads quietly and with respect.

LUATH GUIDES TO SCOTLAND

These guides are not your traditional where-to-stay and what-to-eat books. They are companions in the rucksack or car seat, providing the discerning traveller with a blend of fiery opinion and moving description. Here you will find *'that curious pastiche of myths and legend and history that the Scots use to describe their heritage... what battle happened in which glen between which clans; where the Picts sacrificed bulls as recently as the 17th century... A lively counterpoint to the more standard, detached guidebook... Intriguing.'*
THE WASHINGTON POST

These are perfect guides for the discerning visitor or resident to keep close by for reading again and again, written by authors who invite you to share their intimate knowledge and love of the areas covered.

Highways and Byways in Mull and Iona

Peter Macnab

ISBN 0 946487 16 2 PBK £4.25

'The Isle of Mull is of Isles the fairest,
Of ocean's gems 'tis the first and rarest.'
So a local poet described it a hundred years ago, and this recently revised guide to Mull and sacred Iona, the most accessible islands of the Inner Hebrides, takes the reader on a delightful tour of these rare ocean gems, travelling with a native whose unparalleled knowledge and deep feeling for the area unlock the byways of the islands in all their natural beauty.

South West Scotland

Tom Atkinson

ISBN 0 946487 04 9 PBK £4.95

This descriptive guide to the magical country of Robert Burns covers Kyle, Carrick, Galloway, Dumfries-shire, Kirkcudbrightshire and Wigtownshire. Hills, unknown moors and unspoiled beaches grace a land steeped in history and legend and portrayed with affection and deep delight.

An essential book for the visitor who yearns to feel at home in this land of peace and grandeur.

The Lonely Lands

Tom Atkinson

ISBN 0 946487 10 3 PBK £4.95

A guide to Inveraray, Glencoe, Loch Awe, Loch Lomond, Cowal, the Kyles of Bute and all of central Argyll written with insight, sympathy and loving detail. Once Atkinson has taken you there, these lands can never feel lonely. 'I have sought to make the complex simple, the beautiful accessible and the strange familiar,' he writes, and indeed he brings to the land a knowledge and affection only accessible to someone with intimate knowledge of the area.

A must for travellers and natives who want to delve beneath the surface.

'Highly personal and somewhat quirky... steeped in the lore of Scotland.'
THE WASHINGTON POST

The Empty Lands

Tom Atkinson

ISBN 0 946487 13 8 PBK £4.95

The Highlands of Scotland from Ullapool to Bettyhill and Bonar Bridge to John O'Groats are landscapes of myth and legend, 'empty of people, but of nothing else that brings delight to any tired soul,' writes Atkinson. This highly personal guide describes Highland history and landscape with love, compassion and above all sheer magic.

Essential reading for anyone who has dreamed of the Highlands.

Roads to the Isles

Tom Atkinson

ISBN 0 946487 01 4 PBK £4.95

Ardnamurchan, Morvern, Morar, Moi-dart and the west coast to Ullapool are included in this guide to the Far West and Far North of Scotland. An unspoiled land of mountains, lochs and silver sands is brought to the walker's toe-tips (and to the reader's fingertips) in this stark, serene and evocative account of town, country and legend. For any visitor to this Highland wonderland, Queen Victoria's favourite place on earth.

NATURAL SCOTLAND

Rum: Nature's Island

Magnus Magnusson

ISBN 0 946487 32 4 £7.95 PBK

Rum: Nature's Island is the fascinating story of a Hebridean island from the earliest times through to the Clearances and its period as the sporting playground of a Lancashire industrial magnate, and on to its rebirth as a National Nature Reserve, a model for the active ecological management of Scotland's wild places.

Thoroughly researched and written in a lively accessible style, the book includes comprehensive coverage of the island's geology, animals and plants, and people, with a special chapter on the Edwardian extravaganza of Kinloch Castle. There is practical information for visitors to what was once known as 'the Forbidden Isle'; the book provides details of bothy and other accommodation, walks and nature trails. It closes with a positive vision for the island's future: biologically diverse, economically dynamic and ecologically sustainable.

Rum: Nature's Island is published in co-operation with Scottish Natural Heritage (of which Magnus Magnusson is Chairman) to mark the 40th anniversary of the acquisition of Rum by its predecessor, The Nature Conservancy.

Wild Scotland: The essential guide to finding the best of natural Scotland

James McCarthy

Photography by Laurie Campbell

ISBN 0 946487 37 5 PBK £7.50

With a foreword by Magnus Magnusson and striking colour photographs by Laurie Campbell, this is the essential up-to-date guide to viewing wild-life in Scotland for the visitor and resident alike. It provides a fascinating overview of the country's plants, animals, bird and marine life against the background of their typical natural settings, as an introduction to the vivid descriptions of the most accessible localities, linked to clear regional maps. A unique feature is the focus on 'green tourism' and sustainable visitor use of the countryside, contributed by Duncan Bryden, manager of the Scottish Tourist Board's Tourism and the Environment Task Force. Important practical information on access and the best times of year for viewing sites makes this an indispensable and user-friendly travelling companion to anyone interested in exploring Scotland's remarkable natural heritage.

James McCarthy is former Deputy Director for Scotland of the Nature Conservancy Council, and now a Board Member of Scottish Natural Heritage and Chairman of the Environmental Youth Work National Development Project Scotland.

Scotland, Land and People: An Inhabited Solitude:

James McCarthy

ISBN 0 946487 57 X PBK £7.99

'Scotland is the country above all others that I have seen, in which a man of imagination may carve out his own pleasures; there are so many inhabited solitudes.'

DOROTHY WORDSWORTH, in her journal of August 1803

An informed and thought-provoking profile of Scotland's unique landscapes and the impact of humans on what we see now and in the future. James McCarthy leads us through the many aspects of the land and the people who inhabit it: natural Scotland; the rocks beneath; land ownership; the use of resources; people and place; conserving Scotland's heritage and much more.

Written in a highly readable style, this concise volume offers an understanding of the land as a whole. Emphasising the uniqueness of the Scottish environment, the author explores the links between this and other aspects of our culture as a key element in rediscovering a modern sense of the Scottish identity and perception of nationhood.

'This book provides an engaging introduction to the mysteries of Scotland's people and landscapes.
Difficult concepts are described in simple terms, providing the interested Scot or tourist with an invaluable overview of the country... It fills an important niche which, to my knowledge, is filled by no other publications.'
BETSY KING, Chief Executive, Scottish Environmental Education Council.

The Highland Geology Trail
John L Roberts
ISBN 0 946487 36 7 PBK £4.99
Where can you find the oldest rocks in Europe?
Where can you see ancient hills around 800 million years old?
How do you tell whether a valley was carved out by a glacier, not a river?
What are the Fucoid Beds?
Where do you find rocks folded like putty?
How did great masses of rock pile up like snow in front of a snow-plough?
When did volcanoes spew lava and ash to form Skye, Mull and Rum?
Where can you find fossils on Skye?

'...a lucid introduction to the geological record in general, a jargon-free exposition of the regional background, and a series of descriptions of specific localities of geological interest on a "trail" around the highlands.
Having checked out the local references on the ground, I can vouch for their accuracy and look forward to investigating farther afield, informed by this guide.

Great care has been taken to explain specific terms as they occur and, in so doing, John Roberts has created a resource of great value which is eminently usable by anyone with an interest in the outdoors...the best bargain you are likely to get as a geology book in the foreseeable future.'
Jim Johnston, PRESS AND JOURNAL

FOLKLORE
The Supernatural Highlands
Francis Thompson
ISBN 0 946487 31 6 PBK £8.99
An authoritative exploration of the otherworld of the Highlander, happenings and beings hitherto thought to be outwith the ordinary forces of nature. A simple introduction to the way of life of rural Highland and Island communities, this new edition weaves a path through second sight, the evil eye, witchcraft, ghosts, fairies and other supernatural beings, offering new sightlines on areas of belief once dismissed as folklore and superstition.

HISTORY
Blind Harry's Wallace
William Hamilton of Gilbertfield
ISBN 0 946487 43 X HBK £15.00
ISBN 0 946487 33 2 PBK £8.99
The original story of the real braveheart, Sir William Wallace. Racy, blood on every page, violently anglo-phobic, grossly em-bellished, vulgar and disgusting, clumsy and stilted, a literary failure, a great epic.

Whatever the verdict on BLIND HARRY, this is the book which has done more than any other to frame the notion of Scotland's national identity. Despite its numerous'historical inaccuracies', it remains the principal source for what we now know about the life of Wallace.

The novel and film *Braveheart* were based on the 1722 Hamilton edition of this epic poem. Burns, Wordsworth, Byron and others were greatly influenced by this version 'wherein the old obsolete words are rendered more intelligible', which is said to be the book, next to the Bible, most commonly found in Scottish households in the eighteenth century. Burns even admits to having 'borrowed... a couplet worthy of Homer' directly from Hamilton's version of BLIND HARRY to include in 'Scots wha hae'.

Elspeth King, in her introduction to this, the first accessible edition of BLIND HARRY in verse form since 1859, draws parallels between the situation in Scotland at the time of Wallace and that in Bosnia and Chechnya in the 1990s. Seven hundred years to the day after the Battle of Stirling Bridge, the 'Settled Will of the Scottish People' was expressed in the devolution referendum of 11 September 1997. She describes this as a landmark opportunity for mature reflection on how the nation has been shaped, and sees BLIND HARRY'S WALLACE as an essential and compelling text for this purpose.

'Builder of the literary foundations of a national hero-cult in a free and powerful country'.
ALEXANDER STODDART, sculptor

'A true bard of the people'
TOM SCOTT, THE PENGUIN BOOK OF SCOTTISH VERSE, on Blind Harry.

'A more inventive writer than Shakespeare'
RANDALL WALLACE

'The story of Wallace poured a Scottish prejudice in my veins which will boil along until the floodgates of life shut in eternal rest' ROBERT BURNS

'Hamilton's couplets are not the best poetry you will ever read, but they rattle along at a fair pace. In re-issuing this work, the publishers have re-opened the spring from which most of our conceptions of the Wallace legend come'.
SCOTLAND ON SUNDAY

'The return of Blind Harry's Wallace, a man who makes Mel look like a wimp'.
THE SCOTSMAN

Notes from the North
incorporating a Brief History of the Scots and the English
Emma Wood
ISBN 0 946487 46 4 PBK £8.99

Notes on being English
Notes on being in Scotland
Learning from a shared past

Is it time to recognise that the border between Scotland and England is the dividing line between very different cultures?

As the Scottish nation begins to set its own agenda, will it decide to consign its sense of grievance against England to the dustbin of history?

Will a fresh approach heal these ancient 'sibling rivalries'?

How does a study of Scottish history help to clarify the roots of Scottish-English antagonism?

Does an English 'white settler' have a right to contribute to the debate?

Will the empowering of the citizens of Scotland take us all, Scots and English, towards mutual tolerance and understanding?

Sickened by the English jingoism that surfaced in rampant form during the 1982 Falklands War, Emma Wood started to dream of moving from her home in East Anglia to the Highlands of Scotland. She felt increasingly frustrated and marginalised as Thatcherism got a grip on the southern English psyche. The Scots she met on frequent holidays in the Highlands had no truck with Thatcherism, and she felt at home with grass-roots Scottish anti-authoritarianism. The decision was made. She uprooted and headed for a new life in the north of Scotland.

She was to discover that she had crossed a border in more than the geographical sense.

Loving her new life and friends in first Sutherland and then Ross-shire, she nevertheless had to come to terms with the realisation that in the eyes of some Scots she was an unwelcome 'white settler' who would never belong. She became aware of the perception that some English incomers were insensitive to the needs and aspirations of Highland communities.

Her own approach has been thoughtful and creative. In Notes from the North she sets a study of Scots-English conflicts alongside relevant personal experiences of contemporary incomers' lives in the Highlands. She gently and perceptively confronts the issue of racial intolerance, and sets out conflicting perceptions of 'Englishness' and 'Scottishness'; she argues that racial stereotyping is a stultifying cul-de-sac, and that distinctive ethnic and cultural strands within Scottish society are potentially enriching and strengthening forces. This book is a pragmatic, positive and forward-looking contribution to cultural and politicial debate within Scotland.

Notes from the North is essential reading for anyone who is thinking of moving to Scotland and for Scots who want to move into the 21st century free of baggage from the past.

SOCIAL HISTORY

The Crofting Years

Francis Thompson
ISBN 0 946487 06 5 PBK £6.95
Crofting is much more than a way of life. It is a storehouse of cultural, linguistic and moral values which holds together a scattered and struggling rural population. This book fills a blank in the written history of crofting over the last two centuries. Bloody conflicts and gunboat diplomacy, treachery, compassion, music and story: all figure in this mine of information on crofting in the Highlands and Islands of Scotland.

'I would recommend this book to all who are interested in the past, but even more so to those who are interested in the future survival of our way of life and culture' STORNOWAY GAZETTE

'A cleverly planned book... the story told in simple words which compel attention... [by] a Gaelic speaking Lewisman with specialised knowledge of the crofting community.' BOOKS IN SCOTLAND

'The book is a mine of information on many aspects of the past, among them the homes, the food, the music and the medicine of our crofting forebears.' John M Macmillan, erstwhile CROFTERS COMMISSIONER FOR LEWIS AND HARRIS

'This fascinating book is recommended to anyone who has the interests of our language and culture at heart.' Donnie Maclean, DIRECTOR OF AN COMUNN GAIDHEALACH, WESTERN ISLES

'Unlike many books on the subject, Crofting Years combines a radical political approach to Scottish crofting experience with a ruthless realism which while recognising the full tragedy and difficulty of his subject never descends to sentimentality or nostalgia' CHAPMAN

BIOGRAPHY

Tobermory Teuchter: A first-hand account of life on Mull in the early years of the 20th century

Peter Macnab
ISBN 0 946487 41 3 PBK £7.99
Peter Macnab was reared on Mull, as was his father, and his grandfather before him. In this book he provides a revealing account of life on Mull during the first quarter of the 20th century, focusing especially on the years of World War I. This enthralling social history of the island is set against Peter Macnab's early years as son of the governor of the Mull Poorhouse, one of the last in the Hebrides, and is illustrated throughout by photographs from his exceptional collection. Peter Macnab's 'fisherman's yarns' and other personal reminiscences are told delightfully by a born storyteller.

This latest work from the author of a range of books about the island, including the standard study of Mull and Iona, reveals his unparalleled knowledge of and deep feeling for Mull and its people. After his long career with the Clydesdale Bank, first in Tobermory and later on the mainland, Peter, now 94, remains a teuchter at heart, proud of his island heritage.

'Peter Macnab is a man of words who doesn't mince his words - not where his beloved Mull is concerned. 'I will never forget some of the inmates of the poorhouse,' says Peter. 'Some of them were actually victims of the later Clearances. It was history at first hand, and there was no romance about it'. But Peter Macnab sees little creative point in crying over ancient injustices. For him the task is to help Mull in this century and beyond.'
SCOTS MAGAZINE, May 1998

Bare Feet and Tackety Boots

Archie Cameron
ISBN 0 946487 17 0 PBK £7.95
The island of Rum before the First World War was the playground of its rich absentee landowner. A survivor of life a century gone tells his story. Factors and schoolmasters, midges and poaching, deer, ducks and MacBrayne's steamers: here social history and personal anec-

dote create a record of a way of life gone not long ago but already almost forgotten. This is the story the gentry couldn't tell.

'This book is an important piece of social history, for it gives an insight into how the other half lived in an era the likes of which will never be seen again' FORTHRIGHT MAGAZINE

'The authentic breath of the pawky, country-wise estate employee.' THE OBSERVER

'Well observed and detailed account of island life in the early years of this century' THE SCOTS MAGAZINE

'A very good read with the capacity to make the reader chuckle. A very talented writer.' STORNOWAY GAZETTE

On the Trail of Robert Service
GW Lockhart
ISBN 0 946487 24 3 PBK £7.99

Robert Service is famed world-wide for his eye-witness verse-pictures of the Klondike goldrush. As a war poet, his work outsold Owen and Sassoon, and he went on to become the world's first million selling poet. In search of adventure and new experiences, he emigrated from Scotland to Canada in 1890 where he was caught up in the aftermath of the raging gold fever. His vivid dramatic verse bring to life the wild, larger than life characters of the gold rush Yukon, their bar-room brawls, their lust for gold, their trigger-happy gambles with life and love. 'The Shooting of Dan McGrew' is perhaps his most famous poem:

A bunch of the boys were whooping it up in the Malamute saloon;
The kid that handles the music box was hitting a ragtime tune;
Back of the bar in a solo game, sat Dangerous Dan McGrew,
And watching his luck was his light o' love, the lady that's known as Lou.

His storytelling powers have brought Robert Service enduring fame, particularly in North America and Scotland where he is something of a cult figure.

Starting in Scotland, *On the Trail of Robert Service* follows Service as he wanders through British Columbia, Oregon, California, Mexico, Cuba, Tahiti, Russia, Turkey and the Balkans, finally 'settling' in France.

This revised edition includes an expanded selection of illustrations of scenes from the Klondike as well as several photographs from the family of Robert Service on his travels around the world.

Wallace Lockhart, an expert on Scottish traditional folk music and dance, is the author of *Highland Balls & Village Halls* and *Fiddles & Folk*. His relish for a well-told tale in popular vernacular led him to fall in love with the verse of Robert Service and write his biography.

'A fitting tribute to a remarkable man – a bank clerk who wanted to become a cowboy. It is hard to imagine a bank clerk writing such lines as:

A bunch of boys were whooping it up...
The income from his writing actually exceeded his bank salary by a factor of five and he resigned to pursue a full time writing career.'
Charles Munn, THE SCOTTISH BANKER

'Robert Service claimed he wrote for those who wouldn't be seen dead reading poetry. His was an almost unbelievably mobile life... Lockhart hangs on breathlessly, enthusiastically unearthing clues to the poet's life.' Ruth Thomas, SCOTTISH BOOK COLLECTOR

'This enthralling biography will delight Service lovers in both the Old World and the New.'
Marilyn Wright, SCOTS INDEPENDENT

Come Dungeons Dark
John Taylor Caldwell
ISBN 0 946487 19 7 PBK £6.95

Glasgow anarchist Guy Aldred died with 10p in his pocket in 1963 claiming there was better company in Barlinnie Prison than in the Corridors of Power. 'The Red Scourge' is remembered here by one who worked with him and spent 27 years as part of his turbulent household, sparring with Lenin, Sylvia Pankhurst and others as he struggled for freedom for his beloved fellow-man.

'The welcome and long-awaited biography of... one of this country's most prolific radical propagandists... Crank or visionary?... whatever the verdict, the Glasgow anarchist has finally been given a fitting memorial.' THE SCOTSMAN

SPORT

Over the Top with the Tartan Army (Active Service 1992-97)

Andrew McArthur

ISBN 0 946487 45 6 PBK £7.99

Scotland has witnessed the growth of a new and curious military phenomenon - grown men bedecked in tartan yomping across the globe, hell-bent on benevolence and ritualistic bevvying. What noble cause does this famous army serve? Why, football of course!

Taking us on an erratic world tour, McArthur gives a frighteningly funny insider's eye view of active service with the Tartan Army - the madcap antics of Scotland's travelling support in the '90s, written from the inside, covering campaigns and skirmishes from Euro '92 up to the qualifying drama for France '98 in places as diverse as Russia, the Faroes, Belarus, Sweden, Monte Carlo, Estonia, Latvia, USA and Finland.

This book is a must for any football fan who likes a good laugh.

'I commend this book to all football supporters'. Graham Spiers, SCOTLAND ON SUNDAY

'In wishing Andy McArthur all the best with this publication, I do hope he will be in a position to produce a sequel after our participation in the World Cup in France.

CRAIG BROWN, Scotland Team Coach

All royalties on sales of the book are going to Scottish charities, principally Children's Hospice Association Scot-land, the only Scotland-wide charity of its kind, providing special love and care to children with terminal illnesses at its hospice, Rachel House, in Kinross.

Ski & Snowboard Scotland

Hilary Parke

ISBN 0 946487 35 9 PBK £6.99

How can you cut down the queue time and boost the snow time?

Who can show you how to cannonball the quarter-pipe?

Where are the bumps that give most airtime?

Where can you watch international rugby in-between runs on the slopes?

Which mountain restaurant serves magical Mexican meals?

Which resort has the steepest on-piste run in Scotland?

Where can you get a free ski guiding service to show you the best runs?

If you don't know the answers to all these questions - plus a hundred or so more then this book is for you!

Snow sports in Scotland are still a secret treasure. There's no need to go abroad when there's such an exciting variety of terrain right here on your doorstep. You just need to know what to look for. *Ski & Snowboard Scotland* is aimed at maximising the time you have available so that the hours you spend on the snow are memorable for all the right reasons.

This fun and informative book guides you over the slopes of Scotland, giving you the inside track on all the major ski centres. There are chapters ranging from how to get there to the impact of snowsports on the environment.

'Reading the book brought back many happy memories of my early training days at the dry slope in Edinburgh and of many brilliant weekends in the Cairngorms.'

EMMA CARRICK-ANDERSON, from her foreword, written in the US, during a break in training for her first World Cup as a member of the British Alpine Ski Team.

FICTION

The Bannockburn Years

William Scott

ISBN 0 946487 34 0 PBK £7.95

A present day Edinburgh solicitor stumbles across reference to a document of value to the Nation State of Scotland. He tracks down the document on the Isle of Bute, a document which probes the real 'quaestiones' about nationhood and national identity. The document ends up being published, but is it authentic and does it matter? Almost 700 years on, these 'quaestiones' are still worth asking.

Written with pace and passion, William Scott has devised an intriguing vehicle to open up new ways of looking at the future of Scotland and its people. He presents an alternative interpretation of how the Battle of Bannockburn was fought, and through the Bannatyne manuscript he draws the reader into the minds of those involved.

Winner of the 1997 Constable Trophy, the premier award in Scotland for an unpublished novel, this book offers new insights to both the academic and the general reader which are sure to provoke further discussion and debate.

'*A brilliant storyteller. I shall expect to see your name writ large hereafter.*'
NIGEL TRANTER, October 1997.

'*... a compulsive read.*' PH Scott, THE SCOTSMAN

The Great Melnikov

Hugh MacLachlan

ISBN 0 946487 42 1 PBK £7.95

A well crafted, gripping novel, written in a style reminiscent of John Buchan and set in London and the Scottish Highlands during the First World War, *The Great Melnikov* is a dark tale of double-cross and deception. We first meet Melnikov, one-time star of the German circus, languishing as a down-and-out in Trafalgar Square. He soon finds himself drawn into a tortuous web of intrigue. He is a complex man whose personal struggle with alcoholism is an inner drama which parallels the tense twists and turns as a spy mystery unfolds. Melnikov's

options are narrowing. The circle of threat is closing. Will Melnikov outwit the sinister enemy spy network? Can he summon the will and the wit to survive?

Hugh MacLachlan, in his first full length novel, demonstrates an undoubted ability to tell a good story well. His earlier stories have been broadcast on Radio Scotland, and he has the rare distinction of being shortlisted for the Macallan/Scotland on Sunday Short Story Competition two years in succession.

MUSIC AND DANCE

Highland Balls and Village Halls

GW Lockhart

ISBN 0 946487 12 X PBK £6.95

Acknowledged as a classic in Scottish dancing circles throughout the world. Anecdotes, Scottish history, dress and dance steps are all included in this

'*delightful little book, full of interest... both a personal account and an understanding look at the making of traditions.*'
NEW ZEALAND SCOTTISH COUNTRY DANCES MAGAZINE

'*A delightful survey of Scottish dancing and custom. Informative, concise and opinionated, it guides the reader across the history and geography of country dance and ends by detailing the 12 dances every Scot should know – the most famous being the Eightsome Reel, "the greatest longest, rowdiest, most diabolically executed of all the Scottish country dances".*'

THE HERALD

'*A pot-pourri of every facet of Scottish country dancing. It will bring back memories of petronella turns and poussettes and make you eager to take part in a Broun's reel or a dashing white sergeant!*'
DUNDEE COURIER AND ADVERTISER

'*An excellent an very readable insight into the traditions and customs of Scottish country dancing. The author takes us on a tour from his own early days jigging in the village hall to the characters and traditions that have made our own brand of dance popular throughout the world.*'
SUNDAY POST

Fiddles & Folk: A celebration of the re-emergence of Scotland's musical heritage

GW Lockhart

ISBN 0 946487 38 3 PBK £7.95

In *Fiddles & Folk*, his companion volume to *Highland Balls and Village Halls*, now an acknowledged classic on Scottish dancing, Wallace Lockhart meets up with many of the people who have created the renaissance of Scotland's music at home and overseas.

From Dougie MacLean, Hamish Henderson, the Battlefield Band, the Whistlebinkies, the Scottish Fiddle Orchestra, the McCalmans and many more come the stories that break down the musical barriers between Scotland's past and present, and between the diverse musical forms which have woven together to create the dynamism of the music today.

'I have tried to avoid a formal approach to Scottish music as it affects those of us with our musical heritage coursing through our veins. The picture I have sought is one of many brush strokes, looking at how some individuals have come to the fore, examining their music, lives, thoughts, even philosophies...' WALLACE LOCKHART

' "I never had a narrow, woolly-jumper, fingers stuck in the ear approach to music.

We have a musical heritage here that is the envy of the rest of the world. Most countries just can't compete," he [Ian Green, Greentrax] says. And as young Scots tire of Oasis and Blur, they will realise that there is a wealth of young Scottish music on their doorstep just waiting to be discovered.' THE SCOTSMAN, March 1998

For anyone whose heart lifts at the sound of fiddle or pipes, this book takes you on a delightful journey, full of humour and respect, in the company of some of the performers who have taken Scotland's music around the world and come back enriched.

POETRY
Poems to be read aloud

Collected and with an introduction by Tom Atkinson

ISBN 0 946487 00 6 PBK £5.00

This personal collection of doggerel and verse ranging from the tear-jerking *Green Eye of the Yellow God* to the rarely printed, bawdy *Eskimo Nell* has a lively cult following. Much borrowed and rarely returned, this is a book for reading aloud in very good company, preferably after a dram or twa. You are guaranteed a warm welcome if you arrive at a gathering with this little volume in your pocket.

This little book is an attempt to stem the great rushing tide of canned entertainment. A hopeless attempt of course. There is poetry of very high order here, but there is also some fearful doggerel. But that is the way of things. No literary axe is being ground.

Of course some of the items in this book are poetic drivel, if read as poems. But that is not the point. They all spring to life when they are read aloud. It is the combination of the poem with your voice, with all the art and craft you can muster, that produces the finished product and effect you seek.

You don't have to learn the poems. Why clutter up your mind with rubbish? Of course, it is a poorly furnished mind that doesn't carry a fair stock of poetry, but surely the poems to be remembered and savoured in secret, when in love, or ill, or sad, are not the ones you want to share with an audience. So go ahead, clear your throat and transfix all talkers with a stern eye, then let rip! TOM ATKINSON

Luath Press Limited
committed to publishing well written books worth reading

LUATH PRESS takes its name from Robert Burns, whose little collie Luath (*Gael.*, swift or nimble) tripped up Jean Armour at a wedding and gave him the chance to speak to the woman who was to be his wife and the abiding love of his life. Burns called one of *The Twa Dogs* Luath after Cuchullin's hunting dog in *Ossian's Fingal*. Luath Press grew up in the heart of Burns country, and now resides a few steps up the road from Burns' first lodgings in Edinburgh's Royal Mile.

Luath offers you distinctive writing with a hint of unexpected pleasures.

Most UK bookshops either carry our books in stock or can order them for you. To order direct from us, please send a £sterling cheque, postal order, international money order or your credit card details (number, address of cardholder and expiry date) to us at the address below. Please add post and packing as follows: UK – £1.00 per delivery address; overseas surface mail – £2.50 per delivery address; overseas airmail – £3.50 for the first book to each delivery address, plus £1.00 for each additional book by airmail to the same address. If your order is a gift, we will happily enclose your card or message at no extra charge.

Luath Press Limited
543/2 Castlehill
The Royal Mile
Edinburgh EH1 2ND
Telephone: 0131 225 4326 (24 hours)
Fax: 0131 225 4324
email: gavin.macdougall@luath.co.uk
Website: www.luath.co.uk